Crime and Disrepute

Eastern
Kentucky
University

Sociology for a New Century

A PINE FORGE PRESS SERIES

Edited by Charles Ragin, Wendy Griswold, and Larry Griffin

Sociology for a New Century brings the best current scholarship to today's students in a series of short texts authored by leaders of a new generation of social scientists. Each book addresses its subject from a comparative, historical, global perspective, and, in doing so, connects social science to the wider concerns of students seeking to make sense of our dramatically changing world.

- *How Societies Change* Daniel Chirot
- *Cultures and Societies in a Changing World* Wendy Griswold
- *Crime and Disrepute* John Hagan
- *Racism and the Modern World* Wilmot James
- *Gods in the Global Village* Lester Kurtz
- *Constructing Social Research* Charles C. Ragin
- *Women, Men, and Work* Barbara Reskin and Irene Padavic
- *Cities in a World Economy* Saskia Sassen

Forthcoming:

- *Social Psychology and Social Institutions* Denise and William Bielby
- *Global Transitions: Emerging Patterns of Inequality* York Bradshaw and Michael Wallace
- *Schools and Societies* Steven Brint
- *The Social Ecology of Natural Resources and Development* Stephen G. Bunker
- *Ethnic Dynamics in the Modern World* Stephen Cornell
- *The Sociology of Childhood* William A. Corsaro
- *Waves of Democracy* John Markoff
- *A Global View of Development* Philip McMichael
- *Health and Society* Bernice Pescosolido
- *Organizations in a World Economy* Walter W. Powell

Crime and Disrepute

John Hagan
University of Toronto

PINE FORGE PRESS
Thousand Oaks ♦ *London* ♦ *New Delhi*

For information, address:

 Pine Forge Press
A Sage Publications Company
2455 Teller Road
Thousand Oaks, California 91320
(805) 499-4224
Internet:sdr@pfp.sagepub.com

Production: Scratchgravel Publishing Services
Designer: Lisa S. Mirski
Typesetter: Scratchgravel Publishing Services
Cover: Lisa S. Mirski
Print Buyer: Anna Chin

Printed in the United States of America

94 95 96 97 98 10 9 8 7 6 5 4 3 2

Library of Congress Cataloging-in-Publication Data

Hagan, John, 1946–
  Crime and disrepute / John Hagan.
      p.   cm. — (Sociology for a new century)
    Includes bibliographical references and index.
    ISBN 0-8039-9039-1 (pbk. : alk. paper)
    1. Criminology. 2. Deviant behavior. 3. Crime. 4. Crime—United States. 5. Criminal justice, Administration of—United States.
    I. Title.   II. Series.
    HV6025.H268   1994
    364—dc20   93-49390
                                                                      CIP

Contents

ABOUT THE AUTHOR

John Hagan is Professor of Sociology and Law at the University of Toronto, having taught previously at the University of Wisconsin and Indiana University. He is currently editor of the *Annual Review of Sociology* and a former president of the American Society of Criminology. His recent books include *Structural Criminology,* which received the American Sociological Association Crime, Law & Deviance Distinguished Scholar Award, and *Crime & Inequality,* which is forthcoming from Stanford University Press.

ABOUT THE PUBLISHER

Pine Forge Press is a new educational publisher, dedicated to publishing innovative books and software throughout the social sciences. On this and any other of our publications, we welcome your comments, ideas, and suggestions. Please call or write to:

Pine Forge Press
A Sage Publications Company
2455 Teller Road
Thousand Oaks, California 91320
(805) 499-4224
Internet:sdr@pfp.sagepub.com

Foreword

Sociology for a New Century offers the best of current sociological thinking to today's students. The goal of the series is to prepare students, and—in the long run—the informed public, for a world that has changed dramatically in the last three decades and one that continues to astonish.

This goal reflects important changes that have taken place in sociology. The discipline has become broader in orientation, with an ever growing interest in research that is comparative, historical, or transnational in orientation. Sociologists are less focused on "American" society as the pinnacle of human achievement and more sensitive to global processes and trends. They also have become less insulated from surrounding social forces. In the 1970s and 1980s sociologists were so obsessed with constructing a science of society that they saw impenetrability as a sign of success. Today, there is a greater effort to connect sociology to the ongoing concerns and experiences of the informed public.

Each book in this series offers a comparative, historical, transnational, or global perspective in some way, to help broaden students' vision. This volume does so by examining and seeking new explanations for American's crime problems, which are all the more staggering when viewed in *comparison* to violent crime and imprisonment rates in other Western industrial nations. The comparative focus throws in sharp relief what is unique about crime in America relative to other times and places, and emphasizes the importance of understanding how these problems have developed.

The comparative perspective is additionally useful because it suggests fresh explanations are needed to explain the unique aspects of America's changing and more contemporary crime problems. One of this book's innovations is its development of a new sociology of crime and disrepute that focuses on the criminal costs of social inequality to account for America's experience. A key part of this understanding is that America's changing place in the world economy and the plight of America's cities have combined to make contemporary prospects for upward social mobility, especially through urban vice industries, less promising and more hazardous than was the case for earlier disadvantaged groups in previous parts of this century. Another criminal cost to the growing disparity between rich and poor takes place at the other end of the socio-economic spectrum, in the way white-collar crime is permitted to flourish in the new global economy. The important theoretical link between these very different kinds of crime is further demonstration of why a comparative and historical perspective can form the basis for a better understanding of crime and disrepute in America.

Prologue

The dimensions of America's crime problems are staggering. U.S. rates of violent crime and imprisonment far exceed those of other Western industrial nations—for example, more than quadrupling those of neighboring Canada. A recent National Academy of Sciences report reveals that while the time spent in prison by violent offenders nearly tripled in the United States between 1975 and 1989, violent crime did not decline. The effects have been devastating for minority low-income communities. Homicide is now the leading cause of death for young African-American males, and this death rate soared more than 50 percent during the "War on Drugs" of the mid- to late 1980s. The imprisonment rate for young African-American males is four times that for whites, and it is estimated that three-quarters of black male school dropouts in the United States have come under supervision of the criminal justice system by the time they reach their early thirties.

This book highlights the uniqueness of America's crime problems relative to other times and places, and emphasizes the importance of understanding how these problems have developed. While classical sociological theories provide a base from which this understanding can begin, a new sociology of crime and disrepute that focuses on the criminal costs of social inequality is required to explain unique aspects of America's changing and more contemporary crime problems. This new approach directs attention to processes that divert capital resources away from socially and economically distressed communities. This approach also gives special attention to the development of "deviance service centers" and "ethnic vice industries" organized around drugs, prostitution, and related activities, which are often adaptations to the absence of alternative avenues of social and economic mobility within distressed communities. The new sociology of crime and disrepute seeks to understand the social and economic roles these behaviors often play in the social organization of inner-city American life, and to explain the fact that often activities surrounding ethnic vice industries, especially involving drugs, have become more violent. A key part of this understanding is that America's changing place in the world economy and the plight of America's cities have combined to make contemporary prospects for upward social and economic mobility, especially through urban vice industries, less promising and more hazardous than was the case for disadvantaged groups earlier in this century.

Meanwhile, the new attention that is given to "crimes of the street" must not obscure our simultaneous awareness and attentiveness to "crimes in the suites." There is an important theoretical link between these very different kinds of crime. While the diversion of investment and resources from disadvantaged groups creates conditions in which disreputable and criminal adaptations are sought out and developed, the investment of resources among the advantaged in society provides opportunities for the latter to "take advantage" by disreputable, if not criminal, means. This is especially true in a changing global economy where corporations can be bigger than countries and where corporations often and easily evade efforts of countries to monitor unethical and often illegal entrepreneurial activities. The problems of white-collar crime are truly global in the ways the geographical dispersion of criminal activity can markedly increase opportunities for eluding detection, prosecution, and sanctioning, thus lessening if not eliminating risks of punishment.

America's continuing ambivalence about problems of crime and disrepute is reflected in its loosely structured criminal justice system, its periodic crackdowns on particular kinds of crime, and its recent and extensive reliance on imprisonment. Even white-collar crime has sometimes been singled out for aggressive prosecution—for example, in the immediate post-Watergate era. However, enforcement efforts focus much more selectively and persistently on street crime. Today, this emphasis is so extreme that the United States is a world leader in the use of imprisonment, especially of minority citizens, leading to widespread perceptions of injustice. An important part of the United States coming to terms with its crime problems will require a realization of the uniqueness and extensiveness of these problems. The new sociology of crime and disrepute is placing the uniqueness of the American experience in a comparative and historical perspective that can form the basis for a better understanding of contemporary events and for the evaluation of measures aimed at mitigating problems of crime in America.

Crime and Disrepute

1

The Changing Face of Crime

Crime changes in measure and meaning, across groups and places, through historical time and individual lives. We need think only of our own lives. For most of us adolescence is a turbulent and transient period of change that includes mildly disreputable, if not outright criminal, activity. The discovery of **disrepute**, the disparaged status that is associated with activities that sometimes are called "criminal," and that can bring pleasure as well as pain, can be a marker of the loss of innocence that often distinguishes adolescence. During adolescence, most of us try smoking, stealing, or sampling some other disreputable pleasure that is illegal. These acts are so characteristic of the transition from childhood to adulthood that they are a focus of classic novels from *Huck Finn* to *The Catcher in the Rye,* and the source of a genre of films, dating from *Rebel without a Cause* and ranging from the middle class angst of *Pump Up the Volume* to the ghetto-based anger of *Boys 'n the Hood.*

Sometimes the adolescent pleasure derives from the behavior simply being regarded as disreputable, while the illegality may only consist of being "under age." Most of us were never caught, and if we were, little legal action followed, *unless* we had been caught previously or were otherwise in social or legal disfavor, individually or collectively, with authorities. The ambiguous, transitory, and contingent nature of these experiences reflects the changeable quality of crime.

Early **statutes** defined delinquent behavior as including "sexual immorality or any similar form of vice" (Hagan and Leon, 1977; Sutton, 1988). These statutes might as well have defined a part of adolescence itself. However, not all youth crime is minor, and mild as well as serious youth crime can sometimes have lasting consequences; again, the effects are contingent on background characteristics and social setting. Involvements in delinquency and crime may be sustained much longer among some individuals than others, and in a sense one can speak of these individuals as having criminal careers (Blumstein and Cohen, 1987; Moffit, 1993). Nonetheless, more serious forms of youth crime also tend to peak in adolescence or early adulthood.

In fact, in all industrialized societies, adolescents and young adults are more involved than older adults in crime. On average, crime rises in frequency through the first part of the life span and then declines through adulthood. More specifically, milder forms of youth crime (which in industrialized societies by law are called "delinquency") peak at about fifteen to seventeen years of age (which we now think of as mid- to late adolescence), followed by a steep decline through adulthood. More serious crimes may peak a few years later, but they also decline through adulthood. Crime is in this sense a young person's calling. This change in crime patterns by age is so common in contemporary industrialized societies that it is sometimes called **invariant** (Hirschi and Gottfredson, 1983).

However, in nineteenth-century Europe, when the terms *delinquency* and *adolescence* were not yet invented, crime came later in the life span and declined more slowly (Greenberg, 1985). Individuals typically did not peak in their involvement in crime until their middle and late twenties. They lived shorter and physically more demanding lives, and there were fewer possibilities for adolescent indiscretions. Youths entered dangerous and exhausting forms of employment at early ages (for example, the chimney sweeps, miners, and factory hands of nineteenth-century England), and they had less time and opportunity to engage in crime. This probably postponed the peak in crime to later adulthood, when individuals became less employable and more desperate.

Following industrialization, the average life span lengthened and the period between childhood and adulthood emerged as a physically and socially significant time of maturation and learning. Adolescence came to be understood as we know it today, as a time of turbulence and change, with adolescents granted greater leeway to experiment in their behaviors during this transition. Youth crime was redefined as delinquency and dealt with through the separate procedures of juvenile courts (Platt, 1969). In these courts, young offenders were understood to be more malleable to reform than adults. Some now think this reform movement went too far, that youth should be held more accountable for their acts. Times change, and with them the social conditions that shape behavior and its meaning. Crime changes. A result is that both the behaviors we call criminal, and our understandings of these behaviors, change in ways that require sociological explanation.

One way to better recognize the significance of the linkage between crime and social change is to think about some of the behaviors that most frequently have been called criminal in our society: vagrancy, prostitution, and alcohol and drug abuse. These behaviors were once the principal preoccupations of law enforcement agencies in Western societies, and they continue to consume much law enforcement attention. It is important to understand how and why this is the case.

An Ambivalent Century of Crime

Early Vagrancy and Prostitution Laws

As a society, we are uncertain about many of the behaviors we call criminal. Once we called vagrancy a crime, and locked up large numbers of indigent persons for being so. This labeling of vagrancy as a crime, however, is now generally thought to be inappropriate because vagrancy refers to a condition or subjective state rather than the commission of a definable act.

The origins of statutes that outlawed vagrancy date to a period in fourteenth-century England when religious houses gave assistance to the poor, sick, and feeble. This practice came into question after the Black Plague ravaged England and cut the labor force in half. Feudal landowners of the period were already encountering problems because they were selling their serfs into freedom to raise money in support of the Crusades. The Church also became less willing to assume costs of supporting growing numbers of the poor. A result was the passage of a statute that made it illegal to give or receive such assistance, "Because . . . many beggars . . . refuse to labor, giving themselves to idleness and vice. . . ." This statute forced the poor to accept employment at low wages (Chambliss, 1964).

Vagrancy laws have been revived in other periods and settings. After a period of dormancy, they found renewed use in sixteenth-century England to control persons in the countryside who seemed to threaten emerging patterns of transportation of goods between traders and merchants. Vagrancy laws often were used in the early part of this century in North America to control street populations, and modern analogues of these laws often are considered today by municipal governments to criminalize the homeless. However, as already noted, it is now accepted jurisprudence that vagrancy statutes are liable to indiscriminate use because such laws refer to a condition or subjective state rather than an objective set of behaviors. In effect, this amounts to judging the person rather than an act.

Criminal codes must now be more specific about the behaviors they define as criminal, and many of the persons earlier arrested under vagrancy statutes are today therefore prosecuted under different laws, for example, involving prostitution, alcohol, and drug use. Prostitution became an issue of public debate during the first part of this century, partly as a result of the writings of the *muckrakers,* the news reporters who were so intent on exposing urban corruption during this period (for example, Turner, 1907). Prostitution was not an offense in either English or American common law. At the turn of the century in America, the interest was more narrowly focused on regulating than repressing prostitution. There were well-known areas of prostitution in most large American cities, including New Orleans's Basin Street, San Francisco's Barbary Coast, Denver's Market Street Line, and New York's Bowery and Five Points (Holmes, 1972).

In the early part of this century the muckrakers, purity reformers, and the urban progressive movement joined forces in urging a more repressive approach to prostitution involving criminalization. During a five- to ten-year period at the beginning of the century, "vice commissions" were established in over forty cities and states and the criminalization process began. The Injunction and Abatement Act was passed in Iowa in 1909 to allow the closure of houses of prostitution, and between 1911 and 1915, twenty-one states passed similar laws. The federal government passed the Mann Act, which made it illegal to import aliens for immoral purposes and permitted the deportation of aliens engaged in prostitution.

Along the way, humanitarian reformers such as Jane Addams (1912) sought to focus attention on the "panderers and procurers" and to provide humanitarian aid to women involved in prostitution, but attention shifted instead to punishing prostitutes and ignoring procurement. In the end, the urge to repress prevailed in North America, and its weight fell most heavily on women who practiced prostitution openly and could not afford to be less visible or more discrete in their activities. Note, however, that by punishing the prostitutes and largely ignoring the clients and pimps, criminal law was selectively used to both repress and perpetuate prostitution. In this sense, there was uncertainty of moral purpose, and both regulation and repression prevailed. We return to this point later.

The Chemical Crimes

Meanwhile, America also invoked the criminal sanction to deal with the "chemical crimes" of alcohol and drugs. Both were criminalized in a variety of ways, but the effort to invoke a prohibition on alcohol consumption was perhaps the most ambitious and futile use of the criminal sanction in this century. It left the intriguing question of why the prohibition of narcotics was so much more popular than the prohibition of alcohol among the nation's citizens.

The best answer to this question seems to involve the amount of public certainty that developed about the prohibition of narcotics compared to an ambivalence that accompanied the popularity of alcohol. Early measures to criminalize narcotics had a strong base of support in ethnic and racial prejudices focused on isolated minority groups, such as Chinese, African, and Mexican Americans. It made little difference that the "evidence clearly indicates that the upper and middle classes predominated among narcotic addicts in the period up to 1914" (Duster, 1970). During the first decade of this century narcotics were openly consumed, with hay fever remedies and even Coca-Cola commonly including cocaine as their active ingredient. Patent medicines containing morphine, cocaine, and heroin could be bought in the stores or by mail. Nonetheless, the use of narcotics was soon strongly associated in the public mind with vilified minority groups: the Chinese were associated with opium (Reasons, 1974), southern blacks with cocaine (Musto, 1973), and Mexicans with marijuana (Bonnie and Whitebread, 1974).

Yet it wasn't until after passage of the Harrison Act in the United States in 1914 that the composition of narcotics addicts clearly seemed to change, so that "by 1920, medical journals could speak of the 'overwhelming majority [of drug addicts]' from the 'unrespectable parts' of society" (Duster, 1970:11). As in the case of prostitution, the original legislation did not punish addicts. The Harrison Act imposed a sales tax on narcotics. However, journalists and government agency lobbyists, who sometimes are appropriately called "moral entrepreneurs" (Becker, 1963), gradually persuaded the public to associate narcotics problems with visible minorities. This in turn provided the groundwork for the criminalization of addiction itself. Addicts were an unlikely source of resistance, since they were an increasingly disadvantaged and shrinking part of the population (Mosher and Hagan, 1993).

Well-organized groups such as the Women's Christian Temperance Union and the Anti-Saloon League also attempted to persuade the public that the use of alcohol was closely associated with poverty, crime, and insanity. A "symbolic crusade" was waged in the claimed defense of Protestant small town and rural American values, which were thought to be under attack from the forces of industrialization, including non-Protestant immigrants, and the rise of the city itself (Gusfield, 1963). Again, journalists of the Progressive Era played a major role in condemning the use of alcohol for its part in these changes in American society.

However, the use of alcohol was more popular and developed over a longer period than narcotics, and an organized opposition emerged with support from the labor movement. Temperance forces were able to pass the National Prohibition Act, but wage earners who became the most frequent targets of enforcement were able to organize an opposition and ensure the ultimate failure of Prohibition (Timberlake, 1963:99). Of course, fortunes were made during Prohibition and alcohol continued to be produced, distributed, and consumed. In this sense, the legality and economics of alcohol changed more than its consumption, creating opportunities for the creation of an **ethnic vice industry** that was associated in important, albeit often exaggerated, ways with the assimilation of European immigrants into American society that we discuss further later. The prohibition experience alerts us to a critical role that law can play in the creation of structures that organize criminal behavior.

In sum, the early part of this century was an important period of change in the American response to crime, with continuing changes in the definition of what was called criminal. The famous jurist Roscoe Pound (1930:23) could remark at the end of the second decade of this century that "of one hundred thousand persons arrested . . . , more than one half were held for violation of legal precepts which did not exist twenty-five years before." One of the contradictions of this period, called the Progressive Era, was that its reforms made the criminal law more intrusive into everyday lives, especially of the poor who were most exposed to the police and courts, while also seeking to make the treatment of criminal offenders more orderly and rule-bound, and in the end, more professionally bureaucratic.

From Class Control to Crime Control

A prominent social historian, Eric Monkkonen (1981), suggests that a further important change occurred during this era. He argues that beginning in 1890, urban police forces shifted from a predominant concern with public order offenses of the kinds we have described to an emphasis on the prevention and control of more serious crimes against persons and property. Monkkonen suggests that the period from 1860 to 1890 was characterized by a "class control" style of policing manifested by aggressive action against such offenses as vagrancy, prostitution, and alcohol and drug use and the provision of social welfare services which focused police attention on the lower classes. In contrast, he asserts that from 1891 to 1920 these police forces adopted a *crime control* model, which was reflected in a reduction in non–crime-related services, a decrease in public order arrests, and a concomitant increase in "crime" arrests (for example, street crimes of violence), the net result of which was a diminishment of class control.

However, it remains the case that as we approach the end of this century, a great deal of law enforcement is still focused on the policing of public order crimes, and this disproportionately involves the urban poor (Boritch and Hagan, 1987). We no longer prosecute persons for vagrancy per se, but much contemporary policing still revolves around such problems as prostitution and alcohol and drug use. This probably reflects not only the ambivalence with which we regard these activities, but also the economic role these behaviors play in the social organization of inner-city American life, and the fact that activities surrounding these vice industries have become more violent. In any case, at the end of this century as at the beginning, and now perhaps in an even more concentrated way, sex, alcohol, and drugs are a central part of the social and economic life of America's central cities.

Deviance Service Centers

Indeed, important parts of America's inner cities can be thought of as **deviance service centers** (Clairmont, 1974) organized around **ethnic vice industries** (Light, 1977). The sociological concept of a deviance service center parallels in an ironic way the economic notion of a free enterprise zone, except for the very notable fact that a deviance service center is distinguished by its organization around illegal services and substances that form the base for vice industries. These centers are social locations in which activities otherwise defined as illegal (for example, prostitution, drug and alcohol use) are allowed to develop and serve a clientele from within and outside the community. Such centers have existed throughout this century, but today they are focused in Hispanic and African-American inner-city ghettoes.

This phenomenon is given a historical grounding in the concept of **ethnic succession**, which refers to the fact that, for lack of alternatives, first the Irish, then the Jews, later Italians, and most recently African and Hispanic Americans have sought to move upward in the American social structure through organized vice activities (Ianni, 1972; 1974). However, while earlier groups did so with some success, America's changing place in the world economy and the dire state of America's cities have made contemporary prospects for upward mobility through organized forms of urban vice less promising and more hazardous.

Contemporary accounts of the involvement of juvenile gangs in the vice industries of New York City, Chicago, Milwaukee, Boston, and Los Angeles are discussed in greater detail in later chapters. Here it is enough to note, through the research in New York City neighborhoods by Mercer Sullivan (1989), that this kind of youth crime can have significant reciprocal and redistributive roles in low income neighborhoods. Lacking other sources of legitimate employment and income, youths and other members of low-income communities are drawn to the promise of drug trafficking and related activities that characterize deviance service centers. Sullivan writes:

> The selling of illegal drugs functions much as did the selling of illegal alcohol beverages during Prohibition. Inner-city residents supply criminalized goods and services first to the local population and then to the wider community, as Projectville's Sky Wilson and Juice Baker sold drugs first to peers and then to office workers in the central business district. Inner-city entrepreneurs risk violence and stigmatization in their personal careers in return for a flow of money back to them and into their neighborhoods. Respectability flows out and money flows back in. (241)

Thus, Sullivan also points out that while these activities bring sorely needed additional resources into the inner city, they also play a role in maintaining the inner city on the moral as well as physical periphery of the economic system. Vice industries are not the mobility ladders they once promised to be.

The recurring lesson of our century of crime is that crime is variable, in a definitional as well as numerical sense. Meanings of crime change over time and across social settings, reflecting ambiguous and uncertain sentiments about what is to be called criminal. Changes in legal definition and enforcement modify and create criminal opportunities. The variable meaning of crime is therefore a central issue for society and sociologists as well. This is reflected in sociological approaches that appropriately emphasize change and make it central to the definition of crime as our subject matter.

Defining the Changeable Nature of Crime

The most notable sociological approaches to defining crime have addressed its changeable character. We will consider two forerunners for a continuum approach used in this book to consider the changeable meaning of crime. The first is Thorsten Sellin's cross-cultural approach and the second is Leslie Wilkins's notion of normative statistics.

A Cross-Cultural Approach

Sellin's (1938) early approach to defining our subject matter was more significant for the problems it exposed than for the solutions it provided. Sellin made the telling point that if we are to be scientific in our approach we cannot look to the laws of a country to tell us what is criminal. He argued that every group has its own standards of behavior, which he designated **conduct norms**, and which were not necessarily expressed in law. His central premise was that, "For every person . . . , there is from the point of view of a given group of which [s]he is a member, a normal (right) and an abnormal (wrong) way of reacting, the norm depending upon the social values of the group which formulated it" (30).

However, beyond this enormous source of cultural variation, Sellin further argued that there are normative proscriptions that are *invariant* across all cultures, which he called conduct norms. These were the norms Sellin thought we should make the subject of our scientific work, so that, "such study would involve the isolation and classification of norms into **universal categories** transcending political and other boundaries, a necessity imposed by the logic of science."

Sellin exposed the problem of variability in what is considered crime, but his solution failed because he could not specify what the universal conduct norms were. There is little in law or elsewhere to guide us toward such universals. Instead of suggesting universals, anthropological research informs us about the remarkable diversity in cultural norms. Even the crime of murder can be problematic. Most societies consider murder to be unacceptable, but what constitutes murder varies within and between societies, for example, with regard to killing in self-defense and in war. If there are universals of human behavior, they may be limited primarily to more trivial aspects of everyday life (see Malinowski, 1959). Sellin could not enumerate conduct norms that were both non-trivial and universal, but he did force researchers to acknowledge the nonscientific nature of reliance on criminal codes to define our subject matter.

Normative Statistics

Leslie Wilkins (1964) began with the problem that ultimately undermined Sellin's approach, noting that "at some time or another, some form of society . . . has defined almost all forms of behavior that we now call 'criminal' as desirable for the functioning of that form of society." Instead of looking for invariance or universality, Wilkins then focused on the regularity or frequency with which various forms of behavior occur in any particular society. The result is a continuum of behaviors on which high-frequency behaviors are considered normal and low frequency behaviors are inferred to be deviant. An attractive feature of this approach is that it is represented in the form of a simple bell-shaped curve (see Figure 1.1). Wilkins reasoned that "the model given by the normal fre-

FIGURE 1.1

A statistical approach to the definition of crime and disrepute.
(Source: Wilkins, 1964:47)

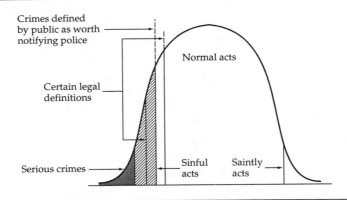

quency distribution shown in this chart represents the distribution of ethical content of human action" (47).

At the outer extremes of this chart are serious crimes and saintly acts. Note that the exact boundaries of these extremes are specified in a conceptual rather than an operational way (that is, there are no exact boundaries), and that the range of deviant behaviors included within legal definitions or considered likely to lead to police notification is similarly open to variation. The point is that this conceptualization allows for the changeable character of crime and disrepute across specific settings, and indeed focuses attention on it.

At the same time, the numerical emphasis of this approach may make the designation of our subject matter seem much simpler than it is. For example, a purely statistical approach will underestimate the role of societal groups in selecting from infrequent acts those that are considered criminal. Not all infrequent acts will be considered criminal. Additional analytical content must therefore be added to this numerically grounded framework.

Crime on a Continuum

In proposing a continuum approach to the definition of our subject matter, we begin with a premise that is well established in Sutherland's classic work on white-collar crime (1949). One of Sutherland's central points in introducing the concept of white-collar crime was that we must include in the range of behaviors we study not only acts formally considered to be criminal by law, but also a range of behaviors that for all practical purposes are treated as crimes. These include the range of unethical business practices that are handled in the civil courts, but are nonetheless regarded as socially injurious and legally penalized. Sutherland argued that these latter considerations make white-collar infractions criminal for social scientific purposes.

Thus, our conceptualization must include not only behaviors that are formally considered criminal by law, but also a range of behaviors that for all practical purposes are treated as crimes, but which may vary in their location in and outside the boundaries of criminal law. That is, we need a definition that considers behaviors that are both potentially and actually liable to criminal punishment. The point is as made by Sellin that we cannot allow nonscientists—such as state or federal legislators and other agents of law enforcement—to determine the terms and boundaries for the scientific study of crime. Instead, the definition of our subject matter must acknowledge that the distinction of crime from other forms of behavior is socially and politically determined.

Our approach therefore begins with a larger range of behavior that sociologists call **deviance**, which consists of variations from social norms. "Crime" is in turn a kind of deviance that is proscribed by criminal law. Forms of crime and deviance can be usefully subdivided along dimensions of socially defined seriousness, three of which are identified in a pyramid-shaped representation outlined in Figure 1.2. A wide range of behaviors varying in seriousness between, for example, such relative extremes as mass murder and public sexuality can be located in terms of the three vertical axes or dimensions of this operationalization.

1. The first of these social dimensions makes central the public ambiguity about various kinds of deviant behavior illustrated in the earlier historical discussion. The key aspect of this dimension is that not all persons or groups, in any given social context, agree or even have strong feelings about the wrongfulness of particular acts. For example, many if not most persons may have no strong feelings about the recent decision of a couple to engage in sexual intercourse in an uncurtained stadium hotel window that was in full view of 50,000 Blue Jay baseball fans at the futuristic Skydome in Toronto. Many watched, but few were concerned about issues of legality. This response illustrates our first dimension of seriousness: the degree of agreement about the wrongfulness of an act. This measure can vary from amusement and disinterest, through degrees of dispute, to

FIGURE 1.2

Kinds of crime and disrepute. *(Source: Hagan, 1977:14)*

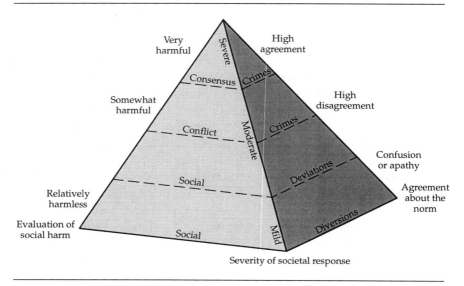

conditions of general agreement. This is a reflection of social agreement about the norm, and it forms one dimension of seriousness.

2. The social response to the act is the basis of our second dimension of seriousness. The penalties for crime and deviance range from feigned or real indifference and avoidance to public humiliations, tortures, dismemberments, and executions, with responses like ostracism, derision, and ridicule in between. The range of response is immensely and imaginatively disturbing. The more severe and strongly supported the penalty prescribed, the more serious is the societal evaluation of the act.

3. The societal evaluation of the harmfulness of the act is our third dimension of socially defined seriousness. Some acts, such as gambling, drug use, and prostitution, seem largely personal in their consequences, and therefore sometimes are designated as "victimless." The sense that these activities may only indirectly harm others diminishes their social salience as crimes, especially compared to acts of confrontation and violence, such as robbery, assault, and murder, where the consequences are more direct and interpersonal. Victimization is more apparent in such acts, although sometimes the distinction

between offender and victim is obscured by circumstances that determine who had first access to the more lethal weapon. Evaluations of harmfulness are therefore often conditioned by considerations of personal and social harm and estimations of the degree of victimization involved. The emphasis here is on perception, so that it is not just the actual harm specific acts impose, but also the harm they are perceived to impose. As Shakespeare pointed out, "There is nothing either good or bad, but thinking makes them so."

Although the three dimensions of socially defined seriousness are operationally and conceptually distinct, they are also closely associated. The same acts that (1) provoke broad agreement as to wrongfulness tend to (2) provoke strong penalties and (3) be regarded as very harmful. These are the most serious acts that are most likely to be called criminal. However, as we move away from these acts we encounter more disagreement about wrongfulness, a more equivocal societal response, and more uncertainty about perceived harmfulness. This is the ambiguity and uncertainty that our continuum approach stresses.

In terms of the pyramid used to visualize this approach in Figure 1.2, the forms of behavior most often treated as crimes are concentrated at the top, and those behaviors least consistently defined as criminal fall toward the bottom. The pyramid shape of this figure purposefully implies that the more serious forms of crime tend to be relatively infrequent, while less serious acts are considerably more common. The pyramid is further subdivided by broken lines into several groupings of crime and deviance. These lines are broken to indicate that the divisions are imprecise, and even porous, with forms of behaviors moving back and forth between groupings. Two broad and overarching groupings consist of criminal and noncriminal forms of deviance, which are further subdivided into consensus and conflict crimes, and social deviations and diversions. Each category can now be described in greater detail.

Categorizing Crime

Our discussion moves from forms of crime socially defined as more serious to the less serious. It is important to emphasize that this ordering does not carry claims to a disinterested or otherwise transcendent morality. The ranking reflects societal evaluations, as misguided as these might sometimes seem. For example, criminologists have often pointed out that unpunished but highly unethical and nonetheless noncriminal business practices can in a moral sense be more serious than individual acts of murder or mayhem.

Consider the recent prosecution of the General Motors Corporation for the production of pickup trucks thought to be defectively, but knowingly, designed in a way that led to deadly gas tank explosions in collisions. This can be understood as a form of homicide by corporate policy, sometimes called *corporate homicide,* that should rank highly on a moral scale of crime; but whether this is regarded as a serious crime, or a crime at all, will depend on public, judicial, and legislative responses to the issues raised by this case. Our continuum approach tries to capture the results of this social process of evaluation, rather than to offer an independent moral judgment of it. That is, our goal is to describe and explain, but not to judge the institutionalization and the violation of the norms of an existing social order, as represented, for example, in a country like the United States. Some of us may not agree with this social ordering, but this makes it even more important to understand the mechanisms by which this ordering occurs.

A further way of emphasizing the changeable form of categorization of crime and deviance within the continuum approach is to note how impermanent, even in a relatively modern setting, the boundaries on what gets called "criminal" can be. Berk et al. (1977) illustrated this point by carefully classifying and counting changes made in the California penal code between 1955 and 1971. They included all kinds of behaviors labeled criminal, giving particular attention to whether the cumulative effect was to bring more or less behavior under criminal control. One result is the graph presented in Figure 1.3, which represents the cumulative change in the behaviors contained in the California code for this period. Note that for no part of the overall period did the state legislature's actions result in a net decline in the volume of activities called criminal. So that even though individual behaviors were removed from the code during this time, the cumulative effect of legislative actions was to increase the coverage of the code. The implication is that the expansiveness of the criminal code that Roscoe Pound observed during the Progressive Era (discussed earlier) was not so unique. We next consider the many varieties of behaviors included in such statutes and within our continuum model.

Consensus Crimes

The crimes that concern many of us the most are crimes of predation that legal philosophers have called **mala en se**, or "bad in themselves." It is easy to overestimate how much crime of this type exists, nonetheless it is the case that for some centuries across Western societies a select group of

FIGURE 1.3

Cumulative changes in criminalization, California Penal Code, 1955–1971. *(Source: Berk et al., 1977:178)*

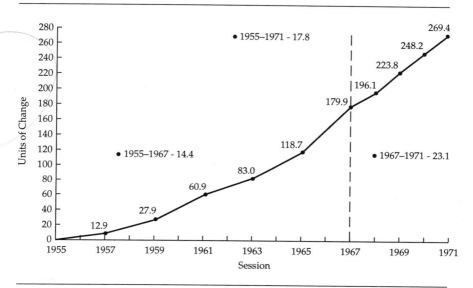

behaviors have rather consistently been treated as seriously criminal. These include the common law crimes of premeditated murder, forcible sexual assault or rape, armed robbery, and kidnapping. Perhaps because of the regularity of the condemnation of such behaviors, an area of research has developed that measures just how consistently behaviors are ranked generally as seriously criminal by the public.

The pioneering study of this kind asked groups of Philadelphia judges, police, and college students to rank the seriousness of crimes. Respondents did this easily and with great agreement both within and across groups (Sellin and Wolfgang, 1964). Subsequent studies replicated these findings across a number of cultural settings (Newman, 1976). Although related work also confirmed these conclusions, there were notable caveats. First, younger and better educated subjects were most agreed in their rankings, while less educated minority respondents were in least agreement, for example, about interpersonal violence between individuals who knew one another (Rossi et al., 1974). Second, when respondents considered that some forms of organizational and white-collar crime also result in physical harm to victims (for example, asbestos poisoning of workers and deaths in car accidents resulting from design decisions), these crimes were ranked as more serious (Schrager and Short, 1978). The dissonance that is audible in these findings hints at the need for the second category of "conflict crimes" included later in our continuum approach.

Considerations of consensus and conflict involve two different conditions. The first involves the general sentiments of the population, as reflected by the proportion of the population as a whole that approves or disapproves of particular behaviors. The second involves the attitudes of particular groups on specific issues, as reflected, for example, by the percentage difference in the proportions of younger and older Americans who disapprove of underage drinking. Using both criteria, *consensus* can be said to exist when a population is generally agreed in its attitudes and when these attitudes are unrelated or only weakly related to group memberships. Alternatively, *conflict* can be said to exist when attitudinal agreement is lower in a population and/or attitudes are related more strongly to group membership. Using these criteria, criminal behaviors can be located relative to one another and with reference to an overall continuum of attitudes toward criminal behaviors. **Consensus crimes** (Toby, 1974) are located toward one end of this continuum, while **conflict crimes**, which we discuss next, are located toward the other (Hagan et al., 1977).

Of course, even the consensus crimes are neither immutably nor permanently criminal. Nonetheless, the fact that some behaviors have been defined with much agreement as crimes makes them of distinct interest, especially to a concerned public. There is substantial normative agreement about these behaviors, and it is therefore understandable to ask why some people choose to challenge this consensus by committing these acts. Some of the theories we consider in the following chapter focus on this question.

Conflict Crimes

Conflict crimes are easily recognized by the controversy that surrounds them. Legal philosophers historically have referred to the behaviors involved as **mala prohibita**, or wrong by prohibition. The uniqueness of these behaviors is that while they are prohibited and punished by statute, the public is uncertain and divided in its thoughts about such statutes, with particular groups often feeling strongly opposed to one another on the issues involved. One concern is that groups often seek advantage over others through such laws, as when political groups seek to criminalize their opponents before and after revolutions and counter-revolutions. The fall of communism in Eastern Europe offered many examples of this, including the election of the former convicted and incarcerated Vaclav Havel to the presidency of the reconstituted Czechoslovakia.

No enumeration of conflict crimes could be exhaustive—they come and go so fast—but some of the more durable examples include the public order offenses (malicious mischief, vagrancy, and creating a public disturbance), chemical crimes (alcohol and narcotic offenses), political crimes (treason, sedition, sabotage, espionage, and conspiracy), minor property offenses (petty theft, shoplifting, and vandalism), and the so-called right to life offenses (abortion and euthanasia). Often the debates that surround these issues are enduring, as with the ongoing and seemingly unending public, legislative, and court debates about abortion in America. The problem, of course, is that there is no consensus on the basic issues, including the permissible perimeters of political protest, the dimensions of public disorder, the consumption of comforting chemicals, the protection of public and private property, and the limits of living and dying. Absent agreement, dissent reigns and is expressed in behavior defined by statute as criminal.

A result may be that those who engage in conflict crimes will be diverse in background and experience and differ in less significant ways from the general population than do those who commit consensus crimes. With this in mind, Turk (1982) points out that ". . . political criminals are extremely diverse in regard to their origins, motivations, character traits, activities, sophistication, and effectiveness" and concludes that "there is probably nothing distinctive about political criminals apart from the fact that they happen to have been identified as current or potential political threats."

Because of this diversity, sociologists are less interested in explaining why individuals become involved in conflict crimes, and more interested in explaining why their behaviors are defined as criminal. Several of the theories we consider in the following chapter address this kind of question about public and state responses to crime.

Social Deviations and Diversions

Social deviations are not considered criminal in the particular context under study, but are nonetheless subject to official control, for example, under juvenile delinquency legislation, statutes defining mental illness, and numerous civil statutes that attempt to control various forms of professional and business activities. Often there is no clear indication of what these official categories include, and while business and professional people may use this ambiguity to escape sanctioning, individuals with fewer resources often cannot do this (Arnold and Hagan, 1992). Sometimes the sanctions are recast as "support and treatment" and are assigned for an indefinite duration, with the presumed purpose to help rather than penalize the persons designated as deviant. However, too often the help is undesired, as, for example, the troubled history of official and unofficial responses to homosexuality illustrates.

Meanwhile, we all personally or vicariously experience the last of our categories, the **social diversions**. These lifestyle variations include fads and fashions of speech, appearance, and play. Sometimes activities otherwise regarded as delinquent or criminal become so common that they are pursued with the casualness of the social diversions and treated as such. My favorite example is found in a description of a few passing moments in a day in the life of the marijuana-smoking surfer, Jeff Spicoli, in the California-based observational study of *Fast Times at Ridgemont High*.

> It was a typical late May morning. The sun was shining. The sound of second-semester typists wafted across the lunch court. Jeff Spicoli was parked out in the Adult School parking lot smoking from his bong. He held a long hit in his mouth, then expelled it slowly, luxuriously, through the window of his blue Malibu. (Crowe, 1981:212)

The essence of social diversions is that they are frequent and faddish, with their disreputable pleasures ranging from harmless habits (for example, talking to plants and animals), through entertaining acts (for example, "mooning" and "streaking," see Aguirre et al., 1988), to dangerous feats (for example, "the Alka-Seltzer Screw," *Playboy Advisor*, 1973:35).

These activities may seem unusual or odd to many of us, nonetheless, we often react with no more than a mixture of amusement and amazement at the time, energy, and resources expended. Some societies regard our tolerance of social diversity as indulgent, and perhaps it sometimes is. The image of Jeff Spicoli likely would evoke stronger responses in other cultural settings, but this is part of what makes crime and disrepute so interesting, variable, and open to change. Much of the fascination of our subject matter is reflected in the likelihood that the social diversions of Ridgemont High are the conflict and even consensus crimes of less tolerant times and places.

Counting Crime and the Distribution of Disrepute

We are finally ready to move beyond the question so often asked of crime and disrepute, "What is it?" to the no less basic questions of "How much is there?" and "Where do we find it?" These kinds of questions lead us to more specifically wonder: Is violent crime increasing? Are Americans uniquely violent? Do some groups of Americans experience more crime than others? Will men continue to be more criminal than women? Answers to such questions require meaningful means to measure crime, which we have seen is an ambiguous and elusive concept. Fortunately, a variety of measures are available and are introduced in our efforts to answer the following questions.

Is Violent Crime Increasing?

There is no doubt that Americans fear crime and sense that it is increasing. Nearly half of all Americans surveyed by the National Opinion Research Center (1987) between 1972 and 1987 answered yes to the question "Is there anywhere near your home—that is, within a mile—where you would be afraid to walk alone at night?" In a more specifically focused survey in which Seattle women were asked to rank on a scale from 0 to 10 how afraid they were of being raped, two-thirds between the ages of nineteen and thirty-five scored above 5, and almost a third scored 10 (Warr, 1985). Although most Americans are never themselves victims of serious crime, their lives nonetheless are much influenced by the fear of it.

There are grounds for such fear, but this fear should also be placed in a perspective that historical comparison can provide. There is widespread agreement that crime rates, and most significantly rates of violent crime, increased in the United States and in many other Western industrial societies during the 1960s and 1970s, declined slightly and briefly in the early 1980s, and then rose and remained at relatively high levels into the early 1990s. However, it is also important to consider how we know this, and to place this finding within a longer term perspective.

First, it is difficult if not impossible to address this issue of change beyond the confines of violent crime. This is because we have so little confidence in the continuity and validity of statistics on anything other than violent crime, most notably homicide, when comparisons are made over time. Community "victimization surveys," which ask respondents to report experiences of crime by members of their households, reveal vast amounts of unreported and therefore unrecorded crime. Victim reported crimes other than homicide often triple the amount of officially recorded crime (see Skogan, 1986).

Meanwhile, analyses of crime over time, especially long periods of time, usually rely on government crime statistics. Two approaches have been taken to confirm the validity of these official statistics for homicide. First, health statistics have been gathered from medical sources that report deaths from homicide. Second, victimization surveys of the kind described already have been compared with official homicide statistics. These efforts are encouraging with regard to homicide: an early victimization survey (Ennis, 1967) found only slightly *fewer* reports of murder than the official data (the disparity is presumably a comment on "how soon we forget" and the inability of the victims to provide a reminder!), while a comparison of data from the Center for Health Statistics and the Uniform Crime Reports over a thirty-six-year period in the United States yields nearly identical trends (Hindelang, 1974). So if only because the bodies are difficult to hide, official homicide statistics have some credibility, and they have been used to suggest some fascinating trends over far longer periods than most of us would otherwise think to consider.

Certainly the most interesting of these trends is the observation of a long-term U-shaped curve in rates of criminal violence. This curve is discussed extensively in the work of Gurr (1979; 1981), but it also can be discerned in the work of Monkkonen (1981), Lane (1980:36), and Gillis (1989). While Gurr (1981:296) is careful in summarizing the evidence for this curve, noting that "The evidence for it is substantial in some societies, especially the English-speaking and Scandinavian countries, but either lacking or contradictory in others," Lane (1980:36) is somewhat less guarded in pointing to the ". . . exciting possibility that there is a single comprehensive explanation for long-term trends in the Western world as a whole over the past two centuries."

One example of the evidence marshaled for this trend is found in English homicide statistics from the thirteenth century to the present traced in Figure 1.4. This trend is predominantly and dramatically downward, with the beginning of an upward turn in the mid-twentieth century. Rates of violent crime were far higher in medieval and early modern England than in the twentieth century, as much as 10 and 20 times higher. This is so despite contemporary increases that began in the early 1960s and that are more familiar to most of us.

Our attention now turns to these more recent times portrayed in Figure 1.5. The homicide rate has peaked two to three times in this century, in 1930 and 1980, and perhaps again in 1990. The century-long low was in the early 1960s, with a more recent lull in 1985. In 1990 the homicide rate was 9.4 per 100,000 population, slightly below the previous peak of 10.4 at the turn of the previous decade. Today's homicide rates per 100,000 residents are about twice their level in the late 1950s, and they combine with population growth to produce total numbers of homicides that are clearly high by historical standards (Reiss and Roth,

FIGURE 1.4

Indicators of homicide per 100,000 population in England, thirteenth to twentieth centuries. Each dot represents the estimated homicide rate for a city or county for periods ranging from several years to several decades. *(Source: Gurr, 1981:313)*

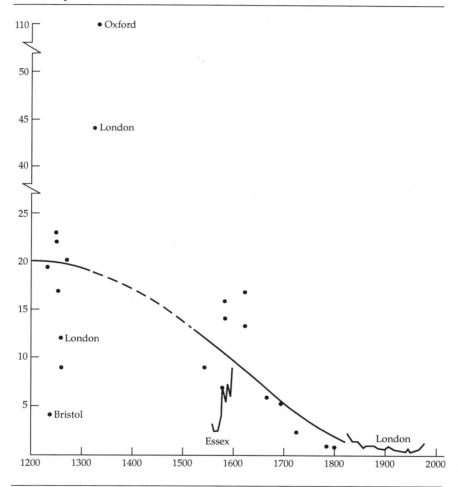

1993:3–4). It is obviously of little comfort but still significant that these rates are about half the level noted in Figure 1.4 for a number of cities during the Middle Ages.

FIGURE 1.5

Age-adjusted homicide rates, by sex and race, United States, 1929–1989. *(Source: Reiss and Roth, 1993:51)*

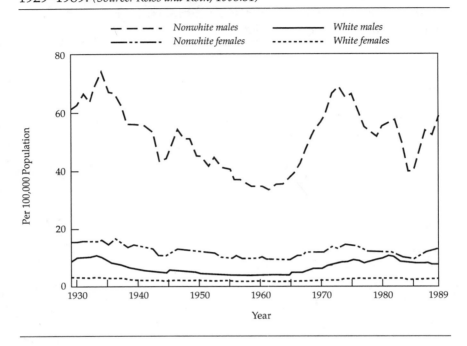

Are Americans Uniquely Violent?

In many respects, Canada is the country generally thought most similar to the United States. Canada and the United States share an English language and cultural heritage, as well as a common border and are one another's largest trading partners. However, they have had rather different rates of violent crime for at least half a century, and, as is reflected in Figure 1.6, for about the last third of this century the absolute and relative difference has grown. For example, the Canadian homicide rate per 100,000 population in 1972 was 1.4, compared to 4.5 in the United States. In 1987, the respective rates were 2.2 and 8.3 (Hagan, 1991a).

Similar differences are apparent when the net of measurement is widened to include the added violent crimes of murder, rape, robbery, and aggravated assault. This comparison reveals that while there were less than 200 violent crimes per 100,000 population in the United States in the early 1960s, and less than 50 in Canada, the respective numbers in-

FIGURE 1.6

Serious violent crime rates, Canada and the United States, 1962–1985. *(Source: Hagan, 1991a:49)*

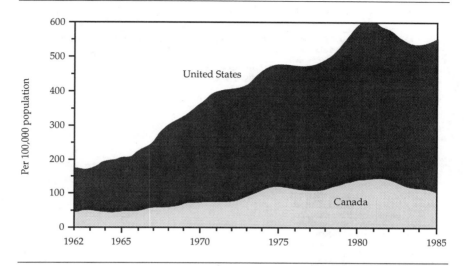

creased to well over 500 in the mid-1980s in the United States, compared to just over 100 in Canada (Hagan, 1991a). Lipset (1989) notes that the citizens of Canada and the United States therefore understandably display a difference in their respective fears of crime.

> Given the differences in rates of violent crime, it is not surprising that Americans are more fearful than Canadians of being unprotected after dark. The Gallup Polls have inquired in both countries: 'Is there any area right around here—that is, within a mile—where you would be afraid to walk alone at night?' In the mid-seventies, 31 percent of the northern population said yes, while 40 percent of those south of the border gave this answer. The gap between the countries was wider, 27 to 45 percent, when Gallup repeated the question in the mid-eighties. (13)

The reality is that, when it comes to serious crime, the United States is more like its southern neighbor, Mexico, and other violent nations of the world than it is like Canada. Indeed, as we can see in Figure 1.7, the United States has rates of violent crime that are substantially higher than other developed nations of the world. World Health Organization figures for the period from 1981 to 1986 indicate that while countries such as the Bahamas and Ecuador had homicide rates higher than the United States,

FIGURE 1.7

Crude homicide rates for selected countries, most recent year for which data are available. Data from the World Health Organization, 1987. *(Source: Reiss and Roth, 1993:52)*

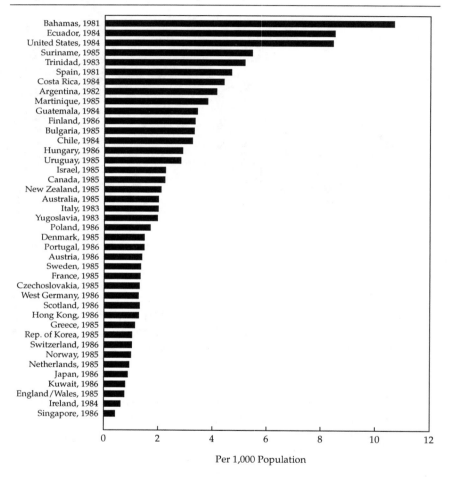

the U.S. rate was nearly twice that of the closest European nation, Spain, and four or five times that of most European and British Commonwealth countries (Reiss and Roth, 1993:53). Similar, if slightly muted, conclusions emerge from reports of crimes of violence in an International Crime Victim Survey (van Dijk et al., 1990). When it comes to the consensus crimes of violence, the United States is a relatively dangerous place.

Do Some Groups of Americans Experience More Crime Than Others?
There is perhaps no more controversial issue in sociological criminology than that of whether class and minority group memberships are linked to crime. Two assumptions are central to this debate. The first is that adverse class and minority group circumstances reflect limited resources and opportunities and adverse experiences that make criminal victimization and violation more likely. The second is that prejudice and discrimination by the police and courts disproportionately target impoverished and minority group members for criminalization. These assumptions are not mutually exclusive and we will argue that they are both correct.

It is clearly the case that persons *prosecuted* for criminal and delinquent offenses are disproportionately persons of color and reduced economic circumstances. It is also clearly the case that some disadvantaged groups are more vulnerable to some kinds of criminal victimization. According to victimization data from the National Crime Survey conducted in the mid-1980s, African Americans experience rates of rape, aggravated assault, and armed robbery that are approximately 25 percent higher than those for whites. In addition, rates of auto theft for black Americans exceed those for whites by about 70 percent, while robbery victimization is more than 150 percent higher. For much of the past half-century, rates of black homicide deaths have ranged from six to seven times those for whites (Hawkins, 1986; Rose and McClain, 1990).

Nonetheless, sociologists began to doubt the meaning of official crime statistics when in the late 1950s they started to do school-based "self-report" surveys to study delinquency. Self-report questionnaires are paper-and-pencil instruments that usually anonymously ask teenage respondents to enumerate their involvements in delinquency (Nye and Short, 1957). Self-report studies often reveal no relationship, or only a weak one, between the occupational status of parents and the delinquency of their teenage children, leading to the suggestion that this relationship may be a "myth" (Tittle et al., 1978; see also Tittle and Meier, 1990).

A source of such a myth could be that official police and court data are biased and reflect the results of prejudice and discrimination. There is evidence of this bias that we consider in detail in Chapter 5. However, there is also evidence that differences between the official and self-report data reflect a mixture of problems, including not only bias but also a difference in the behaviors considered. Self-report questionnaires often tend to focus on minor forms of delinquency (Braithwaite, 1981; Hindelang et al., 1981). When serious forms of delinquency are emphasized, the results of self-report studies often are more consistent with the official data (Elliot and Ageton, 1980; Thornberry and Farnsworth, 1982; Johnson, 1980). Official data sources may also more accurately reflect group differences in behavior when they are focused on more serious crimes.

These issues become most acute when we come to the topic of race and crime and the increasingly harsh fact of American life that young African-American males have a vastly disproportionate risk of encountering the criminal justice system, both as victims and violators. Crime is also a great concern for low-income Hispanic and white Americans, but these patterns are more pronounced, better studied, and more fully documented among African-American youths (Hagan and Peterson, 1994). Among the harsh facts are the following:

- Homicide is the leading cause of death among African-American youths.

- Overall, black Americans account for one third of all arrests and one-half of all incarcerations in the United States.

- About one fifth of all 16 to 34-year-old African-American males are under justice system supervision.

Crimes of violence are especially highly concentrated among black American youths. For example, among 15 to 19 year olds, the gun homicide rate for black males is about 68 per 100,000 population, compared to about 6 per 100,000 for white males (Fingerhut and Kleinman, 1990).

Although there have been variations over time in rates by ethnic status and sex, black rates of homicide have exceeded white rates at least since 1910, and probably longer (Monkkonen, 1993). In general, the pattern is that differences in black and white rates of arrest are greatest for serious crimes involving violence, and smaller for less serious crimes. This is significant in relation to the issue of bias and discrimination, because if it is assumed, as it generally is, that prejudice and discrimination cause less distortion in arrest patterns for more serious crimes, we might expect the reverse of the pattern just described with regard to seriousness: that is, we might expect that differences in arrest patterns between races would be greater for more minor rather than more serious crimes. Yet this is not the case, increasing the certainty that the patterns of victimization and violation reflect much more than enforcement bias. A sense of the magnitude of the difference for homicide in late adolescence and early adult race and sex groupings can be observed in Figure 1.8 (Reiss and Roth, 1993:51). The following more general summary describes racial differences in the experience of crime in post–World War II America:

FIGURE 1.8

Homicide rates, persons ages 15–24 years, by race and sex, 1940–1988. *(Source: Reiss and Roth, 1993:64)*

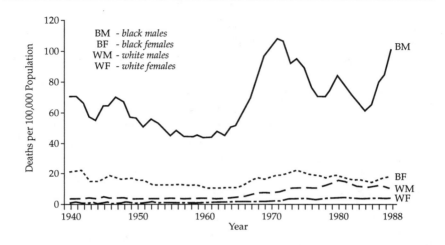

Both blacks and whites generally experienced rapid arrest increases in the 1960s and early 1970s. Black and white trends are most similar for theft and burglary. Black and white crime trends are very different in other respects. Regardless of crime type or year, black arrest rates are substantially higher than white rates. The differences are greatest for the violent crimes of robbery, murder and rape. (LaFree, 1993)

Of particular concern is the most recent spike upward in rates of violence in African-American communities beginning in the mid-1980s. To this point rates of crime more generally were showing signs of decline probably linked to the aging of post-war baby boom youth. Close inspection of Figures 1.5 and 1.8 reveals that white Americans did not experience this same movement upward as African Americans in the late 1980s, but instead experienced a continuing gradual decline. As the following analysis of these trends suggests, this pattern may be linked to a turn in the nature of employment and drug problems confronting America's racial ghettoes in the late 1980s.

The crack cocaine epidemic became national news in 1986. Both the police and the news media believe that crack unleashed an unprecedented wave of violence in poor neighborhoods. . . . [T]his increase in lethal violence was confined to black men between the ages of fifteen and twenty-four, whose chances of dying violently rose by more than 50 percent between 1985 and

1987. Homicide rates did not increase systematically among older black men, and they declined among white men. Since selling crack is mostly an adolescent occupation, the fact that homicides increased mainly among fifteen- to twenty-four-year-olds is not surprising. (Jencks, 1992:183)

The link between drugs and violence in minority communities is anticipated in our discussion of the history of deviance service centers and ethnic vice industries earlier in this chapter, and this theme is pursued further in Chapter 3.

As we also discuss in greater detail in Chapter 3, **race** is one of a number of markers linked to economic disadvantage that concentrates crime in low-income communities. We review evidence in Chapter 3 that high rates of homicide are concentrated not only by race, **gender,** and **age,** but also within low-income community settings. These kinds of findings combine to make the point that criminal violence is a highly concentrated experience in American life.

Will Men Continue to Be More Criminal than Women?

As we have already suggested, criminal forms of deviant behavior are also strongly related to gender. Whether unofficial or official measures are used, men are significantly more likely to be alcoholic (Cahalan, 1970), addicted to illegal drugs (Terry and Pellens, 1970), and involved in the more serious forms of crime (Hindelang, 1978). However, it is also the case that the disparity between the sexes fluctuates, for example, with the type of crime, time, and social setting. For example, while official statistics indicate that males exceed females in crimes against the person by as much as 8 to 1, the ratio for crimes against property is more on the order of two or three to one, and in some areas of property crime this ratio is falling.

Some have suggested that women are increasing their involvement in all types of offenses, and more specifically that a new breed of violent, aggressive, female offender may be emerging (Adler, 1975). On the other hand, it also has been suggested that the new female criminal is more a social myth than an empirical reality (Chesney-Lind and Shelden, 1992), an ideological backlash against the economic and political gains women have made in recent years. The evidence indicates that while some areas of crime are changing, others are much more stable.

A review of official data and self-report surveys on crime and delinquency found the gender gap in crime narrowing for more minor offenses, and that this trend was more notable for youths than adults (Smith and Visher, 1980). This finding is intriguing because it is consistent with the expectation that contemporary changes in gender roles would have more noticeable effects among younger women. However, it is also the case that these changes have occurred within constraints of persisting gender roles, in the sense that females continue to be most highly represented in minor property crimes and some public order offenses (for example, prostitution) that appear to reflect traditional gender roles in relation to crime.

The most interesting change involves minor property crime. Comparing Uniform Crime Reports of arrests for intervals over the past three decades, the percentage of female involvement has increased from an average of 17 percent in the early 1960s, to 27 percent in the early 1970s, to 35 percent by the mid-1980s. Across the same three points in time, the percentage of female arrests for most other crimes has increased only slightly, stayed the same, or declined. The greatest changes are therefore for minor forms of theft and "hustles," including shoplifting, theft of services, falsification of identification, passing bad checks, credit card forgery, welfare fraud, employee pilferage, and street-level drug dealing (Steffensmeier and Allan, 1991:70). Women are becoming more similar to men in the level of their participation in these minor forms of property crime (see also Hagan, Gillis, and Simpson, 1985), but they also remain persistently different in their lower rates of involvement in more serious and violent forms of crime.

Crime Changes

We began this chapter by noting that crime changes in meaning and measurement, across groups and places, through historical time and individual lives. This is at once what makes crime sociologically interesting and difficult to study. It requires that we have a definition of our subject matter that recognizes shifts in what are considered crimes, measures that reveal sources of error and bias in what is treated as crime, an appreciation that crime varies substantially across social groupings and settings, and a perspective that considers how crime changes over historical time and through individual lives. These are the kinds of issues we address in this book.

As we do this we will consider social behaviors that range from being regarded as social diversions and deviations to conflict and consensus crimes. Some behaviors move across these categories within relatively brief periods of time. Forms of drug use are an example. We noted in this chapter that over the course of this century narcotic drugs moved from being common diversions, through being defined as taxable deviations, to explicit treatment as crimes, with varying degrees of social support that have included periods of notable conflict as well as relative consensus. During this century of change, narcotic drug use shifted from being a common and often middle class avocation, to being more restrictively concentrated in minority low-income settings. Notable exceptions have involved periods when cocaine and related drugs have been more broadly consumed and the widespread use of various kinds of drugs by youth from all classes in the 1960s and 1970s. However, the more dominant pattern has involved the emergence in American ghetto settings of an ethnic vice industry built around drugs that can be enormously profitable for some and extremely violent and dangerous for others. These patterns are important, and they are considered in greater length in Chapter 3.

Meanwhile, a broader set of trends is apparent with regard to crime in America. We have seen that despite a long historical trend toward a decline in violent crime since the Middle Ages, violent crime in America is now at high levels that rival previous peaks in this century. Although these high levels of violent crime are paralleled and even exceeded in some developing countries, U.S. rates of criminal violence are among the highest in the Western industrialized world. Low-income and minority communities suffer most from this crime, especially violent crime, which is most highly concentrated among young African-American males, for whom homicide is the most frequent cause of death.

These harsh social facts are in some ways relatively recent developments, but in other ways they are culminations of long-term trends. There is a long and rich heritage of sociological theories that attempt to explain crime. In the following chapter we consider prominent efforts to explain crime using classical traditions of sociological theory.

2

Classical Theories of Crime and Disrepute

We have discussed what crime is, how it is measured, where it is found, and how all of this changes. An obvious next question is how do we explain this phenomenon? Sociological criminology has a rich tradition of theoretical diversity that rivals or exceeds that of any other subfield in sociology. Each of the major traditions of sociological theory—structural functionalism, symbolic interactionism, and conflict theory—is connected to a group of well-articulated explanations of delinquency and crime. Usually these connections are clear and continuing, although in some instances the connections are more tentative, and other categorizations of the theories are plausible (for example, Kornhauser, 1978). Regardless, it is impossible to study crime from a sociological perspective today without considering the classical theories and some of their most prominent derivations and applications.

However, as essential as these traditions may be, they are also inadequate. A major concern is that these traditions have not kept pace with changes in the national and world economy and that they have not sufficiently confronted the altered reality of America's interconnected problems of poverty, race, ethnicity, gender, and crime. We make these points with regard to each of the major theory groups, but not until each is more fully introduced.

The Structural Functionalist Theories

The **structural functionalist theories** tend to see crime and other forms of disreputable behavior as resulting from breakdown or strain in social processes that otherwise produce conformity. The focus is on institutions such as the family and school that socialize individuals to conform in their behaviors to the core values of the surrounding society. The particular concern is with the ways in which these institutions fail in their socialization mission. Wide agreement, or consensus, is assumed by this approach about the core values of society—about what people want from their lives and about how they are expected to behave in achieving these goals.

The thing to be explained in structural functionalist theories, then, is why some individuals, through their criminally disreputable behavior, come to challenge this consensus. The question asked within this grouping of theories is: Why do some individuals come to violate the conforming values that nearly all of us are assumed to hold in common? Specific answers are offered by anomie, subcultural, differential opportunity, social disorganization, control, and social learning theories of crime and disrepute. Some of these answers focus on broad class and group level processes, while others focus more specifically on individuals. Over time, the emphasis in this theoretical tradition has shifted from the group to the individual—a shift, we will argue later, that has made this tradition less relevant to contemporary issues than it could be.

Anomie Theory

The roots of functional theory lie in Durkheim's (1951, originally published in 1897) notion of anomie. Durkheim defined **anomie** in terms of lack of social regulation, and the translation of this concept from Durkheim's writings in French is usually as normlessness. *Normlessness* is usually defined as a form of purposelessness experienced by a person or a class as a result of a lack of standards and values. However, Merton (1938) gave this concept an American stamp by using it to describe the results of a faulty relationship between goals and the legitimate means of attaining them. Two aspects of social and cultural structure were emphasized in Merton's application: culturally defined goals (notably monetary success) and the acceptable means (mostly involving education) of their attainment. Merton emphasized that while in our society success goals are widely (that is, consensually) shared, the means of attaining these goals are not. He noted that anomie can result.

Merton did not mean for his theory simply to explain why some individuals deviate more than others. He was more interested in explaining why disadvantaged **classes** of individuals deviate more than other classes of individuals. He reasoned that members of less economically advantaged classes are most affected by the disparity between shared success goals and the scarcity of means to attain them. Higher rates of crime and deviant behavior among those in less advantaged class groupings are the expected result of this structural inconsistency.

Merton's theory of anomie includes a famous typology of adaptations to inadequate means of attaining goals. Perhaps most important for understanding crime is a category in this typology called *innovation,* which includes various forms of economically motivated crimes. However, also included are *retreatism,* consisting of escapist activities such as drug use; *rebellion,* involving revolutionary efforts to change the structural system that establishes goals and means; and *ritualism,* which describes various forms of overconforming behaviors. The common feature of the separate categories in the typology is that they all represent adaptations to structurally induced failure—that is, a failure that derives from a socially structured lack of access to achievable goals through legitimate means.

Delinquent Subculture Theories

Merton linked his theory of anomie to group-patterned behaviors by emphasizing that his explanation could account for differences in rates of crime and deviance across whole classes. Later sociologists extended this focus on class issues through the concept of **subcultures**. For example, Cohen (1955) suggested that members of disadvantaged classes become potential members of delinquent subcultures when they experience early failures in school. He noted that when assessed against a "middle class measuring rod," working class children often are found lacking. These students experience a growing sense of "status frustration" because they are not prepared by their early experiences inside and outside the home to satisfy middle class expectations. As an alternative, the delinquent subculture offers a group, often gang-based, solution. This consists of an alternative set of group-shared and group-supported criteria, or values, that working class youth can meet.

Subcultural values may often completely repudiate middle class standards and expectations. In this way the delinquent subculture expresses its contempt for middle class values and makes their opposites the criteria for status. The delinquent subculture in effect says to the onlooking middle class society, "We're everything you say we are and worse." The delinquent subculture that results is said by Cohen to be an inversion of middle class society, taking a disreputable pleasure in being "non-utilitarian, malicious, and negativistic." It is important to emphasize that the force of this solution is that it occurs within groups that provide peer support.

Perhaps the classic application of subcultural theory is Hunter Thompson's (1967) journalistic account of a period he spent with the Hell's Angels motorcycle gang. Thompson reports that to understand the Angels it is necessary to acknowledge the stark social fact that they "are sons of poor men and drifters, losers and sons of losers" (332). "Yeah, I guess I am [a loser]," one reflective Angel comments to Thompson, "but you're looking at one loser who's going to make a hell of a scene on the way out" (334). Instead of surrendering meekly to their individual fates, then, the Angels gather in celebration of their "choppers" and one another: "They reflect and reassure one another, in strength and weakness, folly and triumph" (120). Mayhem is an associated part of the Angel lifestyle, but it is their choppers that become the key symbols of the reversal of conventional values and the inverted process by which Angels collectively reclaim their status. For the Angel, "his motorcycle . . . is his only valid status symbol, his equalizer" (119).

In a variation on the subcultural theme, Miller (1958; see also Banfield, 1968) argues that the values of the delinquent subculture are really the "by-product of . . . the lower class system" that has a ". . . distinctive tradition many centuries old with an integrity of its own" (19). Miller suggests that this "lower class culture" is characterized by a set of values—trouble, toughness, smartness, excitement, fate, and autonomy—that bring affected male adolescents into conflict with the law. He concludes that simply, "following . . . practices . . . of . . . lower class culture automatically violates certain legal norms" (18).

Differential Opportunity Theory

Although legitimate opportunities may be restricted in some class settings, there nonetheless may be illegitimate opportunities that are available and that thereby become especially important in channeling individuals into specific forms of delinquency and crime. We introduced this prospect in the discussion of ethnic succession in vice industries and deviance service centers (Chapter 1). Links between vice and ethnicity are discussed further in the "Structural Functionalist Theory" case study (see pages 38–39), which illustrates the structural functionalist approach to crime and ethnicity. In a parallel way, a **differential opportunity theory** developed by Cloward and Ohlin (1960) argues that to understand the different forms that criminal and delinquent behavior can take, we need to consider the different types of illegitimate opportunities available to those who are seeking a way out of disadvantaged class settings. Different types of opportunities and settings produce different subcultural adaptations. Cloward and Ohlin suggest that three types of adaptations predominate: a stable criminal subculture, a conflict subculture, and a retreatist subculture.

1. The *stable criminal subculture* is the best organized. This subculture emerges when there is coordination between legitimate and illegitimate roles and sectors in the community, for example, between

politicians, the police, and the underworld. In the old-style political machines that once dominated American cities, politicians and the police provided protection for privileged forms of illegal enterprise, creating what we have earlier called deviance service centers. Such circumstances could provide a stable base for the development of illegitimate opportunity structures in which individuals could advance from lower to upper levels of an organized criminal under-world. A genre of films about organized crime, from *The Godfather* to *Goodfellas*, has depicted this kind of stable criminal subculture. When legitimate and illegitimate opportunity structures have been linked in this way, the streets have been made safe *for* crime, and reliable upward mobility routes have emerged for criminals. Yet, this is in some ways more a romantic caricature of our urban past than of today's contemporary city, with its more violent and disruptive crime patterns.

2. The presence of violence and conflict are disruptive of both legiti-mate and illegitimate enterprises. As we have noted, when the latter kinds of enterprise have been interconnected, violence and conflict may sometimes have been restrained. However, in the absence of effective interconnections, violence can reign uncontrolled. Cloward and Ohlin see these kinds of disarticulated communities as produc-ing a *conflict subculture*. In these settings street crime is common, and gangs and violent crime prevail.

3. The *retreatist subculture* is made up of individuals who fail in their efforts to make it in both the legitimate and illegitimate opportunity structures. These individuals are "double failures" in Cloward and Ohlin's theory, and they are destined to the chemical crimes of drug and alcohol abuse as forms of escape from their failures.

The structural functionalist theories we have discussed thus far all take their subjects to be much impressed by the **values** they encounter. Valued outcomes, usually because they are unattainable, lead to the delinquent and criminal behaviors to be explained. Over the years, research in this tradition has come to focus on the issue of whether explicit disparities in the values or goals and means of *individuals* actually result in delinquency and crime. The question asked is whether disparities between individu-ally held aspirations and expectations lead to delinquent and criminal out-comes. The emphasis of this tradition on classes, subcultural groups, and community structures has received reduced attention (Cullen, 1988).

Meanwhile, another stream of the structural functionalist tradition has focused on a more general absence of the goals, values, or commit-ment that our society emphasizes. Here the emphasis is again on values and on group-level processes, in this case on the neighborhood or community level. However, while common goals and values are again assumed, it is not taken for granted that these goals and values are so effectively or intensively shared.

Social Disorganization Theory

This theory evolved out of research by Shaw and McKay (1931) beginning in the 1920s in Chicago. They observed that problems such as truancy, tuberculosis, infant mortality, mental disorder, juvenile delinquency, and adult crime clustered in neighborhoods generally near the center of the city. They observed that these problems were more characteristic of the neighborhoods than of the people in them, so that as different ethnic groups moved in and out of the neighborhoods, it was the neighborhoods and not the people who remained troubled. Since these troubles and problems were assumed to be contrary to shared values of the neighborhood inhabitants, they were taken as indications that these neighborhoods were unable to realize the goals of their residents. In other words, they were taken as indications that it was the neighborhoods that were socially disorganized.

Shaw and McKay also sought to determine the sources of this social disorganization by identifying characteristics these neighborhoods held in common. They concluded that poverty, high residential mobility, and ethnic heterogeneity led to a weakening of "social bonds" or controls, in other words to **social disorganization**, that in turn led to high rates of delinquency. Recall that all of this was being said of neighborhoods, not people.

However, as with previous theories, researchers began to be concerned about what these findings meant for understanding individual behavior (Robinson, 1950). One result was a shift in both theoretical and research interest to the individual level, and the development of a control theory (Hirschi, 1969) that focused on the bonds of individual youths to their families, schools, and communities, as measured through survey self-reports of youthful attitudes, experiences, and delinquent behaviors.

Control Theory

Those who have goals and means to attain them are characteristically bonded to institutions (for example, the family and school) that encourage conformity. Alternatively, Hirschi's (1969) **control theory** argues that the absence of such a social bond is all that is required to explain much crime and delinquency. He cites four sources of the social bond:

1. attachment (for example, to family and friends)
2. involvement (for example, in school and related activities)
3. belief (for example, in various types of values and principles)
4. commitment (for example, to achieving goals)

According to control theory, the less attached, involved, believing, and committed individuals are, the less is their bond to society; and the weaker the bond, the greater the likelihood of delinquency and crime. From this perspective, no special strain between goals and means is required to produce deviant behavior; all that is required is the reduction of the constraining social bond that holds crime and deviance in check. A prominent extension of this theory argues that many criminals simply lack self-control (Gottfredson and Hirschi, 1990).

Social Learning Theory

Control theory seeks to explain why, where, and when delinquency and crime most often occur, but it does not attempt to explain its more specific forms. Akers's (1977) **social learning theory** asserts that "the person whose ties with conformity have been broken may remain just a candidate for deviance; whether he becomes deviant depends on further social or other rewards" (66). According to social learning theory, deviant behavior results from a conditioning process that usually involves social groups in which rewards and punishment shape the course of the behaviors they reinforce.

This principle of social reinforcement has interesting implications that move beyond control theory, for example, in explaining how individuals shift from conforming to criminal and noncriminal forms of deviant behavior. An example involves groups with prescriptive norms that allow some drinking and in which most people drink moderately. The excessive drinking of an alcoholic usually will not challenge such a group's controls or norms until it is so far out of hand that he or she no longer is welcome in the group. However, the latter break can pave the way for a move to a group that values and rewards heavy drinking. This *shift* is emphasized in social learning theory, because it illustrates how *differential reinforcement* and not simply the absence of controls can explain the more specific course of criminal and delinquent behavior.

An Overview of Functionalist Theories

Values or beliefs play a key causal role in all the functionalist theories we have considered. These theories tend to argue that the presence of success goals or values without the means to attain them can produce criminal behavior, as can the absence of these goals or values in the first place. It is an emphasis on these values, and the role of the school, family, and other groups in promoting and transmitting them, that ties the functionalist theories together.

There is a trend in the evolution of these theories that, counter to the intentions of many of their early exponents, has involved shifting attention from group, neighborhood, and class level processes to the ways in which individuals encounter these processes. This has had the effect of reducing structural and cultural issues that are the starting point of this theoretical tradition to a place of secondary importance. Instead, the focus has tended to shift to issues of social psychological strain as experienced by individuals and to the loss of control over individuals. Both the group (often called the **macro level**) and individual (often called the **micro level**) dimensions of analysis are important, but they are not often joined in this contemporary work. A result is the decline of a distinctive emphasis in the early functionalist tradition on issues that rise above the individual. One way to finally make this point is to return to an example of the functionalist approach that illustrates the macro, or group, level of analysis by focusing on the succession of ethnic groups that have participated in organized crime in this century in North America (see the "Structuralist Functionalist Theory" case study below).

CASE STUDY

Structural Functionalist Theory: Organized Vice and Ethnicity

The most durable elements of functionalist theories emphasize opportunities and their associations with classes, cultural groups, and communities. Francis Ianni (1972; 1974) effectively captures this contribution by focusing on the involvement of a series of ethnic groups in the history of organized vice in America. Ianni notes that a succession of ethnic groups have come to North America in search of a better life, but without the ready means—education and occupational skills—to attain their goals. Organized involvement in illegal vice industries became their illegitimate structure of opportunity. First the Irish, then the Jews, later Italians, and most recently Hispanic and African Americans have sought out the opportunities of organized involvement in vice industries. Until recently, Ianni notes that ethnic groups have moved into and then out of organized vice as they have gained access across generations to more legitimate means of attaining success. In the past, immigrant groups were able to subsequently move up the social ladder and out of organized crime.

Of course, the part of this history that is best known as well as frequently distorted involves Italian Americans, often focusing on the specter of the *Mafia*. The Mafia was never a single organization in Italy and could not have emigrated en masse to North America. However, this term does denote a set of cultural attitudes and patterns of local criminal organizations and secret societies that did find a new application in North American settings, beginning in the 1920s. The key to this involved the passage of Prohibition and the creation of an illegal alcohol industry that was well suited to a large new immigrant group with restricted legitimate opportunities. Many Italian immigrants had traditionally produced their own wine at home, and this tradition was an opportunity in the making. Home wineries were converted into home stills, and strong family ties and traditions of local organization were transformed into centralized forms of criminal enterprise to collect and redistribute this new source of illegal profits.

This early phase of Italian-American involvement in organized vice was followed by the Depression and the repeal of Prohibition, which required a transition into new areas of illegitimate enterprise, including drugs, prostitution and the expansion of gambling. Prostitution and drugs were often offensive to the cultural values of older members of Italian-American crime families, but by now second-generation members of these families were taking over, and the Italian-American involvement in organized vice became more North American in character. Ianni is able to trace through specific crime families the process across generations by which areas of illegal enterprise changed, and as well the process by which increasing proportions of these families moved out of organized vice and into legitimate areas of economic opportunity. Today the process of ethnic succession is working toward its logical conclusion, with declining involvement of Italians in organized vice and an increasing involvement of Hispanic and African Americans that we discuss in the following chapter. Structural functionalist theories have focused our attention on the latent and unintended consequences of organized vice for the social mobility of a series of ethnic groups in American history, indirectly raising the question of whether this mobility process continues today.

The Symbolic Interactionist Theories

The **symbolic interactionist theories** of crime and disrepute bring a subtle but important shift from an emphasis on values to the ways in which meanings and definitions are involved in explaining criminality. These meanings and definitions are assumed to shape deviant behavior and responses to it. Over time, the symbolic interactionist theories have extended attention from an emphasis on how symbolic meanings and definitions are acquired from coparticipants in deviant behavior, to a focus on the roles that official agencies of social control play in imposing symbolic meanings and definitions on individuals. We begin with the focus on coparticipants.

Differential Association Theory

Edwin Sutherland (1924) is probably the most revered figure in sociological criminology, in major part for his development of the concept of white-collar crime, but also for his symbolic interactionist theory of **differential association**. The latter concept is often misunderstood as referring only to associations among individuals, but it also refers to associations among ideas. Individuals only behave criminally, Sutherland argued, when they define such behavior as acceptable. To be sure, this process of association occurs through individuals, but the process also depends on the association of ideas or definitions.

> The hypothesis of differential association is that criminal behavior is learned in association with those who define such behavior favourably and in isolation from those who define it unfavourably, and that a person in an appropriate situation engages in criminal behavior if, and only if, the weight of the favourable definitions exceeds the weight of the unfavourable definitions. (Sutherland, 1949:234)

This hypothesis was applied by Sutherland in his famous study of white-collar crime. He argued that individuals become white-collar criminals because they are immersed in a business culture that defines illegal business practices as acceptable. Common commercial clichés transmit this ideology within business groups:

"We're not in business for our health."

"Business is business."

"It isn't how you get your money, but what you do with it that counts"

"It's the law of the jungle."

Sutherland explained that ideas become influential because they are transmitted within business groups that are isolated from competing viewpoints, and because "the persons who define business practices as undesirable and illegal are customarily called 'communists' or 'socialists' and their definitions carry little weight."

This theory was extended by a student of Sutherland's, Donald Cressey (1971), who undertook a study of the more specific business crime of embezzlement. After interviewing more than 100 imprisoned embezzlers, Cressey concluded that individuals only committed this crime after they had first justified their acts by redefining them with the following kinds of thoughts:

> "Some of our most respectable citizens got their start in life by using other people's money temporarily."

> "All people steal when they get in a tight spot."

> "My interest was only to use this money temporarily, so I was 'borrowing' it, not 'stealing.'"

> "I have been trying to live an honest life, but I have had nothing but trouble so 'to hell with it.'"

Cressey (1965) believed that the definitional component of his theory had a wide application to white-collar kinds of crimes, suggesting that, "The generalization I have developed here was made to fit only one crime—embezzling. But I suspect that the verbalization section of the generalization will fit other types of respectable crime as well" (15).

Neutralization Theory

An intriguing feature of the symbolic interactionist theories is that they use the same kind of logic and conceptualization to explain crime in the upper and lower reaches of the social hierarchy. Similar assumptions are made for these different groups because key definitional processes are assumed to be the same. Thus, when Matza and Sykes (1961) extended some of the basic premises of Sutherland's differential association theory to explain common delinquency with their **neutralization theory**, they began by noting that there are "subterranean traditions" in the conventional culture that reflect ironic convergences between what are often thought of as dominant and dissident groups. Matza (1964) argues that this is so because, "the spirit and substance of subterranean traditions are familiar and within limits tolerated by broad segments of the adult population" (64).

As an example of such subterranean convergence, Matza and Sykes (1961) point to Veblen's (1899) classic observation in *The Theory of the Leisure Class* that delinquents conform to the norms of conventional society's business sector, rather than deviate from it, when they place a desire for "big money" in their value system. They go on to note that wealth-motivated and entrepreneurial traditions in American society encourage adventure, excitement, and thrill-seeking, which seemingly further promote deviance when compared with such conformity-producing values as security, routinization, and stability. The point is that the former latent values exist side by side with the latter more conventional values.

Further, Matza and Sykes note that the convergences between delinquency and convention do not simply take mild or material forms. They observe that

> . . . the dominant society exhibits a widespread taste for violence, since fantasies of violence in books, magazines, movies, and television are everywhere at hand. The delinquent simply translates into behavior those values that the majority are usually too timid to express. (716)

With the more recent legacy of Bruce and Brandon Lee, not to mention the *Lethal Weapon* and *Terminator* films, it is difficult to suggest that this trend has diminished. More generally, Matza and Sykes (1961) conclude that, "the delinquent has picked up and emphasized one part of the dominant value system, namely, the subterranean values that coexist with other, publicly proclaimed values possessing a more respectable air" (717).

Still, Sykes and Matza also argue that common delinquents, like white-collar criminals, display guilt or shame when confronted with evidence of their acts. Like the white-collar criminal, the delinquent is described by Sykes and Matza as drifting into a deviant lifestyle through a subtle process of justification or neutralization that ultimately makes him or her an "apologetic failure." "We call . . . [their] justifications of deviant behavior techniques of neutralization," write Sykes and Matza, "and we believe these techniques make up a crucial component of Sutherland's definitions favourable to the violation of the law" (667).

There are five specific neutralization techniques Sykes and Matza (1957) suggest are common among delinquents; these involve:

1. "denials of responsibility" (for example, blaming a bad background)
2. "denials of the victim" (for example, claiming that the victim had it coming)

3. "denials of injury" (for example, recasting vandalism as "mischief" or theft as "borrowing")

4. "condemnations of the condemners" (for example, calling their condemnation discriminatory)

5. "appeals to higher loyalties" (for example, citing loyalty to friends or family as the cause of the behavior)

Sykes and Matza suggest that this kind of thinking causes delinquency among disadvantaged youths in the same way that verbalizations and rationalizations cause crime more generally, regardless of age and class position. However, it is still the case that disadvantaged youths are more likely to get caught and punished for their misbehaviors, an issue that is of more recent theoretical concern in a variant of the symbolic interactionist tradition called **labeling theory**.

Labeling Theory

An early form of a labeling theory of delinquency and crime is found in the work of Franklin Tannenbaum (1938). Tannenbaum was struck by the normalcy of much delinquency. He noted that many forms of juvenile delinquency are a common part of adolescent street life—aspects of the play, adventure, and excitement that many later identify nostalgically as an important part of their youth. The problem is that others often do not view these activities in the same way, but rather as a nuisance or threat, and this can lead to summoning the police.

Police intervention can begin a process of change in the way individuals and their behaviors are perceived by others, and ultimately by the individual himself or herself. Tannenbaum suggests that this begins with a gradual shift from the definition of specific acts as evil to a more general definition of the individual involved. The first contact with authorities is a crucial part of this process, because it can constitute a "dramatization of evil" that separates the child or adolescent from peers for specialized treatment. Tannenbaum worries that this "dramatization" can play a greater role in creating the criminal than any other experience. Individuals so signified may begin to think of themselves as the types of people who do evil things—for example, as delinquents. Note that this turns the conventional idea of deterrence on its head by asserting that legal sanctions associated with the police and courts create more problems than they solve. Tannenbaum had a solution of his own, arguing that "The way out is through a refusal to dramatize the evil" (20). He suggested that the less said and done the better.

Labeling theorists have expanded on Tannenbaum's notion of the dramatization of evil, for example, by suggesting concepts to distinguish between those acts that occur before and after the societal response to deviance. Lemert (1951; 1967) does this, using the terms *primary* and *secondary deviance*. **Primary deviance** refers to the initial acts of individuals that call out the societal response, while **secondary deviance** refers to the ensuing problems that arise from the societal response to the initial acts. The primary acts may occur at random or they may be the product of a diversity of initial causal factors. The key point is that these initial acts are thought to have little impact on the individual's self-concept. That is, "primary deviation . . . has only marginal implications for the psychic structure of the individual. . . ." (1967:17).

However, secondary deviance is much more consequential. The dramatization of evil that can signal the onset of secondary deviance can also lead to a traumatization of self-concept, ". . . altering the psychic structure, producing a specialized organization of social roles and self-regarding attitudes" (Lemert, 1967:40–41). Even more significantly, however, Lemert suggests that secondary deviance can bring with it a stabilization of the deviant behavior pattern involved.

> Objective evidences of this change will be found in the symbolic appurtenances of the new role, in clothes, speech, posture and mannerisms, which in some cases heighten social visibility, and which in some cases serve as symbolic cues to professionalization. (1951:76)

Again, as in Tannenbaum's analysis, the implication is that simply "leaving things be" might often be the better course of action.

The effect of not letting things be is to create *Outsiders*, as expressed in the title of two classic books, one a scholarly analysis by Becker (1963) and the other a fictional treatment of adolescence and delinquency by S. E. Hinton (1967). Becker emphasizes that there is a political dimension to the creation of such groups, and that ". . . the rule-breaker may feel his judges are outsiders" (2). This political process is social in that, ". . . groups create deviance, by making the rules whose infraction constitutes deviance, and by applying those rules to particular people and labeling them as outsiders" (9). There is a crucial distinction drawn within this framing of the problem between rule-breaking *behavior* on the one hand, and the disreputable *status* of being called a deviant on the other.

This distinction parallels a more common division often drawn in sociology between *achieved* and *ascribed* characteristics. Achieved characteristics are usually thought of as earned, while ascribed characteristics are typically thought of as inherited or imposed. As used here, behaviors would usually be regarded as achieved, while statuses would more often be treated as ascribed. To clarify this distinction in the study of crime and disrepute, Becker suggests that ". . . it might be worthwhile to refer to such behavior as *rule-breaking behavior* and reserve the term *deviant* for those labeled as deviant by some segment of society" (14). However, the bigger question is in some ways, "who makes the rules?" Becker's early answer to this question, "those groups whose social position gives them weapons and power. . . ." (18), anticipated the conflict theories we consider next. However, his more pressing concern is with consequences for the careers of individuals after the imposition of criminal and disreputable labels.

Becker draws from the sociological study of occupations to suggest that while the concept of "career" usually is used to distinguish success in conventional work, "it can also be used to distinguish several varieties of career outcomes, ignoring the question of 'success'" (1963:24). An analogy is then drawn with more typical occupational careers that involves a sequence of movements from one position to another. "Career contingencies" are the crucial determinants of when and how these movements take place, with a key contingency in deviant careers being whether a disreputable label is imposed. Becker writes that "one of the most crucial steps in the process of building a stable pattern of deviant behavior is likely to be the experience of being caught and publicly labeled as deviant" (31). Labeling theorists more generally assert that the imposition of a disreputable label sets in motion a process in which the individual's self-concept is stigmatized (Goffman, 1961; 1963) or degraded (Garfinkel, 1956) and she or he becomes what others expect. Becker concludes that the labeling process is a self-fulfilling prophecy that ". . . sets in motion several mechanisms which conspire to shape the person in the image that people have of him" (1963:34).

Overview of the Interactionist Theories

The symbolic interactionist theories broaden the focus of the study of crime and disrepute from the functionalist concern with values to include consideration of the ways social meanings and definitions help to produce criminal and deviant behavior in a wide variety of settings. Over time the attention of this set of theories more generally shifted from how meanings and definitions are cultivated by individuals and within groups to the ways in which meanings and definitions are imposed by members and agents of other groups on individuals within groups that become official outsiders.

Although the attention of interactionist theories to issues of meaning and definition is central to the sociological study of crime and disrepute, work within this tradition has not yet developed a longitudinal understanding that fully exploits the potential of the career analogy. Nor have the interactionist theories fully and effectively linked the understanding of deviant careers to the structural contexts from which they emerge, especially those of minority and low income communities that are a focus of contemporary concerns. Nonetheless, the focus on meaning, the alertness to convergence across classes, the attention to labeling processes, and the career analogy are all unique and important, as shown in the following "Vocational Meaning of Crime" case study demonstrating the application of interactionist ideas.

CASE STUDY

Symbolic Interactionist Theory: The Vocational Meaning of Crime

The interactionist theme of convergence between crime and convention is expressed in the title of Peter Letkemann's (1973) book, *Crime as Work*. Letkemann further develops interactionist assumptions by arguing that we should understand crime in terms of the meanings and definitions that the persons who engage in this activity attach to it, rather than simply rely on the statutory labels found in the criminal code and applied by those who attempt to control crime. To develop this "inside" view of the criminal enterprise, Letkemann conducted in-depth interviews with a Canadian sample of skilled and experienced property offenders.

These interviews reveal that criminal code labels can be misleading. For example, a number of the subjects in Letkemann's sample thought of themselves as safecrackers, but this term was not found in their conviction records. These offenders instead were convicted of breaking and entering.

Letkemann found that his sample of skilled and experienced subjects defined their activities and those of their colleagues in terms of several important distinctions. The first of these distinctions involved an emphasis on having a reputation of consistency and reliability among peers. Sutherland in earlier work (1937) referred to members of this group as "professional thieves"—the point being that these individuals sometimes hold and apply work standards that parallel those in more orthodox occupations.

The comparison group in Letkemann's analysis, who are considered but not interviewed, are referred to as "alkies," "dope fiends," and "normals." These offenders combine alcohol and drug use with minor theft, and they are more dedicated to their chosen chemicals than to a criminal craft. Rather than being an "end in itself," property crime is a "means to an end" for these offenders, and they are therefore regarded as less reliable partners in criminal undertakings.

Letkemann's respondents also distinguished between "amateur" and "experienced" criminals. The former were preoccupied with detection, while the latter recognized that their technical skills were readily identifiable and were more concerned about leaving evidence that could lead to conviction. Of course, the skills of the latter group involved specialization, and these respondents spoke of "having a line" that consisted of a generalized work preference and a related repertoire of skills.

Consistent with the aphorism that "prisons are schools of crime," Letkemann found that doing time, especially in selected settings with seasoned specialists, served as a prerequisite to status among these offenders. [A professional safecracker remarked in a related study that he spent time in prison periodically in place of paying taxes (Chambliss, 1972)]. The irony is, as anticipated by labeling theory, that official sanctions can actually increase notoriety and proficiency in the behaviors they seek to extinguish.

Two paths of specialization status are identified among this sample of property offenders involving "surreptitious" and "overt" forms of crime. The surreptitious crimes include burglary generally, and safecracking more specifically. Victim avoidance is a key skill involved in these crimes. Safecrackers must learn techniques for attaining unobserved access to sites with safes. Further technical skills must be acquired in the use of explosives to open the safes. In contrast, the overt crime of bank robbery requires the development of a more social set of skills. Bank robbers confront rather than avoid their victims. It is often thought that such confrontations require no skill because the offender is armed. However, Letkemann argues that the skill involved is in avoiding use of a weapon and the risks that this provokes. The tragically violent film *Reservoir Dogs* and the Woody Allen comedy *Take the Money and Run* illustrate in very different ways the point that social and planning skills are involved in safely bringing off a robbery.

It is debatable how skilled most safecrackers and bank robbers are, and how representative these skills might be of those held by criminals more generally. These points are developed further in the following chapter. Meanwhile, the more basic point of this interactionist account is that some criminals share characteristics with more conventional workers, including continuity in behavior, the development of basic skills, and experience in their respective specializations. This encourages the notion that careers in crime can be studied in ways that parallel other lines of work, for example, in terms of the meanings and definitions that offenders and others attach to sustained involvements in crime, and in terms of the ways career contingencies, such as getting caught, can affect later life outcomes. Meanwhile, Letkemann is certainly correct that, "The model of a criminal as one who takes a craftsman's pride in . . . work, and who applies . . . skills in the most profitable way . . . possible, is very different from the model of the criminal as one who gets kicks out of beating the system and doing evil."

Conflict Theories of Crime and Disrepute

The **conflict theories** pick up where the labeling theories leave off, often focusing on the role of dominant societal groups in imposing legal labels on members of subordinate societal groups. Conflict theories try to explain how and why this happens, focusing on differences of power and wealth in society. In doing so, attention is focused more on the groups imposing criminal labels than on the individuals who receive them.

Group Conflict Theory

There is a link between conflict theory and subcultural as well as labeling theory. The link is that subcultural groups typically are also subordinate groups, and this makes their activities liable to the legal interventions of dominant groups who oppose them and the values they represent. George Vold (1958) recognized this point and focused his early **group conflict theory** of crime on the role of dominant groups in imposing their value judgments by defining the behaviors of others as criminal. So where the functionalist theories assumed a basic value consensus in society, the conflict theories focus on value conflict between opposing groups.

Vold set the perspective of his theory by referring to crime and delinquency as "minority group" behaviors. He applied this argument first to delinquency, asserting that "the juvenile gang . . . is nearly always a 'minority group' out of sympathy with and in more or less direct opposition to the rules and regulations of the dominant majority, that is, the established world of adult values and powers" (211). The police are seen as protecting adult values in struggles against adolescents who seek symbolic and material advantages not permitted to them under the adult code. Vold argues that this is an intergenerational conflict of values in which adults prevail through their control over the legal process.

Vold analyzes four other types of crime from this group conflict perspective.

1. The first involves the kinds of political movements witnessed in recent years in Eastern Europe. He notes that the irony of such events is that "a successful revolution makes criminals out of the government officials previously in power, and an unsuccessful revolution makes its leaders into traitors. . . ." (214). Examples of this point include the contrasting fates in post–World War II Czechoslovakia of Alexander Dubcek, who was exiled to a low-level bureaucratic job in a remote setting for his earlier failed attempts to resist Russian domination through democratization, and Vaclav Havel, who was later elected president after being released from prison.

2. Clashes between business and labor interests during strikes and lockouts constitute a second type of crime considered by Vold. Here he notes that ". . . the participants on either side of a labor dispute condone whatever criminal behavior is deemed 'necessary' for the maintenance of their side of the struggle" (216). The experiences of the late labor leader Cesar Chavez on behalf of migrant farm workers illustrate this point. Chavez experienced periods of both criminal condemnation and cultural celebration for his efforts to improve the lives of migrant laborers through unionization and strikes.

3. Conflicts within and between competing unions are a third type of crime included within Vold's theory. Vold writes that "such disputes often involve intimidation and personal violence, and sometimes they become entangled with the 'rackets' and gang wars of the criminal underworld" (217). Political and legal aspects of these conflicts were vividly documented in government efforts led by Robert Kennedy to expose illegal activities of the Teamsters Union.

4. The last type of crime considered by Vold involves racial and ethnic conflict. Vold observes that "numerous kinds of crimes result from

the clashes incidental to attempts to change, or to upset the caste system of racial segregation in various parts of the world . . ." (217). These crimes can be violent as well as political, as in the continuing bloodshed coincident with the rise and fall of South Africa's racial apartheid, symbolized in the life of Nelson Mandela, and in many episodes of the ongoing fight for civil rights by African Americans, symbolized through the lives of Martin Luther King, Jr., and Malcolm X. Spike Lee's film biography *Malcolm X* portrays a re- markable life experience of crime that moved from the personal to the political and back again, culminating for many with Malcolm's proclamation in the context of the U.S. mistreatment of African Americans that "violence is intelligence."

Vold did not intend that his theory should explain all crimes, advis- ing instead that ". . . the group-conflict hypothesis should not be stretched too far" (219). He did, however, speculate that his theory was relevant to a "considerable amount of crime," and subsequent work has advanced this speculation.

Theories of Crime, Law, and Order

Austin Turk (1969) presents a propositional statement of conflict theory in his book *Crime and the Legal Order*. Turk treats criminality as a status that is conferred by others, so that ". . . criminality is not a biological, psychological, or even behavioral phenomenon, but a social status de- fined by the way in which an individual is perceived, evaluated, and treated by legal authorities" (25). It is critical to know, then, who does the defining. Two groups are involved: "There are those . . . who consti- tute the dominant, decision-making category—the authorities—and those who make up the subordinate category who are affected by but scarcely affect law—the subjects" (33). Criminals are regarded as the sub- jects of lawmaking by authorities.

An innovative aspect of Turk's theory involves a learning process through which the power of authorities is imposed. He writes that ". . . both eventual authorities and eventual subjects learn and continually re- learn to interact with one another as, respectively, occupants of superior and inferior statuses and performers of dominating and submitting roles" (41–42). The result is that authorities learn "social roles of domina- tion," while subjects learn "social norms of deference." However, there is never complete agreement on the lessons to be learned, and subsequent disagreements become conflicts that are interpreted as challenges to authority. From this perspective, ". . . **lawbreaking** is . . . an indicator of the failure or lack of authority: it is a measure of the extent to which rulers and rules . . . are not bound together in a perfectly stable authority relationship" (48). Turk's theory is systematic and propositional in making explicit the conditions in which this conflict is expected to become most intense, thus specifying the situations in which crime rates are expected to be highest. The relative power of the persons involved is a central consideration. Turk reasons that those who are poor and nonwhite have the least power and therefore are expected to have the highest rates of criminalization.

A related theory of law, order, and power is proposed by Chambliss and Seidman (1971), who take a conflict theory of crime to a societal level of analysis. They suggest that societies low in specialization and stratification tend to resolve disputes through compromise and reconciliation that involves relative consensus. However, as societies become more complex and intensively stratified, a "winner takes all" rule-enforcement approach comes to replace reconciliation as a means of dispute resolution. The selection of which rules are to be enforced and against whom becomes crucial. Chambliss and Seidman point out that bureaucratically structured agencies become the focal point in making these decisions in advanced stratified societies. They argue that, in these settings, "rule creation and rule enforcement will take place when such creation or enforcement increases the rewards for the agencies and their officials, and they will not take place when they are conducive to organizational strain" (474). The implication is that the guiding principle of legal bureaucracy is to maximize organizational gains, while minimizing organizational strains.

This principle leads to what Chambliss and Seidman call a *rule of law*: "the rule is that discretion at every level . . . will be so exercised as to bring mainly those who are politically powerless (that is, the poor) into the purview of the law" (268). Chambliss and Seidman reason that this is because the poor are least likely to have the resources to create organizational strains that provide protection against prosecution. This makes it probable that ". . . those laws which prohibit certain types of behavior popular among lower-class persons are more likely to be enforced" (475). The implication is that the poor and minorities form a large component of our official crime statistics, more because of class bias in our society and the dynamics of our legal bureaucracy than because of differences in behavior.

A Social Realist Theory of Crime

Quinney's (1970) **social realist theory** integrates the formulation and application of criminal definitions with the occurrence of criminal behavior. Several sources of criminal behavior are identified, including (1) structured opportunities, (2) learning experiences, (3) interpersonal associations and identifications, and (4) self-conceptions. The key assumption that links behaviors with definitions in this theory is that "persons in the segments of society whose behavior patterns are not represented in formulating and applying criminal definitions are more likely to act in ways that will be defined as criminal than those in the segments that formulate and apply criminal definitions" (21). This involves the first two elements of the theory, opportunities and learning, in a process through which the better off in society are involved in criminalizing behavior patterns that are learned, often in response to differential opportunities, by those who are less well off.

For Quinney, the key to this process involves *conceptions* of crime held by powerful segments of society. These conceptions are portrayed in personal and mass communications that articulate powerful elite definitions of the "crime problem," which in turn become real in their consequences. This is "the social reality of crime," and it takes effect in the following way:

> In general . . . the more the power segments are concerned about crime, the greater the probability that criminal definitions will be created and that behavior patterns will develop in opposition to criminal definitions. The formulation and application of criminal definitions and the development of behavior patterns related to criminal definitions are thus joined in full circle by the construction of criminal conceptions. (23)

This is a broadly integrative theory that brings together the key ideas of labeling and conflict theory with those of opportunity, differential association and learning theories of crime. An overview of this theory is presented in Figure 2.1.

Marxian Theories

A final group of conflict theories incorporate Marxian ideas, which have captured the attention of sociological criminologists at several junctures in this century (Bonger, 1916; Rusche and Kirchheimer, 1939; Greenberg, 1981). A group of English criminologists in the 1970s, Taylor, Walton and Young (1973), joined this tradition by calling for a *New Criminology*. This school of thought sees the criminal law as the product of an alliance be-

FIGURE 2.1

Model of the social reality of crime. *(Reprinted with permission of Little, Brown and Co. Source: Quinney, 1970:24)*

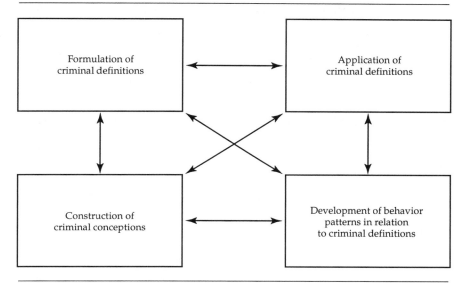

tween business interests and the state. They argue that this alliance is grounded in "an ethic of individualism" which holds *individuals* responsible for their acts, while at the same time diverting attention from the *environmental* structures from which these acts emerge. They argue that this ethic restrains only the disadvantaged classes because it is the "labour forces of the industrial society" that are bound by this ethic through the criminal law and its sanctions. In contrast, "the state and the owners of labour will be bound only by a civil law which regulates their competition between each other" (264). The effective result is a double standard of citizenship and responsibility in which the more advantaged are "beyond incrimination" and therefore criminal sanction as well (see Swigert and Farrell, 1980).

A further application of Marxian ideas in the study of crime and disrepute is provided by Spitzer (1975). Spitzer's theory is premised on the assumption that we give attention to criminal behavior as well as to its disreputable status. He reasons that "we must not only ask why specific members of the underclass are selected for official processing, but also why they behave as they do" (see also Colvin and Pauly, 1983). Spitzer locates a Marxian answer to this question by focusing on historical and structural characteristics of late modern capitalism. He argues that "problem populations" are produced when, because of their behaviors, personal qualities, and positions, groups of individuals threaten the "social relations of production."

These threats disturb, hinder, or call into question crucial components and concepts of capitalist society, which include:

1. modes of appropriating the product of human labor (for example, when the poor "steal" from the rich)
2. conditions under which production takes place (for example, those who refuse or are unable to perform wage labor)
3. patterns of distribution and consumption (for example, those who use drugs for escape and transcendence)
4. socialization processes (for example, youths who refuse to be schooled)
5. supporting and sustaining ideologies (for example, proponents of gay and lesbian lifestyles)

These threats are linked to two sources. The first involves contradictions in the production sphere of society and includes the "surplus population" of the unemployed. The second involves disturbances in class rule that result, for example, from critical attitudes that are said to develop in educational institutions that produce school dropouts and student radicals.

Two broadly defined problem populations result. The first is referred to as *social junk*, which from the perspective of the dominant class may be seen as a costly but nonetheless relatively harmless burden to society. Examples of this category include the dispossessed and the homeless, who may also be aged, disabled, and physically or mentally challenged, as well as sometimes involved with alcohol and drugs. In contrast is Spitzer's second category characterized as *social dynamite*. The uniquely more dangerous feature of this grouping is "its potential actively to call into question established relationships, especially relations of production and domination" (645). This second group tends, according to Spitzer, to be more youthful, alienated, and politically volatile than social junk. However, social junk may also be transformed in some political circumstances into social dynamite, and vice versa. We see this point in our illustration of the application of the conflict theories to explain the pattern of official responses to ghetto riots in the "Conflict Theory" case study on page 55.

Conflict Theory: Ghetto Revolts and the Courts

Spitzer's (1975) concept of social dynamite is exemplified in the 1992 riots that followed the acquittal of Los Angeles police officers accused of beating Rodney King and in the ghetto riots of the 1960s, including the 1965 Watts revolt, the 1967 Detroit rebellion, and the 1968 Chicago riot. These riots posed major challenges to law enforcement authorities that were analyzed from a conflict perspective by Isaac Balbus (1973). Balbus found court authorities in each of the cities conscious of their role in assisting political elites in stopping the "fires in the streets" that had engulfed their cities. Their first concern was to reestablish *order*.

Yet this concern to impose order did not operate alone or without check. Legal procedures were also under close scrutiny during this period, so that a semblance of *formal rationality* also had to be preserved. Considerations of *organizational maintenance* also operated, in that the riots placed heavy pressures of sheer volume on the courts of each city. Balbus argues that these shared concerns about order, formal rationality, and organizational maintenance affected the courts of the three cities in parallel ways, resulting in a similar sequence in the patterned responses of authorities across the cities. This sequence conditioned the fairness of the treatment offenders received.

The beginning phase in each city involved an urgent concern with order that outweighed attention to formal rationality and organizational maintenance. Serious and widespread abrogations of standard procedures characterized the processes of arrest, charging, and bail-setting. For example, judges indiscriminately implemented preventive detention policies by imposing excessively high bail requirements. The intent was to "clear the streets" and keep them clear for the duration of the revolts. However, even here standards of justice were not completely abandoned, and some formal rationality prevailed during this period. Balbus describes the legal response this way: "Although the police and military response was often brutal and led to considerable destruction of life, there was no wholesale slaughter of riot participants. Martial law was *not* declared, and *some* concern for the legality of arrests was exhibited" (234). Balbus explains that a level of legality was preserved, if only out of the desire to formally treat the ghetto rebellion as involving "ordinary crimes" rather than as distinctively different acts of political protest and rebellion.

Meanwhile, although during the revolt the priority was to prosecute virtually all those arrested and to do so on serious charges, in the weeks and months that followed the revolts concerns about formal rationality and organizational maintenance produced convictions on less serious charges and lenient sentences. Balbus notes that this pattern reverses the more typical tendency for dismissal and leniency to decrease with movement through the criminal justice system. He observes that

> . . . we found . . . a striking reversal of the standard model of the criminal process which posits a series of screens whose holes progressively diminish in size and from which the defendants thus find it increasingly difficult to escape; following the Los Angeles and Detroit major revolts, in contrast, the "holes" became progressively larger, and it was much easier to "escape" at the preliminary hearing and trial stages than it was at the earlier prosecution stage.

Balbus argues that it could not have been otherwise. The justice system needed to help authorities put down the riots by providing swift and harsh treatment at the outset of the disturbances, but as time passed the requirements of formal rationality made it difficult to sustain this severe treatment in open court settings or in the face of an overcrowded justice system whose simple maintenance required a reduction in case volume. This application of conflict theory accords a measured "autonomy" to the state in resisting an inclination toward a more pervasive expression of class bias.

Overview of the Conflict Theories

Conflict theories are important in explaining why some forms of social deviance are selectively treated as criminal. A fundamental insight from conflict theory is that activities common among the socially and economically disadvantaged are more likely to be designated criminal than are activities more common among the powerful. Nonetheless, Vold's advice that the conflict hypothesis "not be taken too far" anticipates much of the modern criticism of this group of theories. Vold's advice reiterates the distinction drawn in Chapter 1 between consensus and conflict crimes. This distinction acknowledges that most people, most of the time, across several centuries, and in most nations, rather consistently have called *some* behaviors criminal. Conflict theories have sometimes been understood as dismissing this social fact and as correspondingly discounting the significance of explaining these behaviors. Some recognition of this point is found in the "left realist" strain of the conflict tradition (Young and Matthews, 1992).

It is in part for this reason that Austin Turk (1976) explicitly asserts that "conflict-coercion theory does not imply that most accused persons are innocent, nor that more and less powerful people engage in conventional deviations to the same extent. It does not even imply that legal officials . . . discriminate against less powerful and on behalf of more powerful people" (292). Rather, Turk expresses the view of an increasing number of conflict theorists that there *are* class-linked differences in criminal behavior patterns and that authorities *vary* in their treatment of minority and class groupings across different kinds of social circumstances. It is the attention these theories give to structured inequalities of wealth and power in explaining these patterns that make their contributions important (see Zatz and Chambliss, 1993).

The Classical Theories

Three classical traditions of sociological theory—structural functionalism, symbolic interactionism, and conflict theory—are well represented in sociological criminology. Each tradition makes a distinctive contribution. Structural functionalism emphasizes that the presence of success goals and values without the means to attain them can produce delinquent and criminal behavior, as can the absence of these goals or values in the first place. Symbolic interactionism alerts us to the role of group-enhanced and imposed meanings and definitions in the production of delinquency and crime. The conflict theories further focus our attention on the role of dominant societal groups in imposing legal labels on members of subordinate societal groups. Yet, these theories are inadequate and often outdated.

We noted weaknesses in each of the classical traditions. For example, the structural functionalist theories too often have abandoned their distinctive early attention to macro or group-level processes that generate crime. The potential of the career analogy that is so central to the symbolic interactionist tradition is not yet fully developed or clearly connected to the minority and low-income community contexts in which criminal careers are today most heavily concentrated. The conflict theories too frequently have deflected attention from the explanation of criminal behavior.

Sociological criminology is the beneficiary of a rich tradition of theoretical diversity that has stimulated much research. However, this tradition does not sufficiently acknowledge changes in the national and world economy or effectively confront the fast-changing reality of America's problems of poverty and crime. As well, the classical tradition of sociological criminology gives too little attention to racial and ethnic differences that distinctively pattern criminal behavior in America. The classical theories can contribute to a new understanding of these issues, but to do so these theories must be placed in the changing contemporary contexts that are the focus of the following chapter.

3

A New Sociology of Crime and Disrepute

Crime, Change, and the Classical Theories

Sociological criminology is currently undergoing a transformation linked to societal changes that have outpaced the development of the classical theories. For example, we live in a world of increased technology, trade, and competition, organized in a global economy that was not imagined even two or three decades ago. This is a world economy in which capital investment and labor demands shift quickly, and where jobs often change and are lost faster than neighborhoods, cities, and countries, not to mention individuals, can effectively respond. Our crime problems are influenced by these events.

Gender and domestic relations also have changed enormously. Women are participating in labor markets at dramatically increased levels with associated changes in the formation and reformation of family structures and relationships. These changes have brought economic opportunities for many women, for example, through increased representation in nontraditional occupations and professions. However, a growing number of impoverished single parent female-headed households also reflects an increased economic marginality and vulnerability of many women and their children. Crime is further influenced by these changes.

Tax and welfare policies also have changed remarkably in most if not all advanced capitalist countries. Tax revolts and reductions of welfare supports are common. These have combined with changes in the economy to increase levels of social, and more specifically, racial inequality. These inequalities are linked in the United States to pervasive patterns of residential segregation and to intense concentrations of poverty that have increased the distress of low-income communities and their crime problems.

These changes affect the contours of many of the social problems of our society, but the classical sociological theories of crime and disrepute predate these changes and remain largely unaltered. Much research still focuses on competitive tests that seek to establish which variations within and between the classical theoretical traditions might best account for crime and disrepute. These tests are useful in clarifying distinctive assumptions and strengths as well as weaknesses of the classical theories. However, the social changes noted here signal a new era and a new role for sociological theory and research. In this new era, the leading edge of research no longer consists of clashes within and between the classical sociological theories, but rather between a new sociology of crime and disrepute and a prevailing economic perspective and connected political philosophy that dominate the formation of American social policy.

Perspectives on Inequality

Before introducing the new sociology of crime and disrepute, we first introduce the more entrenched and economically grounded political philosophy with which the new sociological approach often conflicts. This mode of thought is focused on presumed connections between inequality, individualism, and efficiency. It urges that social inequality encourages individual initiative, and therefore is necessary for economic efficiency, or in other words, economic progress and success. Although this view has had sociological adherents in the past, especially within early functionalist sociology (Davis and Moore, 1945), it is more firmly rooted in popularized versions of noninterventionist laissez-faire economics and conservative moral and political philosophy.

The latter thoughtways differ most notably from modern sociology in their inclination to preserve inequalities. When these thoughtways urge that social inequality acts as a motivating force that rewards individuals for life choices that lead to efficient, productive, economic outcomes, little consideration is given to *how much* social inequality might be needed. This encourages a blanket assumption that most or all efforts to reduce social inequality dampen individual initiative and produce inefficient, unsuccessful economic results (for example, see Okun, 1975). Investments in reducing social inequality are thought to be not just costly but, more significantly, wasteful, because they are presumed unproductive if not counterproductive. This firmly rooted skepticism about efforts to reduce social inequality plays a central role in justifying social policies that divert investment from declining communities and disadvantaged individuals.

A contrasting argument is often expressed implicitly if not explicitly in the new sociology of crime and disrepute. This argument is that investment in expanded social as well as economic opportunities can provide a foundation for broadened participation of citizens in the production of economic wealth and the reduction of social costs. The latter costs notably include crime and related forms of social disrepute that impede economic growth and social well-being more generally.

It is essential to emphasize that the alternative economic and political emphasis on individual responsibility, social inequality, and efficiency is not important simply because it contradicts the views of many sociologists, but the more so because it propels government policies concerning inequality and crime. In place of policy interventions that include programs of redistributive government investment, this approach relies more heavily on the discipline and incentives of largely unregulated economic forces, reinforced by severe criminal sanctions, which are a focus of attention in the final chapter of this book. The sociology of crime and disrepute is responding to the challenge of this kind of political and policy orientation in new ways and with a renewed sense of purpose.

First, the new sociological approach is becoming more synthetic. The renewed and more encompassing sociological concern with inequality that is central to this enterprise is restraining theoretical factionalism in relation to other issues. Several ideas introduced later—including the concepts of social and cultural capital and capital disinvestment and recapitalization—help to synthesize this recent work. Second, sociological research methods are becoming more diverse and interconnected, so that, for example, recent research more consistently and coherently links unofficial and official crime data gathered through field as well as survey and archival methods. We draw extensively on ethnographic field research as well as quantitative studies to make this point. Third, sociological analyses of crime and disrepute are becoming more fluid and flexible in moving between questions about individuals and groups, and between issues of criminal behavior and responses to it. In this chapter we emphasize community- and individual-level studies that focus on criminal behavior as well as its control.

More generally, a new sociology of crime and disrepute is becoming more synthetic in consolidating its insights, and less parochial in dwelling on its internal differences. These insights tell us much about the inefficiencies of crime and the costs of inequality. Before turning to this new sociology of crime and disrepute, however, it is important to consider the changing context of inequality, concerns about efficiency, and the connected philosophy of individualism. We then introduce the social and economic concepts that provide a crucial backdrop for a new sociology of crime and disrepute.

Equality, Efficiency, and Individualism

No one can question that the last half century has brought extraordinary social and economic change. However, there is reason to question assumptions made about the relationship between equality and efficiency during this period. Smoothing over the most extreme periods of recession and rapid growth of the past four or five decades, the last half-century can be divided more generally into a "golden age" that roughly covers the third quarter of this century, and a period of economic slowdown that has followed during the last quarter of this century (Glynn and Miliband, 1994).

The Golden Age

Lasting from about 1954 to 1974, the Golden Age was a post–World War II boom that produced economic growth of about 5 percent per year in the advanced capitalist countries (Margolin and Schor, 1990). The gross domestic product per worker, a common measure of labor productivity or efficiency, surged forward during this period, forming a foundation for this trajectory of growth. The economic perspective outlined previously should therefore predict that social and economic inequality also increased. However, income inequality declined during the Golden Age, especially in the United States, Japan, Sweden, and France. This was reflected in several ways. Women increased their participation in the labor forces of the advanced capitalist economies, unemployment remained relatively low in North America and dropped substantially in a number of European countries previously devastated by World War II, and there was a general expansion of health care and education programs. So overall this period of unique economic prosperity was accompanied by declining inequality. This was reflected in the openness of social mobility observed in Blau and Duncan's (1967) classic study, *The American Occupational Structure*.

The Economic Slowdown

However, the last quarter of this century, from about 1974, brought a period in which economic growth decreased by almost half, to levels that (with significant peaks and troughs removed) averaged about 2½ percent per year. The economic perspective outlined previously should therefore predict that social and economic inequality also declined. Instead inequality now increased. The increase in inequality began in the early 1970s in the United States, when unemployment and income in-

FIGURE 3.1

Wage dispersion across the past half-century: difference in the log wage at the ninetieth and tenth percentiles, 1940–1985. (*Source:* Goldin and Margo, 1992:4)

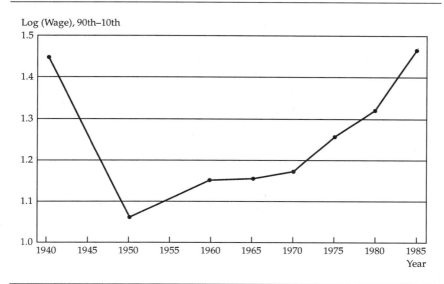

equality began to grow markedly. This is reflected in a graph of the fall and then rise of U.S. income inequality over the approximate last half-century in Figure 3.1. Inequality in earnings increased most dramatically in the United States in the 1980s, but this pattern is observed in other countries where these trends have been studied as well. Reductions in gender inequality also slowed during the 1980s. In general, the poorest women and men suffered the most in this process, experiencing actual declines in real income during the 1980s in Great Britain and the United States (see Glyn and Miliband, 1994). The biggest losses were in the area of manufacturing jobs and among those who stayed or became newly employed in service sector jobs with lower pay and fewer benefits.

During this period when many industries shed jobs quickly, productivity sometimes showed short-term improvement, shareholder profits sometimes increased, and the very wealthy often became more so. However, this often was accomplished through the liquidation of assets, the leverage of debt, and the relocation of work into lower-wage domestic and foreign labor markets where existing production levels were maintained with fewer and/or more poorly paid employees. Major expansions of output did not follow, and these short-term productivity gains usually could not be converted into sustainable economic growth. In particular, the increased inequality did not produce the expected transformation of economic performance.

Some Implications

This experience in part led the World Bank to question the assumed relationship in developing countries between inequality and efficiency, observing that "there is no evidence that . . . income inequality leads to higher growth. If anything, it seems that inequality is associated with slower growth" (1991:137). Glynn and Miliband (1994) extend this lesson to the advanced capitalist countries, concluding that "the general case that increasing inequality improves growth prospects receives no empirical support from the data." This conclusion is supported by findings summarized in Figure 3.2, indicating that countries like the United States, with the most unequal income distribution at the beginning of the

FIGURE 3.2

Inequality and productivity, 1979–1990. *(Glyn, 1992:93)*

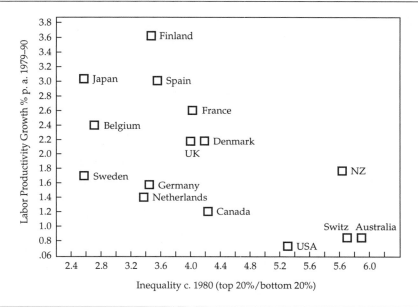

1980s, experienced slower productivity growth during the following decade than did countries like Japan, where incomes have been more evenly distributed. So the assumed relationship between inequality and efficiency, or equality and inefficiency, is not supported by the experience of the last half-century in the advanced capitalist economies.

However, even though the empirical linkage between inequality and efficiency may be doubtful, the connection between these concepts and notions of individual responsibility continues to be strongly held and expressed. This linkage often holds individuals responsible for their social and economic fates, as when social problems such as unemployment are understood as personal problems and responsibilities of the individuals involved. The strength of this connection in the way we think about social and economic life can be traced to the extraordinary impact of the classical economic theorists such as Adam Smith and seventeenth- and eighteenth-century political philosophers of natural rights (Coleman, 1990:301). Yet, it is more often changes in our economy that have altered the prospects of individuals over the past half-century than something for which individuals could be held responsible.

The Dual Economy

An important insight into these changes involves a distinction increasingly drawn between two kinds of jobs in a "dual economy" with "split" or "segmented labor markets" (for example, Averitt, 1968; Hodson and Kaufman, 1982; Baron and Bielby, 1980). These two kinds of jobs are found in a "core or primary labor market" that consists of better-paying and more secure jobs, and a "periphery or secondary labor market" in which wages and job security are much reduced. Core sector jobs classically have been concentrated in the unionized manufacturing sector and have involved the production of autos and aircraft, machinery, iron and steel, nonferrous metals, chemicals, rubber, petroleum, electronics, and other instruments.

During the Golden Age, core sector jobs expanded in number and quality, with a growing union movement often obtaining advances for workers in real wages and job security. However, several notable structural changes signaled a beginning of an end to this era in the late 1960s and early 1970s (Averitt, 1992). First, technological changes demanded a more highly educated labor force made up of increasingly skilled workers. Second, a sustained surge in the consumption of imported manufactured goods forced major changes in domestic production. The new skill requirements increased disparities in wages and employment prospects, while increased consumption of imports introduced foreign competition in wages and eventually in domestic employment itself through loss of core sector jobs. New employment did emerge, but it most often consisted of secondary sector service jobs (for example, the much noted burger flippers) at lower wages and with reduced benefits and security. Secure high-wage manufacturing jobs were permanently lost from the core sector of the domestic economy (Revenga, 1992).

Individuals, cities, states, nations, and geopolitical regions increasingly compete for manufacturing as well as other kinds of jobs in this swiftly changing world economy. It makes little sense to hold individuals so heavily accountable for the circumstances they confront as these changes continue to unfold: for example, as the end of the Cold War reduces the defense industry, as the Pacific Rim countries and the European Community expand their roles in their regional economies and their penetration of the global economy, and as important North American realignments occur through the opening of freer trade with Mexico and Canada. These are structural changes that to date have brought increasing inequality into the American economy and into the lives of individuals who often have little awareness or understanding of these events. A new sociology of crime and disrepute can advance our understanding of the connection of these structural changes to the lives of individuals, for example, through use of the concepts of social and cultural capital we introduce next.

Social and Cultural Capital

The French social theorist, Pierre Bourdieu (1986), uses a gambling metaphor to illustrate what our economic lives would be like if we did not each begin with an accumulation of capital that influences our individual life chances.

> Roulette, which holds out the opportunity of winning a lot of money in a short space of time, and therefore of changing one's social status quasi-instantaneously, and in which the winning of the previous spin of the wheel can be staked and lost at every new spin, gives a fairly accurate image of this imaginary universe of perfect competition or perfect equality of opportunity, a world without inertia, without accumulation, without heredity or acquired properties, in which every moment is perfectly independent of the previous one, every soldier has a marshal's baton in his knapsack, and every prize can be attained, instantaneously, by everyone, so that at each moment anyone can be anything. (241)

Needless to say, the world we inhabit is not simply a game of chance, and to the extent this metaphor has meaning, it might more accurately be represented by a craps game with loaded dice. We acquire at birth and accumulate through our lives unequal shares of capital that incrementally alter and determine our life chances. We acquire this capital through structural and cultural as well as genetic processes, as members of social groups as well as members of biological families. In the gambling metaphor, the game often is weighted, or tilted, in favor of some and against others.

Forms of Capital

The forms of capital require an introduction. The concept of **physical capital** is familiar as referring to tools, machinery, and other productive equipment. Physical capital is a foundation of economic relations. However, economists have added to this the further idea of **human capital**, which refers to the skills and knowledge acquired by individuals through education and training (Schultz, 1961; Becker, 1964). The capital that is embodied in humans is somewhat less tangible than that embodied in tools or machinery, but both involve the creation of resources or power through a transformative process, so that "just as physical capital is created by making changes in materials so as to form tools and facilitate production, human capital is created by changing persons so as to give them skills and capabilities that make them able to act in new ways" (Coleman, 1990:304). Human capital is most often created through education and training.

Social Capital

The creation of **social capital** involves analogous processes that are no less real and probably even more important, even though the product is less tangible than human or physical capital. The creation of social capital involves the creation of capabilities through socially structured relations between individuals in groups. Coleman (1990:305) uses Figure 3.3 to illustrate how the social capital of the family is used by parents to create the skills and capabilities that become the human capital of their children. The nodes represented by the capital letters in this figure constitute human capital, while the connecting lines or links constitute social capital. Coleman reasons that for parents B and C to further the cognitive development of child A, there must be capital in the nodes *and* the links of the diagram. That is, the human capital of parents B and C must be

FIGURE 3.3

Three-person structure: human capital in nodes and social capital
in relations. *(Source: Coleman, 1990:305)*

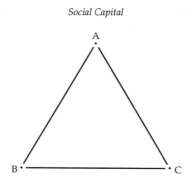

passed on to child A through the social capital represented in the social
structure of the connecting links between A and B, or between A and C,
and for overall maximum effect between A, B, and C. Coleman (1988;
1990) refers to the last of these possibilities as the *closure of social networks,*
and this can more generally refer, for example, to not only the functioning of intact nuclear and extended families but also to well-integrated
neighborhoods, communities, and even nation states. Social groups are
expected to make their maximum contributions to the development of
the various forms of capital when they have this characteristic of closure.

For example, what sometimes is described by social scientists and
philosophers as a loss of community in America is a reflection of an absence of closure in the creation of social capital that affects entire communities. This point is illustrated in Coleman's (1990) account of a
mother's decision to move her family halfway around the world to live
in a setting that provided a more protective form of social capital.

> A mother of six children, who moved with her husband and children from
> suburban Detroit to Jerusalem, describes as one reason for doing so the
> greater freedom her young children have in Jerusalem. She feels it is safe to
> let her eight-year-old take her six-year-old across town to school on the city
> bus and to let her children play without supervision in a city park, neither
> of which did she feel able to allow where she lived before. The reason for
> this difference can be described as a difference in the social capital available
> in Jerusalem and in suburban Detroit. In Jerusalem the normative structure
> ensures that unattended children will be looked after by adults in the

vicinity, but no such normative structure exists in most metropolitan areas of the United States. One can say that families in Jerusalem have available to them social capital that does not exist in metropolitan areas of the United States. (303)

Similarly, Coleman notes that "effective norms that inhibit crime in a city make it possible for women to walk freely outside at night and for old people to leave their homes without fear" (310). More generally, Cohen and Felson (1979) have documented how changes in the social organization of work and labor force participation have moved routine work activities farther from home and altered patterns of guardianship that are a form of social capital involved in the social control of crime.

The concept of social capital therefore draws a clear connection between community-level processes and the lives of individuals. It is important to emphasize, then, that social capital simultaneously involves investment in individuals and in larger social settings. Entire communities and countries, as well as the individuals within them, are locations of the accumulation of social capital. Of course, this is also true of physical and financial capital, which is accumulated by groups (for example, nation states) as well as individuals. Social capital refers to the aspects of structured groupings that increase their capacities for action oriented to the achievement of group and individual goals. Societal and community as well as individual investment is involved, as groups and individuals develop their resources in the pursuit of selected goals.

Cultural Capital

Meanwhile, groups and individuals must also adapt themselves to existing and continuing accumulations of capital that characterize the settings that they inherit and inhabit. Adaptations to these circumstances are expressed through various formations of **cultural capital**. When social capital is abundant in the community and family, these cultural adaptations may easily include the accumulation of the credentials of higher education and even involvements in high culture, for example, including participation in the arts and their supporting institutions, such as museums, the symphony, and the theater. In these community and family settings, social capital is used to successfully endow children with forms of cultural capital that significantly enhance their later life chances (see DiMaggio, 1982; 1987; DiMaggio and Mohr, 1985).

However, in less-advantaged community and family settings without such abundant social and cultural capital, parents are less able to endow or transmit such opportunities to their children. Survival itself is often a struggle, and children and families must adapt to the diminished circumstances and opportunities they encounter. So while many parents who are well situated within secure and supportive social networks may be destined or driven by their capital positions and connected inclinations to endow their children with forms of social and cultural capital that make success in school and later life quite likely, the children of less advantageously positioned and less-driven and controlling parents may more often drift or be driven into and along less-promising paths of social and cultural adaptation and capital formation (Hagan, 1991b).

These forms of adaptation and capital formation are sometimes subcultural in the sense that they involve the cultivation of attitudes and actions that diverge from, or are in actual opposition to, more routine and conforming societal norms and values. However, they are often also the only or best life choices available, and these adaptations can become powerful influences on later life outcomes (Hogan and Astone, 1986; Hagan and Wheaton, 1993). When these choices and adaptations are made within groups, they can gain added salience. Coleman (1990) notes the ironic reversal of purpose to which social capital can be put in this context when he notes that "any organization which makes possible such oppositional activities is an especially potent form of social capital for the individuals who are members of the organization" (303).

It is important to again emphasize that disadvantaging social and economic processes at the societal and community levels can make divergent and oppositional adaptations and formations of social and cultural capital common in particular settings. These settings typically are sites of what we will call **capital disinvestment**. Processes of capital disinvestment are destructive of conventional forms of social and cultural capital, and they often produce subcultural adaptations, which are in effect a form of **recapitalization**, an effort to reorganize what resources are available, even if illicit, to reach attainable goals. As noted earlier, disinvestment processes often are rationalized by dubious economic and political perspectives that causally connect social inequality with economic efficiency. Processes of capital disinvestment and recapitalization occupy a central place in the analytic framework for a new sociology of crime and disrepute.

Capital Disinvestment Processes

Three disinvestment processes that discourage societal and community level formations of conventional social capital involve **residential segre-**

gation, **race-linked inequality,** and **concentrations of poverty.** These processes overlap one another in America, but each is distinct enough to require its own introduction.

Residential Segregation

Despite declines in social inequality and the passage of the Fair Housing Act and other civil rights legislation during the golden age of American economic expansion, the United States has remained a highly racially segregated society. Massey (1990; Massey and Denton, 1993) calls this pattern of residential segregation "American Apartheid" and links it to housing market discrimination against African and Puerto Rican Americans who share a black racial identity.

Massey reasons that whites perceive a protective benefit to segregation because it isolates high levels of black poverty within black neighborhoods. However, this segregation by race and its correlation with income creates ghetto settings that are highly vulnerable to intensified decline during economic downturns that have become more severe in the last quarter of this century. This is because racial segregation sets the stage for the cyclical intensification of problems that combine racial stereotyping and its real world consequences, so that "segregation heightens and reinforces negative racial stereotypes by concentrating people who fit these stereotypes in a small number of highly visible minority neighborhoods . . . thereby hardening prejudice, making discrimination more likely, and maintaining the motivation for segregation" (353).

More specifically, Massey demonstrates with simulation and prediction models that racial segregation concentrates social and economic disadvantage. A consequence is that shifts in black poverty such as those observed during the 1970s have the power to transform poor black neighborhoods very rapidly and dramatically, changing a low-income black community from a place where welfare-dependent, female-headed families are a minority to one where they are the norm, and producing high rates of crime and related problems. In Massey's terms, "segregation creates the structural niche within which a self-perpetuating cycle of minority poverty and deprivation can survive and flourish" (350).

A beginning point in this process is that homes and neighborhoods are sources of social and cultural capital needed to create human capital, and they are built in part on the physical capital of housing. In this sense residential segregation based on housing market discrimination is a societal process of capital disinvestment targeted specifically against black Americans. Skogan (1986b) observes that decisions about freeway networks and their division and redivision of core sections of heavily populated U.S. cities in the 1950s permanently altered racial patterns of residential segregation. Bickford and Massey (1991) even more directly make the point that decisions about public housing have been a federally funded, physically permanent institution for the isolation of black Americans. Bursik (1989) further demonstrates how the politically planned construction of public housing projects has destabilized already unstable neighborhoods, thereby increasing their crime rates. Skogan (1986b) also has described how practices of **redlining** and disinvestment by banks and **blockbusting** by real estate agents have further intensified racial residential segregation.

The effects of segregation began to hit black American communities especially hard during the 1970s, during the period when the loss of core sector manufacturing jobs began. Results of the loss of these jobs initially were felt most intensely in the "rustbelt" of northeastern and midwestern American cities, such as New York City, Chicago, Philadelphia, and Baltimore (Kasarda, 1989). Massey reasons that the results were most devastating in these settings because they were not only primary sites of manufacturing, but also because these were the most segregated cities in America. The loss of core sector manufacturing jobs drove poverty rates up most sharply in these cities where blacks were most segregated residentially. Practices of racial segregation are processes of capital disinvestment that make affected communities extremely vulnerable to economic downturns and social and cultural adaptations involving crime in response to the concentrated poverty that follows.

Racial Inequality

We noted earlier in this chapter that dubious assumptions about the relationship between social equality and economic efficiency combine with strong sentiments favoring individualism to make Americans accept if not support high levels of inequality. For example, inequalities associated with differences in skills are encouraged. However, problems are more likely to follow when inequalities are distributed in a castelike fashion. Blau and Blau (1982) make this premise the core of their discussion of race-linked inequality, observing that "generally, inequalities for which individuals themselves can be considered responsible, even though differential advantages make this a fiction, are held to be legitimate, whereas inborn inequalities that distribute political rights and economic opportunities on the basis of the group into which a person is born are feudal survivals condemned as illegitimate in a democracy"

(118). Race is the ascribed characteristic with which the capital disinvestment of economic inequality is most illegitimately and explicitly associated in American society.

During the Golden Age of the third quarter of this century in the United States, African Americans made substantial gains in the labor market relative to whites. The demand for black workers increased and the racial gap in earnings among younger adults with similar schooling may even have nearly disappeared. However, during the last quarter of this century when core sector manufacturing jobs were lost, African-American economic conditions worsened and wage inequality and unemployment grew. Black college graduates and blacks with high school or less education had the biggest losses in relative earnings, while dropouts had the largest drop in relative employment (Bound and Freeman, 1992).

The earlier declines in racial economic inequality were associated with social policies designed to increase investment in the social and human capital of minority Americans, in large part through the Civil Rights Movement and the War on Poverty. These policies included implementation of employment discrimination provisions of the 1964 Civil Rights Act, affirmative action programs, and court enforcement of antidiscrimination laws. The latter increases in racial economic inequality were associated with an array of actions that included opposition through the courts to affirmative action laws and regulations, as well as a decline in the real minimum wage (Bound and Freeman, 1992). These are policies of capital disinvestment, and they impacted most heavily on young African Americans with low levels of education.

Blau and Blau (1982) argue that when such inequalities are associated with an ascriptive characteristic such as race they produce "a situation characterized by much social disorganization and prevalent latent animosities" (119) that lead in turn to "diffuse aggression." The problem is that, in a situation made more salient by the visible marker of race, "pronounced ethnic inequality in resources implies that there are great riches within view but not within reach of many people destined to live in poverty" (119). The results are socially structured and objectively based subjective feelings of resentment, frustration, hopelessness, and alienation. Blau and Blau suggest that these feelings in turn lead to widespread social disorganization and violent crime. Race-linked economic inequalities are an expression of capital disinvestment in particular groups that in this case most prominently include black Americans, with consequences that often are unplanned and violent.

One likely example of unplanned and violent consequences of capital disinvestment in a large and highly distressed black community involves the Los Angeles riot after the acquittal of the police officers who assaulted Rodney King. A prominent factor in this riot, as it is widely understood, is that conditions in Los Angeles had deteriorated markedly since the earlier Watts riots. The acquittals, then, were sparks or triggering events, while the underlying cause was the capital disinvestment in the distressed black neighborhoods of Los Angeles.

Concentration of Poverty

A third process of capital disinvestment involves the concentration of poverty that began in the cities of the northeastern and midwestern United States in the 1970s and has continued through the last quarter of this century. William Julius Wilson (1987; 1991) in writing *The Truly Disadvantaged* observes that pockets of ghetto poverty have grown during this period in the United States, with substantial increases in the severity of economic hardship among the ghetto poor in these areas, and concentrations of poverty that affect racial minorities more than whites. The nature of this process of capital disinvestment is summarized as follows:

> . . . the social structure of today's inner city has been radically altered by the mass exodus of jobs and working families and by the rapid deterioration of housing, schools, businesses, recreational facilities, and other community organizations, further exacerbated by government policies of industrial and urban laissez-faire that have channelled a disproportionate share of federal, state, and municipal resources to the more affluent (Wacquant and Wilson, 1989:10).

In an assessment of this process in Chicago, Wacquant and Wilson (1989) define extreme-poverty neighborhoods as having 40 percent or more of their residents living in poverty. They find that over 82 percent of the Chicago respondents in this category live in the west and south sides of the city, mostly in neighborhoods that have been all black for a half-century or more. Eight of ten neighborhoods that represent the core of Chicago's historic black belt have 40 percent or more of their residents living in poverty. These "territorial enclaves," as Wacquant and Wilson (9) call them, have undergone a process that has transformed the "traditional ghetto" of half a century ago (for example, Drake and Cayton, 1945) into a "hyperghetto." This process of accelerated decline is encapsulated in "The Results of Capital Disinvestment" case study from an ethnographic account of changes in North Kenwood, one of the poorest black sections on the city's South Side.

CASE STUDY

An Example: The Results of Capital Disinvestment in North Kenwood

In the 1960s, 47th Street was still the social hub of the South Side black community. Sue's eyes light up when she describes how the street used to be filled with stores, theaters and nightclubs in which one could listen to jazz bands well into the evening. Sue remembers the street as "soulful." Today the street might be better characterized as soulless. Some stores, currency exchanges, bars and liquor stores continue to exist on 47th. Yet, as one walks down the street, one is struck more by the death of the street than by its life. Quite literally, the destruction of human life occurs frequently on 47th. In terms of physical structures, many stores are boarded up and abandoned. A few buildings have bars across the front and are closed to the public, but they are not empty. They are used, not so secretly, by people involved in illegal activities. Other stretches of the street are simply barren, empty lots. Whatever buildings once stood on the lots are long gone. Nothing gets built on 47th. . . . Over the years one apartment building after another has been condemned by the city and torn down. Today many blocks have the bombed-out look of Berlin after World War II. There are huge, barren areas of Kenwood, covered by weeds, bricks, and broken bottles.

Source: Arne Duncan, "The Values, Aspirations, and Opportunities of the Urban Underclass" (B.A. honors thesis, Harvard University, 1987, pp. 18 ff.).

Wilson's focus on the concentration of poverty places particular emphasis on historical changes in the demography of northeastern and midwestern cities, structural changes in the economy, and spatial changes in the location of employment opportunities. The demographic migration of young African Americans from the South to northeastern and midwestern cities created a pool of underemployed youth who were particularly vulnerable to three factors: economic downturns, the shift of employment away from central areas of cities, and a decline of core manufacturing sector employment opportunities and their partial replacement with secondary service sector jobs. African Americans relied heavily on core sector blue-collar jobs in manufacturing and could not easily make a transition into the less plentiful service sector jobs that re-placed them (Farley and Allen, 1987; Fagan, 1993). Wilson also suggests that a migration of middle class blacks away from central city locations reduced the availability of conventional role models for minority youth in these ghetto settings. A result is an increased concentration of the most disadvantaged segments of the urban black population—especially, poor, female-headed families with children—in isolated ghetto settings (Sampson and Wilson, 1994).

A key concept in Wilson's discussion of the concentration of poverty is "labor force attachment." The historical, demographic, and economic trends already noted have weakened labor force attachment among the ghetto poor, and Wilson (1991) observes that "a social context that in-cludes poor schools, inadequate job information networks, and a lack of legitimate employment opportunities not only gives rise to weak labor force attachment, but increases the probability that individuals will be constrained to seek income derived from illegal or deviant activities. This weakens their attachment to the legitimate labor market even further" (10).

However, the central point is that the concentration of poverty plays a key role in intensifying the linkage between weak labor force attach-ment and crime. Wilson explains this in the following way:

> I believe that there is a difference, on the one hand, between a jobless family whose mobility is impeded by the . . . economy and the larger society but nonetheless lives in an area with a relatively low rate of poverty, and on the other hand, a jobless family that lives in an inner-city ghetto neighborhood that is not only influenced by these same constraints but also by the behav-ior of other jobless families in the neighborhood.

The latter family confronts the effects of not only their own difficult situ-ation but also the compounding effects of the situation that surrounds them.

The result is a dramatic deprivation of all kinds of capital, from physical and financial to social and cultural. For example, in the hyperghettos studied by Wacquant and Wilson (1989) in Chicago, only 1 in 10 adults has a checking account, only 1 in 10 lives in a home-owning household, and only 1 in 3 is in a household with a car that runs; mean-while, 2 of 3 households have a female head, 1 in 2 families relies on public assistance, and more than 1 in 2 adults are without a job. The ab-sence of financial capital, especially when aggregated and concentrated, is linked to the loss of social capital, and "all and all, then, poverty con-centration has the effect of devaluing the social capital of those who live in its midst" (24). The consequences are devastating because through this process, ". . . the social ills that have long been associated with segregated poverty—violent crime, drugs, housing deterioration, family disruption, commercial blight, and educational failure—have reached qualitatively different proportions and have become articulated into a new configuration that endows each with a more deadly impact than before" (15).

In terms we have used to organize this discussion, the concentration of poverty produces divergent and oppositional adaptations to pervasive deprivations. That is, the concentration of poverty is a capital disinvestment process that produces adaptations, including deviant formations of social and cultural capital that diverge from and oppose convention. These adaptations are ways of obtaining what disinvestment in ghetto neighborhoods and its restriction of access to legitimate opportunities will not otherwise permit. In this sense, deviant formations of social and cultural capital represent adaptive efforts to recapitalize the lives of individuals and the communities in which they live.

Although these may seem to be abstract theoretical ideas, they have very real and immediate meanings for the individuals and communities involved. Much of this is made more concrete and explicit in the renewed ethnographic research tradition on poverty and crime that we consider next.

The New Ethnographies of Poverty and Crime

A number of recent ethnographies document the significance of the process of capital disinvestment and adaptations to limitations of social and cultural capital we have described. These studies characteristically operate on two levels: as studies of communities, and as studies of the life course experiences of individuals. They also typically consider both the behavioral activities of individuals and the effects of responses of authorities to these individuals. These points will become apparent as we review examples of this research.

First, however, it is important to emphasize that the new ethnographies of poverty and crime all give attention to the role of drugs and to what otherwise were referred to in earlier chapters as ethnic vice industries and deviance service centers. This is important because while the processes of capital disinvestment we have described stress the consequences of the diversion and withdrawal of economic and social resources from disadvantaged communities, often in these same communities there is a process of recapitalization that involves the development of deviance service industries.

This process is partly indigenous to communities and partly a product of the actions of external authorities. The key to deviance service industries is that illegal markets emerge whenever desired substances and services—such as narcotic drugs, prostitution, and gambling—are made illegal. Authorities with responsibility for the enforcement of such laws, whether they wish to or not, have the power to regulate the development and operation of these markets, and members of communities that are denied access and involvement to legal markets often pursue these illegal opportunities. For example, we noted in earlier chapters the succession of ethnic groups that have participated in such markets as a mobility mechanism during this century in the United States.

Clairmont (1974) provides a classic description of the development of an ethnic deviance service center in a community called Africville. Africville was a predominantly black community located near Halifax, Canada, until its displacement as part of an urban renewal project. This community was settled by descendants of free refugee blacks who fled slavery in the United States. Over time, Africville experienced the kind of capital disinvestment processes we have described. At the same time, the community was given "functional autonomy" by the adjacent city to develop in almost any way it wished: "that is, not sharing fairly in society's wealth, they . . . [were] allowed by authorities a range of behavior that would not be countenanced elsewhere." A growing bootlegging trade developed during World War I, and eventually a full-scale deviance service center consisting of several vice industries emerged. Clairmont describes the larger process which we have called recapitalization in this way: "minority group members, if oppressed and discriminated against, often find a mode of adjusting to their situation by performing less desirable and sometimes illegitimate services for the majority group."

When deviant services provided by minority group members are concentrated on a majority group clientele, they can provide an external source of financial capital and serve a redistributive function for the minority community. Organization and provision of these services can also recapitalize the financial and even social lives of the individual entrepreneurs involved. In this sense, these activities are adaptive reflections of the accumulations of new forms of social and cultural capital. However, when these services are concentrated internally, and when they run into interference from external authorities and otherwise disrupt and endanger the lives of individuals and the host community, they become disruptive of social and cultural capital, both for the individuals and communities involved. The latter happened in Africville, and the community was ultimately dispersed and relocated in a disinvestment process that was euphemized as urban renewal.

Echoes of this story reverberate throughout the recent ethnographic studies that we now discuss as examples of the processes of capital disinvestment and recapitalization that are central aspects of crime in urban America.

Three New York City Neighborhoods

In an ethnography provocatively titled *Getting Paid*, Mercer Sullivan (1989) and his collaborators interviewed members of cliques about their life histories in three New York City neighborhoods: an African-American public housing project, a Hispanic neighborhood adjacent to a declining industrial area, and a white working class community. The latter predominantly white neighborhood serves as an essential reference point because it did not experience the loss of core sector jobs and more general capital disinvestment that occurred in the comparison minority communities. Various forms of social capital remained intact. The community retained viable legitimate labor market networks that offered opportunities for obtaining jobs through personal contacts. There were still unionized core sector jobs in which adults had some security. Two-parent households were also more viable, and family and community controls were more stable. These are all indications of the kind of closure of social networks that Coleman identifies as a key source of social capital. This had important implications for the life course experiences and prospects of the youth of this neighborhood. For example, when youths in this neighborhood got into trouble with the law, they were more likely to be reintegrated into their families and community, and they were less likely to be permanently marginalized from labor market opportunities. The closure of social networks provided protective social capital.

Access to labor market opportunities is crucial. In the white working class neighborhood, Sullivan found personalized job referral networks that led adolescents to adult employment opportunities, with jobs circulating through friendship, family, and neighborhood-based connections that linked local residents to desirable blue-collar jobs throughout the metropolitan labor market.

Conditions were much different in the Hispanic- and African-American communities studied. Here the consequences of capital disinvestment became strikingly apparent. Sullivan links this process to changes in the world economy we have discussed, including the transition to a post-industrial economy in which lower wage and insecure jobs in the information and service sectors only partly and inadequately have replaced the loss of higher wage and more secure jobs in the manufacturing and industrial sectors. He notes that our cities in effect have exported jobs and imported unemployment in a set of intranational and international realignments that we are only beginning to understand (see also Revenga, 1992).

A result is that the Hispanic- and African-American neighborhoods Sullivan studied were physically isolated from core sector employment. Many of the parents in these neighborhoods had no jobs, while those parents who were employed tended to work in government jobs that recruited by bureaucratic means rather than through personal contacts. That is, these parents had little of the social capital that derives from the closure of social networks and embeddedness in employment networks that can provide others with referrals and leads to jobs. Sullivan found that "without family connections even to low-paying jobs, these youths had to rely on more impersonal methods" (80). In contrast, for white youths, "social ties between residents and local employers reinforced physical proximity to produce a much greater supply of . . . jobs" (104).

These patterns are reflective of a process of capital disinvestment that has corroded the social and cultural capital of these communities and that is associated with a recapitalization of community life around underground economic activities that include drugs and crime. We come, then, to the provocative title of Sullivan's book, which plays on the ghetto jargon of "getting paid" or "getting over" to describe the illegal economic strategies that include the muggings, robberies, and other forms of theft and drug-related crime common to American city life.

Sullivan's point is that these are not intergenerationally transmitted expressions of cultural preferences, but rather cultural adaptations to restricted opportunities for the redistribution of wealth. Put another way, these youth have substituted investments in subcultures of youth crime and delinquency for involvements in a dominant culture that provides little structural or cultural investment in their futures. Their subcultural adaptations represent investments for short-term economic gains. Drawing on the classic analysis of Paul Willis (1977) in *Learning to Labour*, Sullivan argues that this participation in youth crime temporarily achieves a "penetration of their condition." However, he then turns his eye to the life course consequences of these involvements and notes that

> Over time, this penetration becomes a limitation, binding them back into [the social] structure as they age out of youth crime and accept . . . low wage, unstable jobs. . . . Alternatively, some will die; others will spend much of their lives in prisons or mental hospitals. (250)

For these youths, problems connected to youth crime are prolonged into adulthood.

It is important to emphasize the role of the police, courts, and prisons in the development of these youthful criminal careers. Sullivan found in the more stable white neighborhood that parents, using their well-developed social networks and resulting social capital, "sought to manipulate the system—and were often successful in doing so—by means of money and personal connections" (196). In contrast, in both of the minority neighborhoods youths began to move further away from home to commit violent economic crimes and encountered more serious sanctions when they did so. These crimes produced short-term gains, but they also separated minority youths from the legal labor market, stigmatizing and further damaging their social and cultural capital in terms of later job prospects. Of the minority youths Sullivan studied, he writes that "their participation in regular acts of income-producing crime and the resulting involvement with the criminal justice system in turn kept them out of school and forced them to abandon their earlier occupational goals" (64). Court appearances and resulting confinements removed these youths from whatever possibility for closure of job referral networks school might provide and placed them within prison and community-based crime networks that further isolated these youths from legitimate employment.

The Village and Northtown

Elijah Anderson (1990) brings much of this closer to where many of us literally live in his ethnographic study, *Streetwise*. This is a study of a gentrifying community called "the Village" located adjacent to a declining neighborhood referred to as "Northtown." This ethnography is evocative in part because we can so easily recognize in Anderson's descriptions the cultural adaptations so many of us apply in navigating the streets of our changing cities. This analysis is especially insightful when it describes the conflicting cultural demands placed on young black males who are under pressure to put white strangers at ease while simultaneously protecting themselves from some of the same dangers the white strangers fear. Anderson notes that such a youth "is caught . . . in a cultural catch-22: to appear harmless to others might make him seem weak or square to those he feels a need to impress" (177).

Anderson goes on to consider other apparent contradictions, including examples of capital disinvestment that can come from within the minority community itself. For example, he explains the pressures that black professionals experience to residentially abandon neighborhoods that they otherwise seek to assist. Anderson notes that no young black male has an easy time on the streets of a ghetto community, and that "this is one of the reasons many middle-class blacks are deflected from moving into the area. . . . [T]hey do not want such easy confusion of themselves and their children with the black underclass, particularly as it becomes caught up with the working conceptions and stereotypes of others in the neighborhood" (189).

This is a part of the capital disinvestment process that concentrates poverty in visible minority neighborhoods. Another part involves the declining influence of "old heads" in the neighborhood of Northtown. The mentor/protégé relationship between old heads and young boys was for many years a defining feature of the social organization of Northtown. Some readers may identify the residual reflection of such a relationship in the continuing concern of the character created by Spike Lee in his film *Do the Right Thing*, about what the "right thing" was that an older person in the neighborhood was imploring him to do. "Old heads" were respected older women and men of the community who as guides and role models encouraged youths to invest in conventional culture; they represented a source of network closure with the values of this culture that often was otherwise absent.

These cross-generational ties were a crucial source of social capital for the formation of human and cultural capital among neighborhood youths. However, as the depletion of capital investment more generally demoralized such neighborhoods, the authority of old heads and their emphasis on "honesty, independence, hard work, and family values" (70) diminished. So that, "today, as the economic and social circumstances of the urban ghetto changed, . . . boys easily conclude that the moral lessons of the old head concerning the work ethic, punctuality, and honesty do not fit their own circumstances." The result is a form of cultural disinvestment and disengagement, as old heads and young boys go their separate ways, each losing the opportunity of investment from the other, and with the community perhaps losing most of all, as individual-level despair aggregates into community-level decline.

All of the sources of capital disinvestment we have noted are at play in this ethnography, as in the others, and again the underground world of drugs and drug-related crime is the illegitimate opportunity structure that becomes the important avenue of recapitalization, especially for young males. Anderson makes this point by observing that "for many young men the drug economy is an employment agency. . . . Young men who 'grew up' in the gang, but now are without clear opportunities, easily become involved; they fit themselves into its structure, manning its drug houses and selling drugs on street corners" (244). Once committed to these activities, Anderson points out that there are few opportunities or incentives for youths to terminate this involvement during the transition to adulthood that is so important in determining longer-term life chances.

Anderson also extends his analysis to the experiences of young women in ghetto settings. These women also confront a "sea of destitution" and the problem of recapitalizing their lives. They often do so by creating "baby clubs" that invest value in being pregnant or new mothers: "in effect, they work to create value and status by inverting that of girls who do not become pregnant" (126). Anderson writes that

> . . . in cold economic terms, a baby can be an asset, which is without doubt an important factor behind exploitative sex and out-of-wedlock babies. Public assistance is one of the few reliable sources of money, and, for many, drugs are another. The most desperate people thus feed on one another. Babies and sex may be used for income; women receive money from welfare for having babies, and men sometimes act as prostitutes to pry the money from them (136).

In these communities depleted of economic and social capital, where young black women often have the bleakest futures of all, even babies have a short-term asset value in the recapitalization process (127). The long-term consequences of early parenthood are, of course, a much different matter.

Northwest Chicago

A further manifestation of cultural disinvestment that severely disadvantages low-income minority communities involves the kinds of schools described by Felix Padilla (1992) in his study, *The Gang as an Ethnic Enterprise*. This ethnography focuses on Puerto Rican youths living in a neighborhood of Northwest Chicago that has been hit hard by the loss of core sector manufacturing jobs. Many of the first generation parents of these youths originally picked this neighborhood for the access its good public schools provided to valued sources of social, cultural, and human capital. However, by the time their children were passing through them, these schools had become examples of what one secretary of education called "the worst education system of the nation," and what one investigation described as "daytime warehouses for inferior students, taught by disillusioned and inadequate teachers."

During the period of this research, these schools went from one bad situation to another. The first involved tolerating drug-dealing and associated violence in order to retain attendance based funding. The second

involved the implementation of a Safe School Zone law that imposed severe sentences on persons convicted of selling drugs in or around
schools, forcing drug dealing and use out of the schools and into the surrounding neighborhood. Neither response represented an effective investment in the educational needs of these youths. Failing to see a future
in school or in the kinds of secondary service sector jobs it could bring,
these youths turned their gang, the Diamonds, into a drug-dealing,
money-making business and alternate source of employment. In other
words, these youths disinvested in schools that made little investment in
them, and instead reinvested their identities in the cultural symbols and
day-to-day business realities of stealing cars and running, dealing, and
distributing drugs.

Padilla explicitly identifies the Diamonds as an illegal business enterprise. The "mainheads" of this gang purchase large quantities of drugs
wholesale and then hire other gang members to work on commission re-
tailing them on the street. Padillia notes that "the business operated by
the Diamonds parallels an 'ethnic enterprise': a distinctive entrepreneurial strategy historically developed and used by immigrants and their descendants in response to their marginal economic position" (3). However,
the Diamonds are not able to replicate the social mobility of past groups:
"Instead of functioning as a progressive and liberating agent capable of
transforming and correcting the youngsters' economic plight, the gang
assisted in reinforcing it" (163). As one member of the Diamonds notes,
"I got kicked out of school because I was hanging out in the neighborhood selling drugs. And the one thing that sucks about gangbanging is
that you get locked up a lot." Participation in the Diamonds provides
some short-term self-respect but also adds to the longer term employment problems of these youth.

East Los Angeles

Joan Moore's (1991) *Going Down to the Barrio* moves farther across the
country to the American Southwest for what is in many ways a parallel
look at effects of historical and life course changes in the development of
Hispanic gangs in Los Angeles. Again, structural and cultural change are
salient parts of this ethnography. A central theme is that gang members
are not so much rebels, as so often is suggested in classical subcultural
accounts, but more that these individuals are left out of the credentialed,
ordered society built on traditional forms of cultural capital. Put differently, their cultural disinvestment and subcultural identification is an

adaptive rejection of the credential based cultural capital they have had little opportunity to attain.

Moore builds this account from interviews with two samples of adult men and women who were members of two Hispanic Los Angeles gangs, White Fence and El Hoyo Maravilla, during the late 1940s and early 1950s, and in the 1960s and 1970s. By interviewing these two groups retrospectively about their lifetime participation in gangs, Moore is able to explore changes across eras in gang involvements. A central theme is that the loss of core sector manufacturing jobs in the Los Angeles economy led here as in the previous accounts to lower-paying and less secure jobs. For the individuals involved, this meant that the social capital connected to the closure of "kin-based job networks that found decent work for earlier clique members deteriorated" (133). For many youths, the result was to prolong gang involvement into adulthood. Gangs became more highly institutionalized, with young men and women who joined these gangs having less opportunity and encouragement to break their ties to these gangs in early adulthood.

Yet, Moore does not see the gangs she studied as fully divorced from the surrounding culture, especially the surrounding youth culture, and she, like Willis (1977) and Sullivan (1989), sees gang involvement as at least in part a cultural adaptation to their depleted social networks, social capital, and related economic prospects. However, Moore also concludes that "the point is that the youth-culture continuum . . . shifts over time," and that "the gang can be expected to be more deviant as the adolescent subculture in general becomes more deviant" (41). So while the Los Angeles youths studied continued to be influenced in important ways by surrounding cultural trends, they were also increasingly disinvested from conventional cultural goals and reinvested in gangs that had become more durable institutions of socialization that persisted into adulthood.

Perhaps the most striking symptom of cultural disinvestment in Moore's account involves her description of *locura* and its link to increasing involvement in gang violence. Moore defines locura as "the 'craziness' or wildness that is stereotypically associated with Chicano gangs" (62). She finds that 81 percent of the men (and nearly the same proportion of women) active in the 1970s described themselves in this way, compared with 65 percent of the men active in the 1950s [see Willis (1990:103–9) for a parallel account of a similar phenomenon among working class British youth]. She concludes that violence is now endemic to these gangs.

Again like Sullivan, Moore is quite sensitive to the life course implications of these developments and their connection to the surrounding
changes in a deindustrializing economy where well-paying, secure jobs
are increasingly scarce. She notes that ". . . the very culture of defiance at
best dooms the boys to jobs just like their fathers hold, and transfers the
defiant and subversive attitude from school to the workplace" (42).

Moore's sample is not limited to males, and in fact is one-third female, which she indicates is representative of the composition of East Los
Angeles gangs. Moore concludes that girls are subordinated in these
gangs much as they are elsewhere, preparing them for "a lifetime of sub-
ordination as wives" and in lower-level working jobs.

In sum, these Chicano gangs in Los Angeles are more firmly institutionalized and more seriously deviant than they were in the past, and
these gangs have more enduring consequences for the life course experiences of their most recent members.

Milwaukee

John Hagedorn's *People and Folks* reports on interviews with members of
nineteen of Milwaukee's largest gangs. Milwaukee is a prime example of
a deindustrializing city that has experienced a continuing process of
capital disinvestment. Black unemployment was over 25 percent in the
mid-1980s, and the ratio of black unemployed to white unemployed was
the worst in the nation during this period.

Some of the most striking findings about Milwaukee of the 1980s derive from comparisons with communities studied by Spergel (1964) during what we have called the Golden Age several decades earlier. This
comparison reveals that black Milwaukee in the 1980s experienced far
more unemployment and low-wage jobs than was the case in Spergel's
research. When Hagedorn turns to the information he was able to collect
about 260 "gang founders" in Milwaukee, nearly all of whom were between nineteen and twenty-five at the time of his interviews, he finds
that only 10 percent were employed full time, and that nearly three-quarters were still involved with gangs. These are, of course, similar structural conditions and life course consequences as observed in communities already described.

Hagedorn reports that there is strong pressure to remain with gangs
after prison stays that results in a deepening institutionalization of gangs
and their life course consequences. This leads to a provocative assertion
endorsed by Moore that gang members, including those who have experienced imprisonment, are forming an increasing part of a growing ur-

ban "underclass." Some worry that such discussion of connections between class, race or ethnicity, and crime encourages a stereotype of the "undeserving poor" (see Gans, 1990; Marks, 1991; compare with Wilson, 1991). However, Moore underlines this connection in an introduction to Hagedorn's ethnography in which she notes that, as in Milwaukee,

> The more successful East Los Angeles natives continuously migrate out to the suburbs, and the gang members that remain tend to be 'leftovers' from unsuccessful families and/or children of men and women who return to the barrios after a period of imprisonment (16).

Moore calls for more sociological attention to this process, warning that "in both Los Angeles and Milwaukee, circumstances combine to make it increasingly difficult for young men and women to move from juvenile delinquency to adult unemployment" and that "gangs and the emerging underclass are too important to leave to mass media and law enforcement." Little doubt remains after Moore and Hagedorn's ethnographies that the mass media and law enforcement distort gang and class issues.

The New Quantitative Studies of Crime, Class, and Community

The new ethnographies of poverty and crime provide a picture of distressed communities in which capital disinvestment processes have made economic prospects bleak, and in which crime has become a short-term adaptive form of recapitalization for youth whose longer term life chances are further jeopardized by these involvements. A new tradition of quantitative research provides further support for this view of crime in urban America, by focusing on crime at the level of communities, as well as on the development of crime in the lives of individuals over the life course. These studies often further articulate the ways in which community level processes of capital disinvestment affect social networks in the community and the social capital of families and their capacities to assist the formation of human and cultural capital for their children.

Community Effects

Community-level studies done in a number of U.S. cities persuasively link street crime in America to the capital disinvestment processes of residential segregation, racial inequality, and the concentration of poverty emphasized in our earlier discussion and in the new ethnographies of poverty and crime. For example, recent studies in large U.S. cities reveal high levels of homicide victimization for African Americans in tracts with high concentrations of poor families. The same studies show low levels of homicide victimization for both blacks and whites in higher socioeconomic areas (Lowry et al., 1988; Centerwall, 1984; Munford et al., 1976). Since poor black communities are much more distressed economically than poor white communities, and since it is only in higher socioeconomic communities that it is possible to establish real similarity of black and white life conditions, these studies imply that racial differences in homicide rates have their origins in socioeconomic experiences (Short, 1994).

It is surprisingly difficult in community level studies to fully disentangle and uniquely establish the effects of racial segregation, social inequality, and racially concentrated poverty. There is considerable recent evidence of direct effects of the degree, and absolute concentration, of neighborhood poverty on violent crime (for example, Sampson, 1985; Curry and Spergel, 1988; Taylor and Covington, 1988; Williams and Flewelling, 1987; Bursik and Grasmick, 1993b). A review of over sixty studies also suggests the existence of a "positive frequently significant" relationship between unemployment and property crime (Chiricos, 1987:203). This relationship is strongest and most consistent when it is studied with time series data (Cantor and Land, 1985; Land et al., 1994) at the neighborhood level (Land et al., 1990). There is also evidence that measures of general and/or racial socioeconomic inequality, which reflect conditions of relative deprivation, are associated with higher homicide rates (for example, Balkwell, 1990; Crutchfield, 1989; Sampson, 1986). Finally, there is further evidence that, apart from measures of absolute concentration of poverty and relative racial inequality, residential segregation by race leads to higher rates of several kinds of black homicide (Peterson and Krivo, 1993).

However, it is also the case that relationships like those just noted are neither universally found nor completely understood. Jencks and Mayer (1990) suggest the uncertain state of our knowledge when they advise that

> We badly need better studies of neighborhoods' impact on teenage crime. We especially need studies that focus on the effects of very poor neighborhoods, including large public housing projects. We also need studies that follow families as they move in and out of very poor neighborhoods and examine how such moves affect teenagers' behavior (162).

Several researchers have recently noted the further need in such studies to use race-specific measures to assess the impact on minority crime rates of minority experiences of inequality, apart from those of majority group members (Sampson, 1985; Harer and Steffensmeier, 1992; LaFree, Drass, and O'Day, 1992; Messner and Golden, 1992).

In an important recent review of the literature that contains many community-level studies, Land et al. (1990) located a cluster of these kinds of factors (including median income, percent of families below the poverty line, an index of income inequality, percent of black population, and percent of single-parent families) that had a clear causal influence on homicide rates. However, these factors could not be fully decomposed into more specific causal effects. These factors are probably too closely intertwined to be specifically distinguished. One implication is that capital disinvestment processes operate in a more general and interconnected way.

Still, it is important to try to determine more about how capital disinvestment processes might exercise their community- as well as individual-level effects, and important advances are being made along these lines. Much of this work is tied together by an underlying concern with the effects of changing labor markets on youths attempting to make the transition to adulthood in racially segregated and impoverished communities.

Further Labor Market Effects

Greenberg (1979) points out that youths in our money- and media-driven society are under unique pressures to consume. Many youth are under further pressures to express age-linked notions of masculinity, as well as to accomplish the transition to adulthood, all in the absence of adequate access to labor markets. Inadequate availability of employment is perhaps the biggest obstacle to successfully traversing the gap between a troubled adolescence and the entry into a more stable adulthood. This gap is nowhere bigger than for the one-third or more residentially segregated and concentrated inner-city minority youth who are unable to find stable work in the United States.

Allan and Steffensmeier (1989:110) connect several strands of research on labor market conditions and crime by noting that a "lack of suitable employment may contribute to a climate of moral cynicism and alienation that attenuates the effectiveness of social controls." They find that availability of employment produces strong effects on juvenile arrest rates, that low quality of employment (for example, low pay and bad hours) is associated with high arrest rates for young adults, and that generally such effects are stronger in relation to minority (Hispanic and African American) underemployment than in relation to white underemployment (Allan, 1985).

Resulting Disorganization and Aggression

Blau and Blau (1982; see also Messner and Rosenfeld,1993; Messner, 1989) describe the conspicuous connection between race and lack of access to stable and rewarding jobs as resulting in "prevalent disorganization" and as sparking "diffuse aggression," while Sampson and Wilson (1994; see also Bursik and Grasmick, 1993a) conceptualize related concentrations of poverty as producing a "dislocation" and "disorganization" of social control. These theoretical frameworks share with other contemporary sociological approaches a common concern with linking economic and political processes of change to the dislocations they produce in community settings. Sampson and Wilson (1994) write that

> Boiled down to its essentials, then, our theoretical framework linking social disorganization theory with research on urban poverty and political economy suggests that macrosocial forces (e.g., segregation, migration, housing discrimination, structural transformation of the economy) interact with local community-level factors (e.g., residential turnover, concentrated poverty, family disruption) to impede social organization. This is a distinctly sociological viewpoint, for it focuses attention on the proximate structural characteristics and mediating processes of community social organization that help explain crime, while at the same time recognizing the larger historical, social, and political forces shaping local communities.

Diffuseness of aggression and dislocation or disorganization of social control and accompanying social networks are much evident in related community-based quantitative research. In a study of over 150 U.S. cities in 1980, Sampson (1987) found that the scarcity of employed black males relative to black women was directly related to the prevalence of families headed by females in black communities, and that black family disruption was in turn substantially related to rates of black murder and robbery, especially by juveniles (see also Messner and Sampson, 1991).

Simpson (1991) further notes that the major increase in poverty in recent decades has occurred among those living in households headed by a single-parent mother, that in America one-third of these women are black, and that this economic marginalization is an important factor in the violence of young black women as well as men. By 1990, 51 percent of black children compared to 16 percent of white children lived in single-parent families headed by women (O'Hare et al., 1991:19), and there is compelling evidence that class, race, and family disruption have interconnected influences on delinquency (Matsueda and Heimer, 1987). Linkages between poor job prospects, poverty, and family disruption are key sources of the loss in closure of social networks and connected depletions of social capital in minority communities and families.

The structure of community social organization also involves informal social networks and formal institutions that guide and monitor leisure-time youth activities (Bursik and Grasmick, 1993a). Consequences of the loss of this kind of closure in neighborhood social networks are found in the prevalence of unsupervised teenage peer-groups in a community, with large resulting effects on rates of robbery and violence by strangers (Sampson and Groves, 1989). Alternatively, with closely coordinated supervision, gangs in some instances have been connected to external sources of funding from community programs that have successfully reduced gang activity and fear of crime (see Bursik and Grasmick, 1993b; Erlanger, 1979).

Many of these kinds of findings can be synthesized in terms of the concepts of social and cultural capital that we introduced earlier and have used throughout much of this chapter. In conventional circumstances, intact families, informal social networks, and more formal institutions in a community are sources of a closure of social networks and resulting social capital that can be converted into cultural capital to improve the life chances of youth as they become adults. However, in distressed communities these structures and processes are often disrupted and jeopardized. Youths have less access to well-articulated social networks and therefore less hope of finding the stable core sector jobs that will allow them to successfully traverse the gap from adolescence to adulthood: in large part because the economy is not providing them, but also because their communities and families do not have the social networks and capital to help them prepare themselves for such jobs or to find them when they are available. To further understand these problems of capital formation and their consequences in the form of attempted recapitalization through alternative cultural adaptations, we turn next to a tradition of life course research based on the experiences of individuals.

Individual Life Outcomes

If employment problems are in particular a source of family dislocations that result in disruptions in the use of social capital to create human and cultural capital, this should be reflected in life course studies that track individuals from childhood to adulthood. That is, individuals from disadvantaged families and communities should be more at risk of delinquency and crime, as well as employment problems that continue into adulthood. The latter long-term employment problems are of particular concern because they point to problems of crime and poverty that may recur and intensify across generations. This possibility is suggested in the ethnographic studies reviewed earlier, and it is apparent as well in the combined findings from several long-term quantitative studies that follow individuals from childhood and adolescence into adulthood.

For example, in a classic study, *Deviant Children Grown Up*, Robins (1966) followed two St. Louis samples into adulthood: a clinic-based sample of predominantly low-status "severely antisocial children" and a "control group" who were without adolescent behavior problems and were matched with the clinic sample on race, sex, age, intelligence, and socioeconomic status. As adults the clinic sample experienced not only more behavioral problems than the control group, but also more unemployment for longer spells and with more frequent job changes, fewer promotions, depressed earnings, more credit problems, and greater reliance on public assistance.

The Gluecks (1950; 1968) applied a similar matched group design to study white males from predominantly lower-income Boston neighborhoods who, because of their persistent delinquency, were committed to one of two correctional schools in Massachusetts. Sampson and Laub (1990; 1993) reanalyzed these data and reported not only a tendency for the delinquent group to continue to be more criminal as adults, but also that "seven adult behaviors spanning economic, educational, employment, and family domains are also strongly related to adolescent delinquency" (1990:616). These outcomes included greater adult unemployment and welfare dependency among the delinquent sample.

However, research focused on milder forms of drinking, drug use, and delinquency in more predominantly middle class settings reveals fewer problems in adulthood. For example, Jessor et al. (1993) tracked a broadly representative sample of mainly middle class Colorado high school students into early adulthood. Although the authors found some continuity in problem behaviors in adulthood, these behaviors did not affect work and status attainment (see also Ghodsian and Power, 1987; Newcomb and Bentler, 1988). They suggest several plausible reasons for this:

> First, our research involved normal rather than clinical samples, and the extent of their adolescent/youth involvement in problem behavior—even at its greatest—has to be seen as moderate for the most part. Second, our samples were largely middle class in socioeconomic status, and the openness of the opportunity structure for them and their access to 'second chances' have to be seen as far greater than might be the case for disadvantaged youth who had been involved in problem behavior. (Chapter 9)

Jessor et al. optimistically conclude that the course of psychosocial development is not inexorable, that past actions do not necessarily foreclose future options, and that there can be resilience in growth and change: "at least in social contexts that are not malignant" (Chapter 9).

This reference to social context is crucial because it returns our attention to differences in family and community settings of the kinds we have emphasized throughout this chapter. Recall that our argument is that when communities and families can invest network resources and social capital in their youth, it is more likely that these youths will develop cultural and human capital through education and other institutionalized mechanisms that improve their life chances. However, in communities that suffer from capital disinvestment and in families that have little closure of social networks and social capital to facilitate investment in their children, youths are more likely to drift into cultural adaptations that bring short-term status and material benefits, but whose longer-term consequences include diminished life chances. Some of these ideas have been directly tested in a study of nearly 500 youths of varied class backgrounds followed from adolescence to adulthood in Toronto, Canada (Hagan, 1991b).

Class Settings and Subcultural Outcomes

The Toronto study focuses on a range of cultural preferences associated with adolescence, from going to rock concerts to involvements in delinquency. Two subcultures are identified: a "party subculture" focused around partying, rock concerts, and drinking, and a "subculture of delinquency" that involves theft, vandalism, fighting, and running from the police. Both of these subcultures derive salience from their separateness from conventional sources of social and cultural capital, including schools and parents. Identification of youths with these subcultures is linked to weaknesses in the school and family ties, in other words to weaknesses in social capital, that might otherwise direct youths into more reputable cultural domains.

In the Toronto study, the consequences of involvement in the subculture of delinquency, but not of the party subculture, consist of reduced occupational attainments among the sons of working class fathers, but not among daughters or sons with more advantaged class backgrounds. This pattern is consistent both with the findings of Jessor et al. (1993) that relatively minor adolescent deviance has few negative effects among predominantly middle class Colorado youths, and the findings of Robins (1966) and Sampson and Laub (1990, 1993a) of significant longer-term negative socioeconomic consequences of more serious juvenile misconduct in the poorer socioeconomic settings of St. Louis and Boston.

The idea that class in particular might specify the longer-term consequences of juvenile delinquency is not new. In *Delinquent Boys*, Cohen (1955) cites Hollinghead's classic study, *Elmtown's Youth*, to emphasize "the importance of parental status in obtaining special consideration in school activities and on the job through 'connections' and other means of exerting pressure" (111). Hollingshead (1949) was indeed emphatic, observing that "class control tends to result in the manipulation of institutional functions in the interests of individuals and families who have wealth, prestige, and power" (452). The implication is that social network and capital resources produce cultural capital not only by directing youths toward long-term socially and culturally rewarding investments in education, but also by protecting youths from consequences of adolescent experimentation and indiscretion.

Goode (1978) similarly has argued that "the relative resources of individuals or groups in prestige processes may have considerable effect on who gets how much public praise or dispraise," so that "juvenile delinquents of upper-middle class families often avoid much loss of respect" (252). This avoidance of consequences is the "openness of the opportunity structure" and the "access to second chances" that Jessor et al. (1993) identify as compensation for the disreputable involvements of middle class youths.

As we have suggested before, an important way youths from disadvantaged class backgrounds become locked into downward trajectories is through contacts with the police and courts. There is evidence of this in the Toronto study and elsewhere. Being caught by the police and caught up in the criminal justice system are especially hazardous for youths from disadvantaged backgrounds because becoming embedded in crime can produce not only future criminality, but also later problems in finding employment. These problems can be further conceptualized in terms of the structure and process of criminal embeddedness.

The Costs of Criminal Embeddedness

We have seen that for most individuals the key to a successful transition from adolescence to adulthood is finding a job. The personal contacts of individuals, friends, and families, and the network of relations that flow from these contacts, are important sources of social capital used in finding jobs and making job changes (Granovetter, 1974, 1985; Coleman, 1990:302). Youths from advantaged class backgrounds are more likely than others to have the social capital that derives from being "socially embedded" in job networks, and that makes finding and changing jobs easier. This embeddedness facilitates the closure of job finding networks.

However, if early employment contacts can enhance the prospects of getting a job and subsequent occupational mobility, connections into crime seem likely in a converse way to increase the probability of unemployment. For example, criminal involvements of family and friends are more likely to integrate young people into the criminal underworld than into referral networks of legal employment. And youthful delinquent acts are likely to further distance actors from the job contacts that initiate and sustain legitimate occupational careers. Criminal embeddedness in the delinquent group and the criminal underworld is a liability in terms of prospects for stable adult employment.

This embeddedness is compounded by the effects of becoming officially labeled and known as a criminal offender, especially in distressed community settings where few core sector jobs are available in any case. This process of separation and stigmatization can be more subtle than the more conventional process of social embeddedness in that it can eliminate possibilities before they become apparent, operating through the absence rather than the presence of social ties to assist and protect minority youths. Delinquent youths run a high risk of becoming criminally embedded in contexts that isolate them from the closure of social networks and the accumulation of social capital that can derive from legitimate employment in whatever jobs are available.

These risks are reflected in a recent analysis of youths tracked from childhood through adulthood in a London working class neighborhood (Hagan, 1993). This study reveals that intergenerational patterns of criminal conviction make youths especially prone to subsequent delinquency and adult unemployment (Hagan and Palloni, 1990; Hagan, 1993; see also Ward and Tittle, 1993). Other studies similarly show that working class males with conviction records are uniquely disadvantaged in finding employment (Schwartz and Skolnick, 1964), and that a criminal arrest record can have negative effects on employment as much as eight years later (Freeman, 1991; Grogger, 1991). Sampson and Laub's (1993a:168) long-term study of predominantly lower socioeconomic status Boston delinquents indicates that "incarceration appears to cut off opportunities and prospects for stable employment in later life." Criminal sanctions can cause further problems by making offenders who are already disadvantaged more defiant (Sherman, 1993). This is one more way in which the social and cultural capital of such youths is further jeopardized.

Much of what we have learned in this chapter about capital disinvestment processes and the impact of social and cultural capital on life course experiences can be synthesized in a final discussion of community- and individual-level involvement in the illegal economy of drugs.

Capital Disinvestment and Embeddedness in the Criminal Economy of Drugs

As we saw in the ethnographic studies considered earlier, during the same approximate period of capital disinvestment when access to legitimate job networks linked to core sector jobs declined in many distressed minority communities, networks of contacts into the world of drugs and drug-related crime proliferated, paving the way for many youths to become embedded in the criminal economy. Fagan (1993) finds in field studies with over a thousand participants in the Washington Heights and Central Harlem neighborhoods of New York City that this criminal economy employs large numbers of individuals in support roles (for example, lookouts and renting storefronts or apartments) as well as drug sales and in a greatly expanded sex trade. This activity can assume an important role in the neighborhood economy, with white collar as well as blue-collar customers bringing cash into the community, and at least some of the funds being redistributed within the neighborhood. This criminal economy is a contemporary institutionalized link to the deviance service centers and ethnic vice industries of America's past.

However, today's illegal drug industry is also much more competitive, violent, and unstable than in the past. Where drug distribution was once centralized through relatively circumscribed networks of heroin and later cocaine users who retailed drugs on the street, the more recent experience with crack has involved a less regulated market with violent competition for territory and market share (Williams, 1989). As well, while entry-level roles and the market for drugs more generally have increased, the redistribution of profits has declined. This contrasts with an earlier period when marijuana sales predominated. Drug income now is less often invested in local businesses, and profits more often are concentrated among individuals elsewhere in the city and outside the country (see also Ianni, 1974).

Yet, low-level participation in the drug economy, despite its poor career prospects and declining returns to the community, is still a cultural adaptation with compelling short-term capital attractions. In the absence of better sources of employment, drug selling is a primary route to gaining material symbols of wealth and success in the neighborhood.

The drug industry also offers the hope, however illusory, of self-determination and economic independence, as contrasted with the petty humiliations and daily harassment faced in secondary service sector jobs (Fagan, 1993).

This is likely why 1 in 6 African-American males born in 1967 in Washington, D.C., is estimated to have been arrested for drug selling between 1985 and 1987, with rates of actual participation in drug selling presumably being much higher (Reuter et al., 1990:46). Street-level sellers are estimated to have incomes ranging from $15,000 to $100,000 annually (Williams, 1989). A Boston study concludes that disadvantaged youths during the economic boom of the mid-1980s would have had to take sharp reductions in income to move from drug selling to legal jobs (Freeman, 1991). Drug selling is simply more profitable per hour invested than legitimate employment (Reuter et al., 1990). So the illegal drug industry is an important source of social and economic capital for individuals. Unfortunately, this capital is quickly depleted, with excess earnings dispersed through loosely articulated family and social networks, consumption of drugs, and conspicuous spending. And we have seen that imprisonment and unemployment further jeopardize the capital position of youths involved in drug selling.

Capital disinvestment processes and changes in the illegal drug industry also have influenced the lives of many minority women. The increasing number of female-headed households and families has placed new demands on minority women to generate income. The disappearance through deaths and imprisonment of numbers of young adult males may also have relaxed barriers to female participation in street-level drug selling. And the emergence of crack escalated the demand for drugs. These factors have increased the participation of minority women in drug use and sales and also in prostitution (Fagan, 1993).

The ethnic vice industries and deviance service centers that surround drugs and drug-related crime pose great policy dilemmas in the New York City neighborhoods that Fagan studied. As exploitative and corrosive of the community and individuals as these activities may be in the long term, their short-term benefits are often difficult for neighborhood residents to resist.

> First, since neighborhood residents benefit from the redistributive aspects of drug selling, this undercuts their efforts at formal and informal social control. Residents may be less willing to disrupt drug selling since some directly benefit, and especially when economic alternatives do not compete well or the risks are not acute or immediate. As suppliers of a commodity to others in the city, funds flow into the neighborhood and are recirculated to

some extent before accumulating to individuals. What will happen if this circulation is interrupted? Unless risks increase from drug selling or living in its milieu, it is unreasonable to ask people to act against their economic well-being. (Fagan, 1993)

In the end, these are the kinds of dilemmas that continuing social inequality and capital disinvestment provoke.

The New Sociology of Crime, Inequality, and Disrepute

A new sociology of crime and disrepute focuses attention on the criminal costs of social inequality. It does so against the backdrop of a common belief that social inequality encourages individual initiative and is therefore economically efficient. This belief is challenged by the last half-century of economic development in the advanced capitalist nations, when declining social inequality accompanied economic expansion, and increases in social inequality were joined with reduced economic growth. Meanwhile, increased social inequality and reduced economic growth are both associated with increases in crime, especially in America's low-income minority communities.

Structural changes have brought increasing inequality into the American economy and into the lives of individuals who live in its most distressed communities. Three interconnected processes of capital disinvestment—residential segregation, racial inequality, and the concentration of poverty—have intensified the crime problems of these communities. These disinvestment processes are encouraged by the unsubstantiated belief that efforts to increase social equality are wasteful and that they diminish economic efficiency. Meanwhile, capital disinvestment impairs the closure of social networks and the formation of social and cultural capital in distressed communities and families, and it indirectly encourages subcultural adaptations. These adaptations are in effect forms of recapitalization, that is, they represent efforts to reorganize what resources are available, albeit usually illicit, to reach attainable goals.

Often these efforts at recapitalization occur through involvement in ethnic vice industries and the formation of deviance service centers, the sometimes free enterprise zones of crime. One of the most enduring of these illicit industries involves illegal drugs. This illicit enterprise has sometimes provided an external source of financial capital that serves a redistributive function in distressed ethnic communities and that has recapitalized the economic and social lives of the individuals involved. However, the more recent American experience, especially with crack, is more violent, exploitative, and disruptive than past experiences with drugs. Furthermore, as consumption of such drugs has become more concentrated within minority communities, drug sales have brought in and redistributed reduced amounts of money from outside these communities, and have encountered mounting interference from external authorities. The results are increasingly disruptive and dangerous to the communities and individuals involved. These points are confirmed by a growing number of ethnographic and quantitative studies.

The new sociology of crime and disrepute is more eclectic methodologically and theoretically than in the past. It borrows broadly from the classical traditions of sociological theory about crime, and it applies qualitative as well as quantitative research methods to study the causes as well as reactions to crime. This more synthetic trend in sociological criminology provides an antidote to prevailing economic and political assumptions about inequality, efficiency, and crime. This sociological view suggests that expanded social as well as economic opportunities can provide a foundation for broadened participation of citizens in the production of economic wealth and a reduction in the social costs of crime.

It is important to emphasize that although the new sociology of crime and disrepute helps to explain increasingly concentrated problems of street crime in low-income and distressed minority communities, this approach also raises new issues that are as yet unaddressed and therefore unresolved. For example, it is unclear to what extent distressed white communities differ from distressed minority communities in their crime-related problems of social and cultural capital; this is probably in part unclear because there are few, if any, white communities that are comparably distressed. Meanwhile, it is also unclear how and to what extent disadvantaged rural areas might differ from disadvantaged urban areas. Moving farther afield, it is also unknown how and to what extent distressed parts of American cities differ in their crime and related problems from comparable parts of cities in other nations. And, it will be important to learn more about differences between the ways illegal drug and other enterprises operate, and with what kinds of consequences now, as compared to in the past, as well as in other national settings.

There is much to be learned by extending the historical and comparative horizons of our research. Much of the value of the new sociology of crime and disrepute is the quality of the questions that it provokes about the changes that are occurring within American society and in relation to other settings. These are questions and changes that can no longer be ignored.

4

White-Collar Crime in a Global Economy

The topic of white-collar crime forces us to confront important issues in sociological criminology. The term itself was introduced by Edwin Sutherland (1940) more than half a century ago and is probably the most popularly used criminological concept in everyday contemporary life. Attention to the topic of white-collar crime forces us to reconsider many common assumptions about crime.

For example, once the relevance of white-collar crime is acknowledged, it is no longer so easy to take for granted the way in which most crime is defined. Instead we should ask: why is so little public and statutory attention paid to "crimes in the suites" compared to "crimes of the street"? Nor can the official data collected by agencies of crime control be accepted so uncritically. Instead we should wonder: why is it that so little white-collar crime is officially treated as criminal? Nor can it so conveniently be assumed that the poor are more criminal than the rich. Instead we should grapple with the question: just how much upperworld crime is there? These issues intersect in one very stubborn difficulty encountered in researching white-collar crime: the difficulty of "studying what we cannot see" (Mann, 1985; McBarnet, 1991). White-collar crime often is difficult to see because its perpetrators' subtlety and sophistication often leave its victims without knowledge that they have been victimized.

The sociological study of crime takes on new form and substance when the topic of white-collar crime is made a central part of our thinking. One example involves the concept of social capital, which takes on new implications when we consider white-collar crime. In the previous chapter we emphasized that *lack* of access to social capital can be **criminogenic**. Here the problem may be too *much* social capital, especially in the form of trust. The trust that derives from successfully becoming embedded in powerful occupational and corporate networks can be a source of freedom and, therefore, power to commit large-scale white-collar crimes.

The problems of white-collar crime are global. They are spread by the increasingly international scope of financial enterprise and the advantages that the geographical dispersion of criminal activity can provide for escaping detection, prosecution, and sanctioning. This point and others are made in this chapter by considering separately issues involving class, crime, and the corporations; the social organization of work; and the apprehension, prosecution, and punishment of white-collar crime.

Class, Crime, and the Corporations

White-collar crimes often are committed through and on behalf of corporations. The involvement of corporations in crime has been recognized at least since the early part of this century when E. A. Ross (1907) wrote of a new type of criminal "who picks pockets with a 'rake-off' instead of a jimmy, cheats with a company prospectus instead of a deck of cards, or scuttles his town instead of his ship." However, it was not until after the Great Depression that Edwin Sutherland (1940) finally attached a lasting label to these offenders in his influential paper on white-collar crime. Sutherland proposed in this paper that **white-collar crime** be defined "as a crime committed by a person of respectability and high social status in the course of his occupation."

Occupation or Organization?

From this point on (Geis and Meier, 1977; Shapiro, 1980; Wheeler and Rothman, 1982), there has been considerable confusion about the role of **occupation** and **organization** in the study of white-collar crime. For example, Wheeler and Rothman (1982) note that two influential works, Clinard's (1952) and Hartung's (1950) studies of black-market activities during World War II, defined white-collar crime in two rather different ways. Clinard defined white-collar crime occupationally, as "illegal activities among business and professional men," while Hartung included an organizational component, defining such crimes as "a violation of law regulating business, which is committed for a firm by the firm or its agents in the conduct of its business." A distinction is still often drawn today (see Coleman, 1985:8) between "occupational crime—that is, white-collar crime committed by an individual or a group of individuals exclusively for personal gain," and "organizational crime—white-collar crimes committed with the support and encouragement of a formal organization and intended at least in part to advance the goals of that organization."

The problem is that the occupational and organizational components of many white-collar crimes cannot be easily separated. Clinard and Yeager (1980) make this point with the example of a Firestone tire official who aided his corporation in securing and administering illegal political contributions benefiting the corporation, but then embezzled much of the funds for himself. The mixture of occupational and organizational aspects of white-collar crime can have international repercussions. As this book is being written, a former executive of the U.S. General Motors Corporation is under investigation by the U.S. Justice Department for stealing trade secrets by taking plans for a new GM small car to his new employer, the German Volkswagen Corporation. It should not be surprising that organizational white-collar crime is often international crime, since large offending corporations are often multinational in their operations and can have incomes that exceed those of individual countries.

Locating white-collar offenders in terms of their ownership and authority positions in occupational and organizational structures is a key part of the class analysis of white-collar crime (Geis, 1984; Hagan and Parker, 1985; Weisburd et al., 1990). Sutherland's emphasis on "respect" and "status" in defining white-collar crime only begins to open up the issue of class position and its role in the understanding of white-collar crime. A key element of class is the power to commit major white-collar crimes. This power derives from the ownership and authority positions individuals occupy in occupational and organizational structures that often span international boundaries.

From White-Collar Crime to Corporate Homicide

However, as Sutherland recognized, the problem is not only one of our conception of white-collar offenders and their class positions, but also one of our conception of white-collar crime itself (compare with Shapiro, 1990). Often our confused conceptions seem mundane, so mundane that they pass unnoticed. For example, the *New York Times* published two stories in the same edition, one that warned and possibly discouraged its readers from "pirating" computer software (Lewis, 1989), and another which informed and likely encouraged its readers to acquire newly designed devices to copy audiotapes (Fantel, 1989). The contradiction probably was unnoticed, but the latter story nonetheless began with the mildly apologetic and perhaps not entirely facetious suggestion that

> among the higher animals and human beings, larceny seems to be an innate trait held in check by social conditioning. But inhibitions fail, and the primal impulse asserts itself when it comes to tape recording. Even decent folk,

who refrain from pocketing silver spoons, think nothing of taping copy-righted music. (27)

Sutherland (1945) insisted that insofar as there exists a "legal descrip-tion of acts as socially injurious and legal provision of a penalty for the act," such acts are, for the purposes of our research and understanding, crimes (compare with Tappan, 1947). This is the case even though many such acts go undetected and unprosecuted. For example, many stock and securities frauds can be prosecuted under securities statutes as well as under criminal law. The former are often "quasicriminal" statutes. Yet the behaviors prosecuted under either body of law may be identical. It is often an act of prosecutorial discretion that determines whether these be-haviors are defined clearly and officially as crimes. Sutherland insisted that such acts of official discretion were not relevant to the categoriza-tion of these behaviors for the purposes of research. In either case, the behaviors were to be regarded as criminal. Such a position can make a major difference in terms of the relationship observed between class and crime.

Consider the issue of deaths and accidents that result from events in the workplace. Occupational deaths far outnumber deaths resulting from legally defined murder (Geis, 1975). Occupational deaths generally rank third after heart disease and cancer as a source of mortality, accounting for many times more deaths than murder as ordinarily understood. The National Safety Council of the United States estimates that 14,000 people a year are killed in industrial accidents (Coleman, 1985:6). While it can-not be assumed that all or most such deaths result from the intentions of employers to see employees die, there nonetheless is good reason to believe that the majority of such deaths are not the result of employee carelessness.

One estimate (Reasons et al., 1981) holds that more than one-third of all on-the-job injuries are due to illegal working conditions, and that about another quarter are due to legal but unsafe conditions. At most, a third of all such accidents are attributed to unsafe acts on the part of em-ployees. Meanwhile, there are numerous well-documented examples of employers intentionally, knowingly, or negligently creating hazards. These include failing to follow administrative orders to alter dangerous situations and covering up the creation and existence of such hazards. For example, Reasons et al. discuss the case of a petroleum company that was fined $15,000 for violating safety regulations when three men died while cleaning out a tank containing toxic fumes. The men were not pro-vided with protective equipment nor were they trained to recognize the need for such equipment.

Another example involves administrative decisions within the Johns-Manville Corporation that led to many deaths and illnesses from asbestos poisoning (see the "Health Effects" case study below). Swartz (1978) notes that asbestos had been recognized as a serious health hazard since the turn of the century. Nonetheless, people working with it were not informed, and the government bureaucracy and medical community ignored the hazard. At the Johns-Manville plant in Manville, New Jersey, company doctors regularly diagnosed lung diseases among the asbestos workers, but never told the workers that their lung problems were related to asbestos. The Johns-Manville case is not a problem unique to the United States. As the accompanying excerpt from a Canadian royal commission report indicates, the problems of asbestos poisoning are well documented in other countries as well. The asbestos industry is not unique in this respect. Ermann and Lundman (1982) argue that many similar deaths occur in other industries and throughout the world. Swartz (1978) concludes that these deaths should be recognized as a form of murder that result from corporate policy, or what is sometimes called **corporate homicide**.

CASE STUDY

Health Effects of Asbestos in a Canadian Province

Residents of Ontario have more than the normal run of reasons to share the international feelings of apprehension that asbestos has aroused. This province is the scene of what we document in this Report to be a world-class occupational health disaster: the Johns-Manville plant in Scarborough, in the Municipality of Metropolitan Toronto. This plant, between 1948 and 1980, manufactured asbestos-cement pipe, using a mixture of two kinds of asbestos: chrysotile and crocidolite. At various times during its existence, this plant also manufactured asbestos-cement board, using only chrysotile, and asbestos insulation materials, using chrysotile and a third kind of asbestos called amosite.

As of 1983, the death toll from asbestos exposure in this plant, as measured by the number of claims awarded by Ontario Workers' Compensation Board, was 68. This lone plant, whose annual employment never exceeded 714 workers, has already occasioned more deaths from industrial disease than the entire Ontario mining industry, which annually employs over 30,000 workers, occasions from industrial accidents in an average four-year period.

The death toll at this plant, which closed in 1980, offers harsh testimony to the nature of long-latency disease. It has mounted gradually and inexorably because individual deaths are separated from the beginning of the exposures that caused them by some 10 to 30 or more years. The dimensions of the disaster have therefore been growing over time; for example, between August 1981 and August 1982, the middle year in the existence of this Commission, 5 more ex-employees died of mesothelioma, a rare cancer that is specifically associated with asbestos exposure. It is a tragically safe assumption that, among those who worked in this plant, asbestos-related deaths will continue to occur, and that hence the disaster has yet to run its course. . . .

The asbestos-induced disaster at this plant ranks with the worst that have been recorded in the international epidemiological literature on asbestos. It places the name Scarborough on an unenviable list with Charleston, South Carolina; Rochdale, England; and a handful of other places. The Scarborough plant accounts for half of all the asbestos deaths and disabilities that have been compensated by the Ontario Workers' Compensation Board. The remainder have been occasioned by exposure in a wide variety of work situations and industrial processes, for example, wartime gas mask manufacturing, brake manufacturing, and ship-building. The Ontario employers whose workers suffered asbestos disease and death are spread throughout the province; excluding Johns-Manville, only two have given rise to more than five awarded claims.

There is indeed reason to be apprehensive about asbestos in Ontario.

Source: Report of the Royal Commission on Matters of Health and Safety Arising from the Use of Asbestos in Ontario. Province of Ontario, *1984* *(reproduced with permission from the Queen's Printer for Ontario).*

Class and Crime, One More Time

This chapter does not attempt to debate the fine points in the definition of corporate homicide or to establish with any precision how many such homicides occur. It is enough to note that such deaths occur in considerable numbers and that while the consequences of these deaths have only been briefly considered for employees, corporate homicides also involve many additional numbers of consumers and the general public (see, for example, the case study "Corporate Homicide and the Ford Motor Company" on page 108). The National Product Safety Commission of the United States estimates that 20 million serious injuries and 30,000 deaths a year are caused by unsafe consumer products (Coleman, 1985:7). Corporate homicides seem likely to rival in number or even exceed those deaths resulting from homicide conceived in more traditional terms. Of more immediate interest here is the meaning of corporate homicide, and crimes like it, for the relationship between class and crime.

To pursue this interest, a fundamental point must first be made about more conventional forms of crime and delinquency. There is increasing evidence that a relatively small number of offenders accounts for a rather large proportion of serious street crimes (Greenwood, 1982; Wolfgang, 1972). The difficulty of including such persons in conventional research designs has probably obscured the relationship that exists between disadvantaged class positions and this type of criminality.

A parallel point applies to many kinds of white-collar crime. For example, crimes such as corporate homicide may occur with high incidence, but low prevalence, among highly selected subpopulations—that is, among particular employers in particular kinds of industries. The Johns-Manville Corporation and the asbestos industry is an example that has already been noted. Again, it may be difficult to pinpoint such employers in conventional research designs, and this may obscure the relationship observed between advantaged class positions and this type of criminality.

Implicit in the preceding references to street crimes and corporate homicides is the high likelihood that crime is not a unidimensional concept. That is, these are different kinds of crime that likely have different connections to the concept of class. Among adults, class probably is related negatively to making the direct physical attacks involved in street crimes of violence (Nettler, 1978), and class probably is positively related to causing harms less directly through criminal acts involving the use of organizational and corporate resources. The successful upperworld criminal rarely indulges in common crimes: why should she or he when more lucrative expropriative strategies are so easily available? (Braithwaite, 1993:223).

Similarly, among juveniles it may be that some common acts of delinquency (for example, forms of theft that include the illegal copying of computer software) are related positively to class (Cullen et al., 1985; Hagan et al., 1985; Hagan and Kay, 1990), while less frequent and more serious forms of delinquency are negatively related to class (Braithwaite, 1981; Colvin and Pauley, 1983; Elliot and Ageton, 1980; Hindelang et al., 1981; Kleck, 1982; Thornberry and Farnsworth, 1982).

Corporate Homicide and the Ford Motor Company

An interesting illustration of how important definitions of crime and deviance can be is found in the prosecution, albeit unsuccessful, of the Ford Motor Company for reckless homicide resulting from design and marketing decisions made about its subcompact car, the Pinto. Swigert and Farrell (1980) have charted the process by which notions of corporate homicide have gained legal recognition, with particular reference to the Ford Pinto case. They note that until recently, the dominant precedent, first established in the 1909 case of *People* v. *Rochester Railway and Light Company*, has been that corporations are incapable of forming the criminal intent that is necessary to constitute a provable crime like homicide against a person. Also, in many state and federal statutes, homicide is defined as the criminal slaying of "another human being," with "another" referring to the same class of being as the victim. These precedents and statutes together have acted to diminish the plausibility of the idea that corporations can, in a criminal sense, kill people. Instead, corporate misbehavior has been viewed as entailing a diffuse, impersonal kind of cost to society that should be understood in economic (that is, civil) rather than moral (that is, criminal) terms. This kind of thinking, it can be noted, allows corporate decision makers to disassociate their actions from their harmful consequences for individuals; in other words, to *neutralize* potential feelings of guilt. In more practical terms, the difference amounts to that between civil claims of unsafe-product liability and criminal charges of homicide.

However, the indictment of the Ford Motor Company and the trial that followed constituted official recognition of a new public harm—homicide by a corporation. Columnists Jack Anderson and Les Whitten (cited in Swigert and Farrell, 1980:170) brought the issue into full public view when, on December 30, 1976, they charged that:

> Buried in secret files of the Ford Motor Company lies evidence that big auto makers have put profits ahead of lives. Their lack of concern has caused thousands of people to die or be horribly disfigured in fiery car crashes. Undisclosed Ford tests have demonstrated that the big auto makers could have made safer automobiles by spending a few dollars more on each car.

Swigert and Farrell argue that this kind of press attention was a part of a reconceptualization in the public mind of the harm that can result from corporate acts. As these harms were *personalized* in press accounts, they argue, charges of criminal homicide became more plausible.

In the beginning, Swigert and Farrell note, more attention was given in news stories to the Pinto's mechanical defect, its faulty fuel-tank design, than to the issue of personal harm; furthermore, the two issues were kept separate. For example, in the Anderson–Whitten column quoted above, a harm-oriented statement, "lack of concern [of the big auto makers] has caused thousands of people to die or be horribly disfigured in fiery car crashes," was set apart from the defect-oriented comments that "in most American-made cars, the fuel tanks are located behind the rear axle. In this exposed position, a high-speed rear-end collision can cause the tank to explode, turning the car into a giant torch." Over time, however, more attention was given to the personalization of harm, and the mechanical defect and personal harm issues increasingly were fused. On February 8, 1978, for example, the *Washington Post* (cited in Swigert and Farrell, 1980:173–74) reported that punitive damages were awarded to a "teen-ager who suffered severe burns over 95 percent of his body when the gas tank of a 1972 Pinto exploded." As the two issues were combined, mechanical defect ceased to compete with personal harm as an appropriate definition of the problem. "This public recognition of personal harm," Swigert and Farrell suggest, "was ultimately reflected in the grand jury decision that the Pinto-related deaths of three Indiana teenagers were like homicide (180)."

However, while the grand jury and the state of Indiana saw grounds to indict, the trial jury, after listening to ten weeks of testimony and deliberating three days, returned a verdict of not guilty. The question that remains, then, is whether it will continue to be possible for large corporations to neutralize their guilt in the causation of individual harms, even deaths, as civil liabilities (that is, as a cost and risk of doing business) or whether a new attitude toward corporate activities might prevail. Swigert and Farrell cite several court cases that suggest the latter and quote the president of the National District Attorneys' Association as predicting that "a psychological barrier has been broken, and the big corporations are now vulnerable (177)." Time will tell.

It has sometimes appeared that measures of status are not related to crime and delinquency at all (Tittle et al., 1978). However, the study of white-collar crime and delinquency provides increasing reason to believe that measures of class are connected to crime and delinquency in interesting, albeit complicated, ways.

Finally, it is important to address an issue of motivation that often has confused analysts of class and crime. It is sometimes suggested that the scale and significance of white-collar crime calls into question the emphasis placed on social and economic inequality in accounting for criminal behavior. Braithwaite (1993) responds to this by suggesting that inequality in contemporary society simultaneously causes

Crimes of *poverty*	Crimes of *wealth*
motivated by *need*	motivated by *greed*
for goods for *use*	enabled by goods for *exchange* (that are surplus to those required for use)

The focus here is not on needs per se, but on needs as they are conceived and perceived by persons in differing positions of advantage and disadvantage. Among the poor, the need is for use, often in daily living; while among the better off, the need is for exchange, often in achieving social position and status as well as greater economic wealth. However, in both circumstances, issues of inequality and power may be involved in motivating criminal involvement.

White-Collar Crime and the Social Organization of Work

Still, not all white-collar crimes are committed by white-collar persons. For example, much embezzlement is committed by relatively low-status bank tellers (Daly, 1989). Weisburd et al. (1991) suggest that "ordinary people" are committing white-collar crimes in increasing numbers. The implication is that new and perhaps more sophisticated "expropriative strategies" are spreading downward through the social structure (compare with Cohen and Machalek, 1988; Braithwaite, 1993:222). Weisburd et al. reason that this may be happening because ordinary people now have greater access to the white-collar world of "paper fraud," including the use of computers in the growing service industries of banking and finance. They conclude that, "in this sense, lying and cheating are truly the weapons available to us all, . . . the IRS form, the phony invoice, the fraudulent application, or the hidden agreement that leads to mutual though illegal advantage are mechanisms for the commission of a virtually limitless number of crimes" (184).

Treason of the Clerks?

When one considers individuals who are detected and apprehended for some kinds of white-collar crimes, such as bank embezzlement, broadened patterns of participation do seem to emerge. For example, nearly half of the bank embezzlers included in the previous study are women. Most of these women are involved in low-level service positions, such as tellers and cashiers, that provide ample opportunities for the kinds of small scale embezzlements that are often prosecuted through the criminal justice system. Daly (1989:790) calls these "highly monitored, money-changing" jobs. Significantly, many of the crimes committed by these women can be traced to family based needs, such as medical care for a child. This kind of need is more characteristic of women who embezzle than it is of men who do so (Zeitz, 1981).

Samples of officially processed white-collar offenders are helpful in locating such crimes that have largely gone unnoticed in past work. Such samples make the point that some kinds of crime are increasing among women, as occupational roles involved are more available to them; however, these crimes also are a function of the marginal incomes many jobs provide women, the pressures the occupational incumbents experience, and the amount of employer and state control to which these employees are subjected.

Meanwhile, focusing on these officially apprehended and sanctioned offenders can also be misleading. The sense that white-collar crime is so surprisingly middle and underclass in composition emerges only when officially apprehended white-collar criminals are considered, and when the scale of involvements is not brought into the picture. As the data collected by Weisburd et al. helpfully show, you still need capital and organizational position to become a big-time white-collar criminal (Braithwaite, 1993:222).

So it still appears that white-collar crime is positively related to class position, and it is reasonable to ask why this should be so. The answer in part involves the social capital and power derived from ownership and authority positions in the occupational and organizational structures of modern corporations. These positions carry with them a freedom of action and from control that can be criminogenic. That is, to have large amounts of social and cultural capital and the power it can provide is to be *entrusted* with freedom from the kinds of constraints that may normally inhibit crime. The element of trust is a key part of the social capital that white-collar criminals often abuse. Susan Shapiro (1984) illustrates this point with a case study that describes the fraudulent activities of the infamous Equity Funding Corporation of America ("The Fallible Foundations of Trust").

The Fallible Foundations of Trust

Consider the experience of over 10,000 stockholders, many of them venerable institutional investors—endowments, foundations, banks, insurance companies, and pension funds holding the assets of millions of individuals—who owned stock worth about $228,000,000 in the nation's most rapidly growing financial conglomerate, the darling of Wall Street, the Equity Funding Corporation of America (EFCA). In order to increase the value of stock held by corporate insiders and to borrow money and acquire other companies, EFCA inflated its reported income by about $85,000,000 by recording nonexistent commission income on corporate financial statements. To generate needed cash, the company borrowed funds off the books through complicated bogus transactions involving foreign subsidiaries. To lend an illusion of production to one of its life insurance subsidiaries, company officials created $2 billion worth of fictitious insurance business and then sold the bogus policies to other insurance companies (a process called "reinsurance") in order to generate more cash. They obtained still more funds by killing off some of the nonexistent policy-holders and filing claims for death benefits. In order to create tens of thousands of fictitious policy-holder records, corporate executives and mangers held "fraud parties," working through the night to fill out bogus forms. They later created a Beverly Hills office where clerks, supplied with blank credit and medical report forms and lists of common male and female names, manufactured files from scratch.

But EFCA officials were not content to mislead banks and stockholders about the financial condition and prospects of the corporation or to defraud the life insurance companies that reinsured their bogus policy-holders. Officials and lower-level employees also engaged in considerable self-dealing, diverting corporate funds and resources for their personal benefit. These schemes included excessive (often outlandish) salaries, stock bonuses, and entertainment allowances; inflated expense account vouchers; free medical and psychiatric treatment under the guise of routine life insurance examination; outright embezzlement; corporate subsidies for personal vacations, rented Rolls Royce limousines, stereo equipment, home furnishings, and legal fees for a divorce; the diversion of legitimate corporate checks and payments to personal bank accounts; unauthorized commission income; fraudulent stock option arrangements; and insider trading. In the last instance, EFCA president Stanley Goldblum, in a unique position to be aware of the impending collapse of the corporation, sold about $1,500,000 worth of personally owned, over-valued EFCA shares—much of it just days before the New York Stock Exchange halted trading in EFCA stock—to an unsuspecting public.

These malefactions—both corporate and individual—were committed over a period of almost ten years, by dozens of witting and unwitting conspirators, before the knowing eyes of perhaps seventy-five company employees, and with the complicity or, at best, the incompetence of the company's accountants and auditors. The victims of the Equity Funding fraud had not placed their trust in some risky fly-by-night business venture. They had chosen a favorite among the "cream of this country's business and financial community" (Dirks and Gross 1974, 4), a stock listed on the New York Stock Exchange, touted by *Fortune* magazine, and singled out by the *Institutional Investor* as "one of the likely star performers in 1973" (Dirks and Gross 1974, 4).

Two months after the *Institutional Investor* article had made its predictions, EFCA was in Chapter X bankruptcy and what was to become perhaps "the largest fraud-induced bankruptcy proceeding in the history of finance" (Dirks and Gross 1974, 4). EFCA's stockholders (as well as the twelve hundred holders of $22,000,000 of EFCA debentures and four banks owed $50,000,000 plus interest) paid dearly for their trust. Stockholders ultimately received twelve cents for every dollar.

Source: Susan Shapiro, The Wayward Capitalists, *Yale University Press, 1984.*

Organized White-Collar Crime

The organizational form of the corporation is crucial to understanding much white-collar crime (Ermann and Lundman, 1978; Hagan, 1982; Reiss, 1981; Schrager and Short, 1978; Wheeler, 1976). As Wheeler and Rothman (1982) succinctly note, the corporation "is for white-collar criminals what the gun or knife is for the common criminal—a tool to obtain money from victims." Pontell and Calavita (1993) make a similar point even more succinctly when they observe that "the best way to rob a bank is to own it."

Of course, the importance of the corporation is not restricted to the world of crime. From the industrial revolution on, it has become increasingly apparent that "among the variety of interests that men have, those interests that have been successfully collected to create corporate actors are the interests that dominate the society" (Coleman, 1974). This reference to men in particular is not accidental, for corporate entities are disproportionately male in employment, ownership, and control. Our interest is in developing an understanding of the link between the power of the corporate form and the criminogenic freedom that this powerful structure generates.

The corporation itself is a "legal fiction," as H. L. Mencken aptly observed, "with no pants to kick or soul to damn." That is, the law chooses to treat corporations as "juristic persons," making them formally liable to the same laws as "natural persons." Some of the most obvious faults in this legal analogy become clear when the impossibility of imprisoning or executing corporations is considered. However, there are more subtle differences between corporate and individual actors with equally significant consequences.

For example, the old legal saw tells us that the corporation has no conscience or soul. Stone (1975) describes the problem well:

> When individuals are placed in an organizational structure, some of the ordinary internalized restraints seem to lose their hold. And if we decide to look beyond the individual employees and find an organizational "mind" to work with, a "corporate conscience" distinct from the consciences of particular individuals, it is not readily apparent where we would begin—much less what we would be talking about.

Stone goes on to suggest some interesting ways in which the corporate conscience and corporate responsibility could be increased (see also Nagorski, 1989). However, the point is that these mechanisms, or others, have not been put in place. Corporate power in this sense remains unchecked, and it is in this sense criminogenic.

The problem is in part the absence of cultural beliefs to discourage corporate criminality (Geis, 1962). C. Wright Mills (1956) captured part of the problem in his observation that "it is better, so the image runs, to take one dime from each of ten million people at the point of a corporation than $100,000 from each of ten banks at the point of a gun." Nonetheless, there is some evidence that cultural climates vary across time and regimes. For example, Sally Simpson (1986), who studied antitrust violations in the United States between 1927 and 1981, found that such violations were more common during Republican than Democratic administrations. However, even when condemnatory beliefs about corporate crime have been strong, there have been too few controlling mechanisms in place to impose their controlling influence effectively.

Consider, for a moment, the internal structure of a typical modern corporation, as illustrated by Woodmansee's description of the General Electric Corporation (cited in Clinard and Yeager, 1980; see also Shearing et al., 1985). Note the complexity of this enterprise and its gender stratification.

We begin by describing the way GE's employees are officially organized into separate layers of authority. The corporation is like a pyramid. The great majority of the company's workers form the base of the pyramid; they take orders coming down from the above but do not give orders to anyone else. If you were hired by GE for one of these lowest level positions, you might find yourself working on an assembly line, installing a motor in a certain type of refrigerator. You would be in a group of five to 50 workers who all take orders from one supervisor, or foreman, or manager. Your supervisor is on the second step of the pyramid; she or he, and the other supervisors who specialize in this type of refrigerator, all take orders from a General Manager.

There are about 180 of these General Managers at GE; each one heads a Department with one or two thousand employees. The General Manager of your Department, and the General Managers of the one of two other Departments which produce GE's other types of refrigerators, are in turn supervised by the Vice President/General Manager of the Refrigerator Division. This man (there are only men at this level and above) is one of the 50 men at GE responsible for heading GE's Divisions. He, and the heads of several other Divisions which produce major appliances, look up to the next step of the pyramid and see, towering above, the Vice President/Group Executive who heads the entire Major Appliance Group. While there are over 300,000 workers at the base of the pyramid, there are only 10 men on this Group Executive level. Responsibility for overseeing all of GE's product lines is divided between the ten. At about the same level of authority in the company are the executives of GE's Corporate Staff; these men are concerned not with particular products but with general corporate matters such as accounting, planning, legal affairs, and relations with employees, with the public and with government.

And now the four men at the top of the pyramid come into view; the three Vice Chairmen of the Board of Directors, and standing above them, GE's Chief Executive. . . . Usually, these four men confer alone, but once a month, 15 other men join them for a meeting. The 15 other members of the Board of Directors are not called up from the lower levels of the GE pyramid; they drift in sideways from the heights of neighboring pyramids. Thirteen of them are chairmen or presidents of other corporations, the fourteenth is a former corporate chairman, and the fifteenth is a university president.

Could the board of directors of this corporation exercise the kind of control over its employees that individual actors are expected by law to exercise, for example, over their dependents? Stone (1975) points out that top officers and directors, theoretically, are liable to suit by the corporation itself (via a shareholders' action) if they allow a law violation to occur through negligence. However, Stone then cites a frequently noted antitrust case to make the point that, legally, little is expected from corporations in the way of control over their individual actors. In dismissing the claim made in a case against the Allis-Chalmers Corporation, the judgment (*Graham* v. *Allis-Chalmers Mfg. Co.*, 188 A.2d 125, 130[Del. 1963]) indicates that ". . . absent cause for suspicion there is no duty upon the directors to install and operate a corporate system . . . to ferret out wrongdoing which they have no reason to suspect exists." The effect of this kind of decision is to reinforce the power of top management to keep itself uninformed about the very details of illegal activities that the public interest may require they know.

An example of executive disengagement from crimes is hinted at in a well-known E. F. Hutton check-kiting scheme. In this case, the Hutton brokerage firm admitted operating a scheme that obtained billions of dollars in interest-free loans from dozens of banks from 1980 to 1982, by systematically overdrawing its bank accounts and purposely delaying the clearing of its checks. Hutton paid a $2 million fine and agreed to make restitution to the banks that lost money. However, a central question that remains is how high up in the executive structure of Hutton did knowledge of this improper overdrafting scheme go? The chairman of a U.S. congressional subcommittee that investigated the matter noted that "there is no tape of somebody confessing, but a look at the circumstantial evidence indicates that people at Hutton headquarters were encouraging this activity" (*The Toronto Star* 22 September 1985:B1). It is, of course, possible that such schemes were encouraged without the need for top officials to know the exact ways and means by which they were accomplished.

A Criminogenic Market Structure

How widespread is this use of "executive influence from afar" and "executive distancing and disengagement" in corporate criminality? Two intriguing studies (Baumhart, 1961; Brenner and Molander, 1977) suggest that the problem is large. The latter of these studies reports that the percentage of executives who indicate an inability to be honest in providing information to top management has nearly doubled since the earlier research, done in the 1950s. About half of those surveyed thought that their superiors frequently did not want to know how results were obtained, as long as the desired outcome was accomplished. Furthermore, the executives surveyed "frequently complained of superiors' pressure to support incorrect viewpoints, sign false documents, overlook superiors' wrongdoing, and do business with superiors' friends" (Brenner and Molander, 1977).

The last set of findings suggest not only a growing freedom at the top of organizations from the need to know and accept responsibility for criminal activity below, but also a growing pressure from the top down that is itself criminogenic. Farberman (1975) has referred to such pressures in the automotive industry, and in other highly concentrated corporate sectors, as constituting a "criminogenic market structure." The crime-generating feature of these markets is their domination by a relatively small number of manufacturers who insist that their dealers sell in high volume at a small per-unit profit. Dealerships that fail to perform risk the loss of their franchises in an industry where the alternatives are few. A result is high pressure to maximize sales and minimize service. More specifically, Farberman suggests that dealers in the car industry may be induced by the small profit margins on new cars to compensate through fraudulent warranty work and repair rackets. The connection between these findings is that the executives of the automotive industry can distance themselves from the criminal consequences of the "forcing model" (high volume/low per-unit profit) they impose. The result is an absence of control over repair and warranty frauds at the dealership level.

Farberman also points out that corporate concentration can be criminogenic in that it diminishes the corrective role competition can play in restraining criminal practices that increase the costs of production. Asch and Seneca (1969) conclude from their research that high concentration is in particular related to higher rates of crime in consumer goods industries. This receives further support from Clinard and Yeager's (1980) finding that the oil, auto, and pharmaceutical industries appear to violate the law more frequently than do other industries. Particular types of crime, such as collusion and antitrust activity, may also be more common in highly concentrated industries (Coleman, 1987).

A striking microlevel example of collusion in a setting that restricts competition is reported by Wayne Baker (1984). In a study of trading in the pits of securities markets, Baker observed that traders organized themselves in tightly knit social groups that jealously guarded their pits. As a result, they often did not "hear" better bids shouted by traders who visited from other pits, and they juggled trades to exhaust the capital of outsiders.

High Profit Crimes

The scale of the crimes that access to corporate resources makes possible is unique. Shapiro (1984:9) reports that while an average robbery nets its perpetrator $338, offenses investigated by the Securities Exchange Commission cost their victims, on average, over $400,000.

In an intriguing study, Wheeler and Rothman (1982) categorized white-collar offenders into three groups: (1) those who committed offenses alone or with affiliated others using neither an occupational nor an organizational role (individual offenders); (2) those who committed offenses alone or with affiliated others using an occupational role (occupational offenders); and (3) those who committed offenses in which both organization and occupation were ingredients (organizational offenders).

The results of this study indicate in a variety of ways the enormous advantages accruing to those who use formal organizations in their crimes. For example, across a subset of four offenses, the median "take" for individual offenders was $5,279, for occupational offenders $17,106, and for organizational offenders $117,392. In a parallel Canadian study, Hagan and Parker (1985) report that securities violators who make use of organizational resources commit crimes that involve larger numbers of victims and are broader in their geopolitical spread. Why the organizational edge? Wheeler and Rothman (1982) answer with an example.

> Represented by its president, a corporation entered into a factoring agreement with a leading . . . commercial bank, presenting it with $1.2 million in false billings over the course of seven months; the company's statements were either inflated to reflect much more business than actually was being done, or were simply made up. Would the bank have done this for an individual? Whether we conclude that organizations are trusted more than individuals, or that they simply operate on a much larger scale, it is clear that the havoc caused when organizations are used outside the law far exceeds anything produced by unaffiliated actors.

Just as the organizational form has facilitated economic and technological development on a scale far beyond that achieved by individuals, so too has this form allowed criminal gains of a magnitude that men and women acting alone would find hard to attain.

The Globalization of White-Collar Crime

Often the international scope of business and finance expands the potential for profitable white-collar crime. The Bank of Credit and Commerce International (BCCI) scandal discussed in the case study on page 120 is a highly publicized recent example of the danger of some globalized white-collar crimes. Meanwhile, many U.S. corporations regularly make remarkable untaxed profits by manipulating their books to show capital gains in their foreign subsidiaries. A favorite practice is to underprice products sold to foreign subsidiaries, which are then resold for largely untaxed or lower-taxed profits (Harvard Law Review, 1976). These practices are illegal, but they are difficult to control and poorly monitored by the Internal Revenue Service.

International price-fixing provides another example. This practice was pioneered in the oil industry by companies like Exxon, Shell, and British Petroleum long before the Organization for Petroleum Exporting Countries (OPEC) attracted worldwide attention with its oil cartel. Detailed and far-reaching agreements controlled the price of international oil in the period leading up to World War II, and some believe that these agreements lasted much longer (Coleman, 1985:28–29).

In another example, the drug and pharmaceutical industry has often taken advantage of markets in developing countries to "dump" products that have been found unsafe in industrialized nations with tougher drug-safety laws (Braithwaite, 1984). One of the better known instances involved the Dalkon Shield intrauterine contraceptive device that was sold overseas for a considerable period after being declared unsafe in the United States. The risks associated with these products are rarely disclosed by the marketing companies, and when side-effects and other problems are revealed, they typically are worded to meet minimum disclosure requirements of the country involved.

Possibly even more disturbing is the way in which new drugs that are too costly or risky to test in highly regulated countries are tested in developing nations. Oral contraceptives were first given clinical trials, for example, by the Searle corporation in the 1950s in Puerto Rico. Similar practices were followed in testing later methods of contraception in a series of less developed countries, and often on samples drawn from the poorest groups within these countries. Informed consent is rarely required in these countries and the risks of lawsuits are minimal.

Banking beyond Boundaries and the BCCI Affair

The Bank of Credit and Commerce International (BCCI) played a substantial role in world narcotics trafficking by helping to obscure the sources of illegal profits made in the drug trade and by helping to move huge amounts of money illegally across national boundaries. This bank was chartered in Luxembourg in 1972 by Agha Hasan Abedi, a Pakistani who stressed his goal of providing services to the Third World. By the late 1980s, BCCI had become the seventh largest private bank in the world, holding $23 billion in assets and operating in 72 countries. In addition to taking over several American banks, BCCI is reputed to have had among its powerful customers Colombian drug lords, dictators like Duvalier, Somoza, Saddam Hussein, Marcos, Noriega, as well as the Abu Nidal terrorist organization and perhaps Western intelligence agencies (Passas and Groskin, 1993). Although the Federal Bureau of Investigation and the Drug Enforcement Administration had developed suspicious intelligence about BCCI by the late 1970s, it was not until the late 1980s that serious efforts were made to prosecute BCCI activities.

These efforts were built around Operation C-Chase, an undercover sting operation to develop evidence about money laundering operations linking the United States and Central and South America. Undercover agents in this operation posed as "investment fund managers" who would offer "professional money laundering services" to drug traffickers. BCCI was targeted by this operation when it eagerly offered its advice about additional ways of moving money to safe havens while circumventing U.S. bank secrecy laws requiring reports on such transactions. BCCI was in part apparently motivated to do this by losses it was experiencing in its treasury and loan operations. The undercover operations led in 1988 to indictments of eleven BCCI officials and coparticipants, and in 1992 five of the BCCI officials received prison sentences of from three to twelve years.

Many factors may explain the length of time taken to complete these prosecutions, but two key and related difficulties involved BCCI's ability to mount a massive legal defense effort involving prominent political figures, and the international scope of the transactions involved. Clark Clifford, a Washington insider who advised U.S. presidents from Truman to Carter, led a defense team of over 50 lawyers from 20 different law firms costing more than $45 million (Passas and Groskin, 1993). This defense team was able to take great advantage of the fact that many of the BCCI violations were undertaken outside the United States. Key witnesses were located overseas where money laundering was not a crime and relevant extradition provisions were nonexistent. Essential information was made unavailable by laws protecting the confidentiality and secrecy of foreign banking operations. And foreign governments withheld their cooperation in facilitating U.S. prosecutions, perhaps for fear of embarrassing their own officials or prominent Americans.

BCCI was a global scandal that involved the movements of extraordinarily large amounts of money from and for criminal purposes and by criminal means. It was a scandal that continues to be difficult to fully expose in part because of the breadth of its operations and the power of the persons it directly and indirectly involved. Passas and Groskin (1993:19) conclude that "there are a number of high level and well known figures who could be damaged by such revelations and they come from many different political, ideological, geographical, racial and economic groups." The sheer scale of these white-collar crimes as well as the prominence of the participants provided protection from prosecution.

Source: Nikos Passas and Richard Groskin, "BCCI and the Federal Authorities: Regulatory Anesthesia and the Limits of Criminal Law," paper presented at the 1993 annual meeting of the Society for the Study of Social Problems, Miami Beach, Florida

---

Braithwaite (1984:265–70) reports that drug companies have developed highly rationalized strategies for bringing new drugs to market in developed and more highly regulated countries by moving through staged series of less controlled settings. Figure 4.1 outlines a scheduled strategy for a hypothetical new drug. This schedule might begin with preliminary marketing and clinical testing in a country such as Paraguay, where new product registration generally can be accomplished within a month. Then some clinical testing might be undertaken in a developed country such as Belgium, where new drug approval can often be completed in six to eight months. This approval can then be used to obtain entry into a large market in a developing nation such as Brazil,

FIGURE 4.1

Diagram of international registration for a hypothetical new pharmaceutical drug. (*Source: adapted from Braithwaite, 1984:269*)

January 1991	June 1991	January 1992	June 1992	January 1993	June 1993

• 1 month • Paraguay
(Preliminary Marketing & Testing)

• 6 months • Belgium
(Clinical Testing & Approval)

• 2 months • Brazil/Mexico/Philippines
(Larger Scale Marketing)

• 6 months • Great Britain

• 3 months • Australia, New Zealand, Sweden, Germany

• 9 months • United States

• • Rest of World

with subsequent efforts to obtain approval and entry into more lucrative but controlled markets of developed countries. In effect, this process makes Third World people "guinea pigs" for the developed nations, in a marketing strategy designed to maximize economic profits and minimize legal risks.

A further way in which foreign markets are maintained and expanded is through the payment of various kinds of bribes. These bribes are especially effective in developing countries where individual politicians are easily convinced to relax laws for multinational corporations. However, the bribery scandals involving the Lockheed Aircraft Corporation in the 1970s further revealed a range of developed as well as developing countries where such payments were common. These countries included the Netherlands, Japan, West Germany, and Italy, as well as the Philippines, Turkey, Mexico, Colombia, and Venezuela. In the Netherlands, the husband of the Dutch queen received payments, and in Japan the former prime minister was implicated. These kinds of practices continue to receive much publicity in Japan, where efforts to reform political practices have proven particularly problematic.

Finally, no discussion of the internationalization of white-collar crime is complete without some mention of the illegal activities undertaken by and through governments (Halperin et al., 1976). Often these activities are launched at the behest of corporate interests, especially in response to concerns about the security of foreign investments. From the Bay of Pigs to the Iran-Contra affair, the U.S. government has demonstrated a continuing willingness to enter into embarrassingly unethical and illegal military adventures. The largest of these involved the CIA's secret wars in Southeast Asia during the 1960s and 1970s. Thousands of armed mercenaries were financially supported by the U.S. government in military actions that explicitly contravened laws forbidding such practices. Despite the public outrage that ultimately condemned these activities, the U.S. government resumed its use of mercenaries in Nicaragua within a decade.

This section has sought to make the point that the structure of the modern and often multinational corporation allows a power imbalance to prevail in which those individuals at the top experience a relative freedom, while those lower down often experience pressure applied from the top that encourages various kinds of white-collar crime. The same point can be made with regard to the use of political power in government. The point has also been made that the corporate form itself can be used effectively to perpetrate "bigger and better crimes" than can be achieved by individuals acting alone, and that these crimes can have an

international reach, often involving governments. Access to corporate resources is a unique advantage of class positions involving ownership
and authority in business organizations. It is in this sense that it can be
said that the social organization of work in the world of the modern corporation can itself be criminogenic. The power of high political office can
be similarly criminogenic, as illustrated in the classic case of Watergate
discussed in the case study below.

CASE STUDY

Explaining "Watergate"

The American experience called "Watergate" is a chronology of
events that spanned the period from June 12, 1972, to August 8,
1974. The outline of these events is familiar to many readers,
beginning with the unsuccessful break-in at the Democratic
National Committee headquarters in Washington's Watergate
complex, and including the payment of cover-up money to
silence participants. The most comprehensive view of executive
activity during the course of these events is provided in the
Presidential Transcripts (1974), the abridged 1,200-page record of
selected White House conversations. We can use these transcripts
to consider explanations of the Watergate crimes. Of course, a
problem in using these materials is that they are known to be
incomplete. However, we will argue that in spite of the self-
serving potential of the transcripts, they actually provide support
for an explanation of Watergate that is far from flattering (Hagan,
1975).

At least five rationalizations, or neutralizations, of the Watergate cover-up were offered in the course of Nixon's conversations. They include:

1. the protection of national security: ". . . the whole thing was
   national security" (125)

2. the protection of the presidency: ". . . it isn't the man, it's the
   office" (267)

3. support of the defendants: ". . . this was not an obstruction of
   justice, we were simply trying to help these defendants"
   (339)

4. loyalty: "Well, the point is, whatever we say about Harry
   Truman, etc., while it hurt him, a lot of people admired the
   old bastard for standing by people" (359)

5. the country's future: "If there's one thing you have got to do,
   you have got to maintain the presidency out of this. I have
   got things to do for this country" (673)

The most important of these rationalizations, judging from the
attention it received from the participants, was the assertion that
administration agents were simply trying to "help" defendants
by offering them cash payments. However, discussions relating
to the support rationalization reveal that its importance was as
an excuse, or justification, rather than as a cause for the payments
being made. For example, in the March 21, 1973, conversation in
which the decision was made to pay Howard Hunt "hush
money" (133), the discussion was entirely tactical.

> **President:** That's why for your immediate things you have no
> choice but to come up with the $120,000, or whatever it is.
> Right?
>
> **Dean:** That's right.
>
> **President:** Would you agree that that's the prime thing, that
> you damn well better get that done?
>
> **Dean:** Obviously he ought to be given some signal anyway.
>
> **President:** (Expletive deleted), get it.

Several weeks later, on April 14, the support rationalization
appears for the first time, with little effort to deny its justificatory
character. Here the former president reports: "Support, well, I
heard something about that at a much later time" (242). Later in
the same conversation (272), the ad hoc character of the rationalization becomes even more obvious.

> **Haldeman:** What Dean did, he did with all conscience in
> terms . . . [of] the higher good.
>
> **President:** Dean, you've got to have a talk with Dean. I feel
> that I should not talk to him.
>
> **Ehrlichman:** I have talked to him.
>
> **President:** What's he say about motive. He says it was a hush-
> up?
>
> **Ehrlichman:** . . . He says he knew, he had to know that people
> were trying to bring that result about.

Similar discussions surround the remaining neutralizations. In
each case, the rationalization is introduced in a justificatory con-

text. The concerns are tactical: the avoidance of legal prosecution, political embarrassment, and moral blame. These concerns relate more to the consequences than to the causes of upperworld crime.

The actors involved in Watergate proved unconstrained by either moral ties or by a set of operating principles that were themselves unclear. A careful reading of the *Presidential Transcripts* reveals few references to, or considerations of, societal values. Occasional mention is made of the Nixon administration's "commitment" to "law and order"; however, the references are in passing (362), and obviously not a matter of extended consideration. Repeatedly, the rights and obligations of the executive branch (for example, the limits of "executive privilege," the meaning of "national security," and the scope of "high crimes and misdemeanors") were debated in terms of a vague Constitution and undecided public opinion. Similarly, the situational controls operative at the time of the initial Watergate offenses were inadequate. White House aides were able to manipulate funds and personnel for criminal political purposes with little expectation of detection. One reason why there was so little expectation of detection, of course, was that the criminals in this case were people who controlled the institutions of legal control (who could have been better positioned to deviate than those who controlled the FBI, the Justice Department, and so forth?). Furthermore, once "caught," punishment became problematic in an atmosphere confused by promiscuous discussions of pardons. The uncertainties surrounding these events emphasize the enormous amount of trust placed in high elected officials, and the porous nature of the controls operative in these upperworld settings.

If there is a message to the policy-minded in the Watergate experience, it is that checks and balances on power are crucial. Upperworld vocations, particularly politics and business, often carry with them a measure of trust and a corresponding freedom to deviate that is unparalleled in the criminal underworld.

White-Collar Crime and Legal Sanctions

Given the distribution of trust, freedom, and pressure that has been associated with the structure of the modern corporation, and the power this gives to those who run it, a question that recurs is: what does the law do to remedy the potential for abuse? This question raises issues of legal liability and the enforcement of law.

Civil and Administrative Sanctions

"We have arranged things," writes Christopher Stone (1975), "so that the people who call the shots do not have to bear the full risks." This, in a nutshell, is the consequence of the limited liabilities borne by modern corporate actors.

> Take, for example, a small corporation involved in shipping dynamite. The shareholders of such a company, who are typically also the managers, do not *want* their dynamite-laden truck to blow up. But if it does, they know that those injured cannot, except in rare cases, sue them as individuals to recover their full damages if the amount left in the corporations' bank account is inadequate to make full compensation. . . . What this means is that in deciding how much money to spend on safety devices, and whether or not to allow trucks to drive through major cities, the calculations are skewed toward higher risks than suggested by the "rational economic corporation/free market" model that is dreamily put forth in textbooks. If no accident results, the shareholders will reap the profits of skimping on safety measures. If a truck blows up, the underlying human interests will be shielded from fully bearing the harm that they have caused. And then, there is nothing to prevent the same men from setting up a new dynamite shipping corporation the next day; all it takes is the imagination to think up a new name, and some $50 in filing fees. (Stone, 1075)

It may be conceded that large corporations are not quite so free as the small corporation in the example to dissolve and reconstitute their operations.

However, the separation of shareholder and management interests gives rise to a related problem of liability. Given that corporate officers gain their primary rewards through salaries, the effects of damage judgments are indirect, and judging from experience, limited. Stone (1975) reminds us that in 1972, for example, the Ford Motor Company suffered fines and penalties of approximately $7 million for a violation of the U.S. Environmental Protection Act. Yet the salaries of the chief executives of this company increased dramatically in following years. There is no record of shareholders successfully altering such patterns by changing management in the wake of lawsuits. There are also indications that companies such as the Johns-Manville Corporation have filed for protection under federal bankruptcy laws in the United States to limit their potential liability from lawsuits.

A variety of studies indicate that efforts to regulate corporate and white-collar crime through the use of administrative law characteristically involve regulators essentially bargaining enforcement with the regulated. Yeager (1991) found this to be the case in his analysis of enforcement of the Environmental Protection Act. For example, he found that large firms were more successful in appealing the terms of their pollution control permits to administrative law judges, often because of these corporations' greater technical capabilities to press their cases on legal and technical grounds. When other tactics failed, years of delay were gained by the bigger and better defended firms.

Such findings parallel other studies in a tradition of research that dates to Kolko's (1963) classic analysis of the federal Meat Inspection Act of 1906. More recently, Lynxwiler et al. (1983) found larger companies obtaining similar advantages through their use of technical expertise and threat of legal appeals with field inspectors for the federal Office of Surface Mining Reclamation and Enforcement. Among other advantages, the larger companies also experienced smaller fines. Hawkins (1983) also found larger companies better able to negotiate outcomes with field inspectors charged with enforcement of water pollution regulations in Great Britain. Yeager (1994) concludes that "in bargaining over what is to be the reality of regulation, law inescapably reflects and reproduces the favored status of major producers."

These findings raise difficult issues of how the law is used to control white-collar crime. The simple fact is that administrative and civil remedies are often ineffective. We turn now to criminal sanctions, beginning with the decision making that goes into the prosecution of white-collar cases. The following section draws heavily on interviews from a study of U.S. federal courts and U.S. attorney offices.

Prosecuting White-Collar Crimes

A key issue in white-collar crime law enforcement involves the way in which resources are organized. In the United States, most of this law enforcement occurs through U.S attorney offices associated with the federal courts. This is in part because many white-collar crimes are defined by federal statutes, but also because most state courts are organized almost exclusively to respond to cases brought to them by local police, which in turn respond mainly to the large and steady flow of complaints of citizens. This **reactive** form of law enforcement seldom involves much white-collar crime.

In contrast, the federal courts have much greater potential for selectively determining the composition and size of their caseloads, although they do not always develop this potential. The federal courts receive the bulk of their case referrals from federal agencies (for example, the Federal Bureau of Investigation, the Drug Enforcement Agency, and the Internal Revenue Service), which have greater responsibilities for white-collar law enforcement; but they are not limited to agency input. Some U.S. attorney offices attached to federal courts have their own investigative agents. Furthermore, by working closely with federal prosecutors, the enforcement agencies can play a more creative role in **proactively** determining which areas of enforcement the court will emphasize.

As a result, federal courts sometimes devote considerable attention to the prosecution of upperworld as well as underworld crime. Hagan and Bernstein (1979) illustrate this point with excerpts from interviews, first with an assistant U.S. attorney in a proactively organized office.

> [T]he way I operate is I basically initiate grand jury investigations where I think it is appropriate. The ___ case, which was a major securities sales fraud case, is a very good example of that. Basically my philosophy is that the resources here are limited. . . . You can never prosecute all the crimes that are being committed, and you can never prosecute all the white-collar crimes. Going into the decision-making process for me are the following: (1) I want it to be obviously a case with federal impact—that is, a federal problem that we are looking at, and not a local state problem; (2) that the impact is broad; and (3) for me particularly I prefer to make cases in areas where nothing has been done. In other words, to focus on an industry or problem where there has not been a criminal prosecution. . . . So, I will pick an area such as securities fraud where there was a lot of good information about serious abuses but no criminal prosecutions and begin a grand jury investigation. And that resulted in the ___ case being brought and successfully prosecuted. And there are other areas. . . . I will just focus on areas where there really hasn't been federal criminal enforcement, areas which have a consumer impact, and develop cases in those areas.

Yet many U.S. attorneys take a different view, as illustrated by the following response encountered in a much more reactive U.S. attorney's office, using the reactive and proactive concepts just introduced.

> For the most part, they [the enforcement agencies] are the experts. They know whether there is a crime and they know how to prove it. They will get the facts and bring us a package and there it is. I don't know the FBI in Chicago, but I would imagine . . . more [the U.S. Attorney] sitting down

with the FBI and saying, "Okay, I want to go after political corruption, let's go get it." . . . We are basically a reactive agency and before setting priorities we have to consider that. We can't just shut down our reactive side and go proactive and say "I'm sorry we can't accept complaints now because we are too busy doing this." We have to respond to the needs of all agencies and enforce the law.

The latter approach produces a caseload composed largely of conventional underworld (that is, street) crime.

Making a U.S. attorney's office more proactive in orientation involves the creation of new types of cases, cases that U.S. attorneys emphasize can be expensive and protracted in development.

It is damn hard to . . . successfully prosecute these kinds of cases. They [U.S. Attorneys] shouldn't go in unless they know how to do it and they frequently don't know how to do it.

It would be nice to investigate let's say public corruption. "Okay, FBI, I want you to go out and develop snitches in all the HEW places where they might be taking bribes". . .but God knows how much time [that would take] and we don't have the resources to do that.

It is difficult—it is a very difficult process of trying to do everything that should be done and yet still allowing yourself to free up enough resources to do the cases that are more difficult and need to be done but aren't so obvious. There's always a balancing act that is very difficult.

In most areas of white-collar crime it is difficult to develop the evidence that is required to secure convictions, because the victimization is diffuse and the targets (for example, in many financial, environmental, and political corruption cases) do not know they have been victimized. One respondent comments in Hagan and Bernstein's (1979) research that, "it's not like a bank robbery where you have eyewitnesses that didn't take part in the crime, but merely saw it happen. You don't have that in official corruption . . . [here] the only people that know about the crime are involved in the crime." A means must therefore be developed for "turning witnesses" and securing their "cooperation" in the prosecution of a case.

The ways of eliciting cooperation from defendants in white-collar cases often involve threats of coercion, as suggested by the following excerpt from Hagan and Bernstein's field interviews.

Q: How do you urge cooperation from defendants?

A: We threaten to send them to jail. It's the most effective way we've ever done it. We make a good, solid case on them and hang it over their head like a hammer.

Q: And what are the mechanics of doing that, how exactly do you present it to the defendant?

A: We tell them "if you don't cooperate, we will convict you. And we will do it in a way that will make you look—we'll do it so well that you would get really good jail time, a solid big chunk of time."

Q: At what stage do you do this?

A: Well, we are willing to make deals with people in a whole host of ways running all the way from giving them a "pass" to they just don't get prosecuted at all in return for testifying.

Q: Do you usually indict them first?

A: We make deals at all stages. . . . We talk to them before indictment in the very big cases. Then we have all kinds of pleas like a guy has committed a felony. We'll let him plead to a misdemeanor and won't prosecute . . . a whole range of things all the way 'til he pleads to the principal count . . . to charging him with exactly what he did and saying nice things about him at sentencing.

Concessions are also promised in many white-collar cases, with the standard operating rule of "first in, best out."

Q: Is there anything that suggests that one defendant should get a better deal than another?

A: Yes. As soon as I heard there was an investigation into an area in which I knew I was criminally involved, I would run to the U.S. Attorney's Office and say, "Look, I will tell you all about it."

Q: You mean you reward those who come first?

A: Well, typically you have to work it—it's kind of a callous way to approach it, but you have to work "first in, best out." That is the way you have to do it. It is unfortunate, but say you've offered a deal to somebody and he rejects it and the next guy takes it; well, if you go back to the first guy or he comes back to you, he's no longer the first. So he doesn't get as good a deal as the first in. It's the way you have to work and the defense lawyers know it.

Federal prosecutors emphasize the importance of communicating their intentions and actions, as well as the consequences of those actions, to the community of defense lawyers and to judges as well. An assistant U.S. attorney in Hagan and Bernstein's study observes that "the bar has got to be conditioned to flipping people. You can't do it by yourself. You have got to have a sophisticated defense attorney on the other side who knows when it is in their client's interest to cooperate." Another assistant U.S. attorney remarks of the judiciary, "I would say most judges understand that in order to expose official corruption you do have to give some concessions to people who are involved. Again, because only those people who are involved know and can testify about it."

Perhaps even more interesting, however, is the way this practical need is coordinated with the principles of sentencing: cooperation is treated as a sign of contrition and thus predictive of rehabilitation. Of course, this may be more rationalization than reason, as suggested in the following excerpt from one of the previous assistant U.S. attorney interviews.

> I would say the judges do give some consideration simply because it does show contrition and judges are going to disagree with me on this but, when a federal district court judge gets to the point of passing sentence upon people, he is acting not only as a representative of the people but he is also acting as a law enforcement officer, because whatever sentence he gives may bring about cooperation and may cause him [the defendant] to tell the U.S. Attorney about other criminal activity.

This prosecutor at least seems more concerned with the results than with the rationalization of concessions in prosecuting white-collar crime.

Sentencing White-Collar Criminals

This brings us to the issue of sentencing. What happens to the white-collar offenders who are held criminally liable and processed through the criminal justice system? Are they liable to as severe sanctioning as others? Or, do concessions at the sentencing stage result in white-collar lenience? Notions of "equality before the law" are perhaps nowhere more subjective in meaning than in their application to the sentencing of white-collar offenders (Hagan and Albonetti, 1982). This is reflected in the kinds of comments made by judges about the sentences they impose for white-collar crimes. For example, it is reflected in the suggestion that white-collar offenders experience sanctions differently than other kinds of offenders, in the assertion that different kinds of sanctions are appropriate in white-collar cases, as well as in the view that signs of contrition among white-collar offenders, especially in the form of guilty pleas, should be rewarded with concessions in sentencing.

It is especially common for judges to suggest that white-collar offenders experience sanctions differently than other kinds of defendants. This view is well summarized in Mann, Wheeler, and Sarat's (1980) conclusions after interviewing a sample of judges who have tried such cases that, "most judges have a . . . belief that the suffering experienced by a white-collar person as a result of apprehension, public indictment and conviction, and the collateral disabilities incident to conviction—loss of job, professional licenses, and status in the community—completely satisfies the need to punish the individual." This belief persists in the face of findings from a recent study by Benson (1989:474) that "although they commit the most serious offenses, employers and managers are least likely to lose their jobs after conviction for a white-collar crime." The argument for white-collar leniency endures in the minds of judges and others: the defendant, having suffered enough from the acts of prosecution and conviction, does not require a severe sentence.

What kinds of sentences, therefore, are judged appropriate for white-collar offenders? In white-collar cases, judges articulate what they see as a recurring problem—how the goal of general deterrence may be accomplished without doing (perceived) injustice to the individual offender. A judge interviewed by Mann et al. (1980) suggests the mental conflict this dilemma stimulates.

> The problem is the tension between use of incarceration for its deterrent factors, and the inclination not to use it because it is too excessive given the non-criminal record of the [white-collar] offender. From the individual standpoint there are good arguments against sentencing; from the societal interest of deterring crime there are some good arguments for using the sentence. . . . The tension between those two values is very acute.

Mann et al. (1980) conclude that most judges seek a compromise in resolving this dilemma. "The weekend sentence, the very short jail term, and the relatively frequent use of amended sentences (where a judge imposes a prison term and later reduces it) are evidence of this search for a compromise."

It is important to acknowledge the disputed role of fines in sentencing white-collar offenders. Posner (1980) asserts that "the white-collar criminal . . . should be punished only by monetary penalties." His argument is that if fines are suitably large they are an equally effective deterrent and cheaper to administer, and therefore socially preferable to imprisonment and other "afflictive" punishments. It has already been noted that corporate entities are liable to little else than fines. However, Mann et al. (1980) find judges to be skeptical of the effectiveness of fines. They report

> a conspicuous absence of responses by judges that a fine was the appropriate sanction to be imposed on a defendant. . . . Where fines were used in conjunction with another sentence it was generally the other sentence . . .

that was thought to have the intended deterrent effect. Where the fine was used alone, the idea that the commencement of the criminal process against the defendant was the punishment seemed to be more important in the judges' minds than the fine itself.

The sense that emerges is that judges are acutely aware of the issues of deterrence, disparity, and discrimination in the sentencing of white-collar offenders, and that they attempt to respond to these issues by fashioning sentences that combine sanctions in a compromise fashion. Consistent with this view, Hagan and Nagel (1982) found, in a sentencing study in the Southern District of New York, that judges attempted to compensate for the shorter prison terms given to white-collar offenders by adding probation or fines to their sentences. Similarly, fines were most frequently used in conjunction with prison and probation sentences. In any case, all of these findings suggest the likelihood that white-collar offenders are advantaged by the specific types of combinations of legal sanctions that are imposed on them.

Nonetheless, both in the United States and elsewhere, there is some evidence that the mid-1970s brought a new and somewhat harsher attitude toward white-collar crime. Katz (1980) speaks of a "social movement against white-collar crime" that began in the United States in the late 1960s, and the evolution of public opinion documents an increasing concern with the occurrence of such crimes (Cullen et al., 1982; Schrager and Short, 1978). This new concern seems at least in part to have been a response to incidents such as the American experience with Watergate. It was illustrated by the proactive prosecutorial policies of several U.S. attorneys (Hagan and Nagel, 1982), and in the increased prosecution of large-scale securities violations (Hagan and Parker, 1985).

So, there *appears* to have been a move toward tougher legal treatment of white-collar offenses. Of course, charges must be laid before sanctions can be imposed, and we have seen that the power of corporations and of persons in high social class positions to obscure and displace guilt can make prosecutions problematic (see also Benson et al., 1988). Nonetheless, Wheeler et al. (1982) have sought to demonstrate that policies like those already described have led to the more severe sentencing of high-status white-collar offenders. Hagan and Palloni (1986) concur in reporting an increased use of imprisonment of white-collar offenders after Watergate, but also indicate that the length of these prison sentences was unusually short. A Canadian study of the enforcement of securities laws in Ontario (Hagan and Parker, 1985) reveals a similar pattern of tradeoffs in the severity with which white-collar offenders are treated.

A major difficulty in the area of white-collar crime is that organizational complexity can be used to obscure guilt and to pass blame for criminal wrongdoing downward in the class structure of the organization (Braithwaite, 1984). Sometimes another layer of complexity is added by the multinational spread of the crimes involved. Hagan and Parker (1985:314) make this point with the following quote from an investigator in a securities case:

> The principals in [___] were involved in a tremendous scam that was taking place in the Netherlands, the Antilles and in the Bahamian Islands, and places like that, and they [agency investigators] put a tremendous amount of work in it, spent all sorts of money trying to prove what had gone on and they [the agency] went to the Attorney General's department and . . . no criminal charges were laid. You know, it was a matter of economics. Because it would have meant bringing witnesses from practically all over the country, all over the world, to give evidence.

Overall, treatment of white-collar offenders seems to have been lenient in the past. There is no unambiguous evidence that this situation changed markedly during or since the era of Watergate.

Perhaps the most closely watched prosecution and sentencing of white collar criminals to date involved the insider trading scandals that rocked Wall Street in the 1980s. Several individuals, including Ivan Boesky and Michael Milken, were at the center of these activities. Their connected crimes are presented as examples of patterns discussed in the case study below.

CASE STUDY

The Prosecution and Sentencing of Two Wall Street Criminals

Michael Milken and Ivan Boesky were at the center of an insider-trading ring that involved billions of dollars and that threatened to destroy public and investor confidence in Wall Street. Their cases are intriguing not only because they involve core aspects of the ethics of business and banking, but also because they display so many characteristic elements of the prosecution and sentencing of white-collar crime. The story of these Wall Street criminals is told in a number of books, including most notably James Stewart's (1991) best-seller, *Den of Thieves*.

To begin, the cases against Milken and Boesky were in part possible to develop because the Southern Federal District Court, which is situated in Manhattan and which includes Wall Street, had a U.S. Attorney, Rudolph Giuliani, who adopted a very proactive prosecutorial orientation. While his predecessor, John Martin, was more reactive and exercised a "caution that bordered on paralysis" (Stewart, 1991:289), Giuliani shifted office resources and personnel into areas such as drugs, organized crime, and white-collar crime that attracted much media attention. Giuliani freed up resources for the investigation and prosecution of Boesky and Milken through the fraud unit of his office.

Boesky and Milken were found guilty of a number of crimes that for several reasons actually reveal little of the criminal activities in which they were involved. These crimes involved using companies and partnerships in such practices as trading confidential financial information to gain windfall stock profits and managing blocks of secretly and illegally accumulated stocks to manipulate stock prices. Although there was much publicity about these cases, because they were plea bargained, the cases never went to trial and the full details of the actual crimes were not revealed.

The plea bargains involved in these cases illustrate the patterned use of concessions and coercion noted in the text to prosecute white-collar cases. Boesky was used to obtain the evidence needed to convict Milken of conspiring in a complicated insider trading scheme. In exchange for pleading guilty to only one felony, Boesky agreed to provide evidence himself and to arrange a face-to-face meeting with Milken in which he would wear a body mike to record incriminating information. The evidence collected was indirect but nonetheless helpful in developing the government's case.

> Nothing Milken said would be a 'smoking gun' at any future trial, but the tape would be useful probative evidence. Milken had never denied the existence of their scheme; he'd never denied that Boesky owed him money. The discussion of the payment, and how it could be characterized as an investment banking fee, plainly suggested a cover-up. The whole discussion made little sense unless Boesky's version of the conspiracy were, in fact, true (Stewart, 1991:336–37).

Boesky in exchange was sentenced to three years in prison, of which he served only eighteen months, followed by four months in a halfway house.

Unlike Boesky, Milken had nobody more important than himself to turn in. As a result he was indicted on 98 counts of racketeering and securities fraud, and he eventually pled guilty to six felonies. At sentencing, the prosecutors depicted Milken as the mastermind for "a pattern of calculated fraud, deceit and corruption of the highest magnitude," and concluded that, "Milken's crimes of greed, arrogance and betrayal," were part of a "master scheme to acquire power and accumulate wealth" (Stewart, 1991:516–17). Milken was sentenced to ten years in prison, of which he served three, and one billion dollars in fines and penalties. Stewart's investigative reporting concludes that this left Milken with an extraordinary fortune still intact, "one that would place him high on any list of the richest Americans" (1991:524).

High Crimes and Misdemeanors

This chapter has sought to outline some of the important ways in which the study of white-collar crime alters our views of major issues in sociological criminology. We have made the point that the relationship between class and crime is more complicated than frequently assumed, that fundamental aspects of the social organization of work have much to do with the kinds of white-collar crime that are experienced, and that the sanctioning of white-collar crime is unique in its purposes and often lenient in its consequences. The analysis presented in this chapter suggests that crime in the suites deserves greater attention relative to crime in the streets, that some of the neglect of white-collar crime is a result of a tendency to treat much of this activity as noncriminal or quasi-criminal, and that there is likely much more white-collar criminal activity than we realize.

The study of white-collar crime can bridge a gap that is too frequently apparent between the study of crime and other social processes. It can do so by bringing our attention to issues of inequality and power that are centrally involved in this kind of crime. Such issues are equally important to the study of other kinds of crime, and the study of white-collar crime in this way serves a further role in renewing our attention to fundamental processes that should focus criminological work more generally.

5

Criminal Injustice in America

Introduction

The American criminal justice system is unique in a number ways. First, it is a loosely integrated system, which often makes it difficult to determine the results of its operations with much precision. For example, at any given point in time, as we will see later in this chapter, it is uncertain exactly how many inmates are detained in the separate local, state, and federal correctional institutions of the United States.

Second, the American criminal justice system is highly politicized, with criminal justice policies often becoming a part of electoral politics. If patriotism is the last refuge of scoundrels, as Samuel Johnson suggested, political campaigns focused around issues of law and order may not be far behind, and American society has experienced much of both.

Third, the criminal justice system labors under a legacy of racial suspicion and distrust that is a product of America's history of slavery, lynching, and the discriminatory use of the death penalty, especially by white juries (Sellin, 1935; Wolfgang and Riedel, 1973). It also suffers the legacy of patterns of law enforcement, following Reconstruction and extending well into this century, in which the harsher punishment of African Americans, especially for crimes against whites, legally perpetuated a racial caste system (National Research Council, 1989).

Fourth, although the civil rights revolution of the 1950s and 1960s reduced or outlawed some of the most egregious forms of racial injustice in America, young black males continue to encounter the criminal justice system at alarmingly high rates. They often encounter this system first as juveniles and then as adults, and they do so both as victims and violators. It is little consolation that this now may occur with more attention to due process than was the case earlier in this century.

At the same time, and in the context of growing fears of crime, many citizens have lost confidence in the American criminal justice system and have grown skeptical of its efforts to rehabilitate offenders. This loss of confidence has coincided with the emergence of a new emphasis on incapacitation, retribution, and deterrence as guiding principles in a system that imprisons an extraordinarily large proportion of the nation's population. As a result, the American criminal justice system less often rehabilitates offenders than it perpetuates and intensifies effects of residential segregation, racial inequality, and concentrated poverty discussed in earlier chapters. The American criminal justice system stubbornly concentrates resources on the punishment of minority youth. This is so despite the fact that American society attaches great symbolic importance to notions of justice and equality before the law.

The Multiple Meanings of Criminal Justice

The concept of justice is a powerful symbol in America. The criminal law and its enforcement are expected to reflect fundamental principles that define the very kind of society in which we live. For example, American society places a premium on the principle of equality of opportunity, and the American system of criminal justice similarly emphasizes equality before the law. The symbolic significance of this emphasis is reflected in the inscription of the latter principle above the courthouse steps leading to the U.S. Supreme Court Building in Washington, and in the blindfolded goddess of justice that frequently is associated with the law and its enforcement in American courts.

However, the concepts of justice and equality turn out to be more complicated and contradictory in their contemporary applications than this symbolism implies. Philosophers from Aristotle to Rawls (1971) have struggled to provide absolute and fixed meanings to these concepts. However, these efforts are only partly successful because conceptions and perceptions of justice, like those of crime, vary along dimensions of time, place, and location in the social structure from which they derive. This does not mean that American criminal justice is standardless, or that there are no standards by which American criminal justice can be measured. But it does mean that standards such as equality before the law are variable and subject to change, and therefore open to political debate, just as we saw in Chapter 1 with regard to crime.

Numerical, Subjective, and Proportional Equality

For example, numerical equality is often distinguished from proportional and subjective meanings of equality before the law (Nettler, 1979). **Numerical equality** encourages efforts to make punishments correspond in fixed ways to specific crimes, while **proportional** and **subjective** conceptions of equality vary punishments according to objective and subjective characteristics of offenders and their circumstances. The appeal of numerical equality includes a sense of certainty and uniformity and has resulted in contemporary calls for determinate sentencing laws that require judges to give exactly the same sentences to offenders convicted of the same crimes. As we will see later in this chapter, these fixed sentences have coincided in recent years with escalating prison populations containing large numbers of young minority offenders.

Alternatively, greater adherence to subjective or proportional standards of equality might result in a different volume or composition of persons sent to prison. For example, under a standard of subjective equality it could be hoped that a judge might treat embezzlement as deserving more severe punishment when committed by an elected public official or a high-ranking corporate executive than when committed by a low-paid bank teller. If a fine was to be imposed, it could be hoped that a standard of proportional equality would vary the amount of this penalty according to the proportionate ability to pay (that is, as measured by income and assets) as well as the amount taken. Past reliance on subjective and proportional equality did not always or perhaps even often realize these hopes, but as we indicate below, more recent reliance on numerical equality has produced disturbingly punitive results.

The multiple meanings of justice and equality are only one source of political conflict that today pervades criminal justice policy. Often these and other conflicts are left unresolved in a system of loosely coupled criminal justice agencies that evade and resist one another's influence, as well as the direction of any single governing set of policies or principles. However, occasionally, the system and its various agencies become more tightly coupled around the more coordinated pursuit of selected political goals, such as drug law enforcement. It is important to understand the social organization of this system, in both its loosely and tightly coupled forms.

The Social Organization of Criminal Justice

System and Process

Sociologists talk about a criminal justice process as well as a criminal justice system. The **criminal justice process** involves the sequence of decisions that confront an accused person while moving through the stages that lead from the discovery to the punishment of a crime—for example, the stages of arrest, charging, pleading, setting bail, convicting, and sentencing. The interconnections of these decisions and the actors who make them constitute the **criminal justice system**. The latter system has characteristics of a hierarchy, in the sense that the organizations and officials that make up the system can be ordered roughly in terms of their final authority to review decisions made by others. However, this order also often is evaded and subverted by managing the flow of information and people in the system, so that the system is much less coordinated than the notion of a hierarchy would imply.

Albert Reiss (1971) identifies seven component systems in what is often called the criminal justice system. Referring to each of these components as a system makes the point that the larger system is characterized by much autonomy among its parts, which include:

1. The *citizen law enforcement system,* made up of individual and corporate actors who report cases as victims, complainants, and witnesses.

2. The *public law enforcement, or police, system,* which controls decisions about discovering crimes, investigating complaints, making arrests, pressing warrants, and booking offenders.

3. The *defendant system,* made up of citizens accused of crimes and their defense counsel.

4. The *public prosecution system,* which controls decisions about filing the information, making the charge, securing the evidence, plea bargaining, and forming the strategy for prosecution.

5. The *misdemeanor and felony courts,* where substantive and procedural questions of law and adjudication must first be resolved.

6. The *correctional system,* consisting of the organizations responsible for the custody and rehabilitation of convicted offenders.

7. The *appellate judicial system,* which has the power to stay the actions of others pending review, and the sole power to grant or deny appeals.

Loosely Coupled Justice

There is important variation in the extent to which criminal justice systems within the United States and elsewhere are connected or coupled internally. This is also true of schools, churches, hospitals, and many other kinds of formal organizations (Meyer and Rowan, 1977). Nonetheless, many commentators have called particular attention to a looseness that characterizes American criminal justice policies and operations. For example, Gibbs (1986:330) writes that "American penal policy is a mishmash," while Eisenstein and Jacob (1977) observe that even at the highest levels of decision making in this system "the judge does not rule or govern, at most, he manages, and often he is managed by others." The same impression is conveyed by Reiss (1971:114–20) when he speaks of the American criminal justice system as a "loosely articulated hierarchy of subsystems." Reiss goes on to suggest that this hierarchy is so loosely articulated that "the major means of control among the subsystems is internal to each," with the result that "each subsystem creates its own system of justice." Jerome Skolnick (1966) makes this point in the title of his classic study of policing, *Justice without Trial*.

It can be argued that this degree of looseness in criminal justice policies and operations is necessary to provide "individualized" treatment for suspects and offenders (see Hagan et al., 1979; Gibbs, 1986), but this explanation is likely too simple. Another source of the looseness that characterizes the American system of criminal justice may involve its historical roots in the American frontier, where Quinney (1970:55) notes that local authorities were free to develop their own law enforcement policies or to ignore the problem of crime altogether, and where Inciardi (1975:88) notes that law enforcement "lacked form and cohesion." More generally, the loose coupling that is characteristic of the American system of criminal justice may be a way of accommodating the diverse political interests that impinge on the system, while at the same time preserving a sense of autonomy and an impression of impartiality for the judiciary.

In any event, it is important to emphasize that this looseness is certainly not a universal feature of criminal justice systems around the world. For example, totalitarian regimes of the right and the left are often characterized by tightly coupled criminal justice systems and subsystems linked to specific societal crime-related concerns—most notably the desire to maintain political power and social order. Meanwhile, a case study presented later in this chapter (pages 159–160) offers an illustrative comparison of the U.S. and German criminal justice systems, which reveals that democratic societies as well can be characterized by tightly coupled operations. The looseness of the American system may not be entirely unique, but neither is it universal.

Chaos or Diversity

The looseness of American justice system operations often gives them an haphazard appearance. This appearance of randomness is often conveyed, for example, in media portrayals of the justice system as chaotic and, most importantly, in many studies of the justice system that reveal great difficulty in finding variables that can explain much of the variance in decisions to arrest, prosecute, and sentence offenders. For example, the single finding that is consistent throughout the large research literature on judicial sentencing is that whether legal (for example, the seriousness of the offense and the offender's prior record) or extralegal factors (for example, race and class) are the focus of analysis, the unexplained variance in sentencing looms large. This observation even holds in studies of sentencing where the two types of variables are combined (for example, Hogarth, 1971; Hagan and Bumiller, 1983; Myers and Talarico, 1987).

These kinds of findings often characterize what organizational theorists call a **loosely coupled system**. The imagery of loose coupling is meant to convey an impression of entities, in this case court subsystems, that are responsive to one another, but that at the same time maintain independent and diverse identities as well as evidence of operational separateness (Weick, 1976). Meyer and Rowan (1977) add to this conception a collection of characteristics often associated with loosely coupled formal organizations—(1) organizational elements are only loosely linked to one another and activities; (2) rules are often violated; (3) decisions often go unimplemented, or if implemented have uncertain consequences; and (4) techniques are often subverted or rendered so vague as to provide little coordination.

Many of these characteristics are manifested in the criminal justice system, so that, for example, as the literature on sentencing noted earlier suggests, many of the consequences of this loose coupling can be recognized at the level of individual sentencing decisions. At this level of analysis, Glassman (1973) suggests that entities such as court subsystems may be considered loosely coupled to the extent that (1) they share few influences in common, (2) the influences they share differ substantially in their degree of influence, or (3) these shared influences are weak in comparison with other influences also in operation.

For example, when a prosecutor recommends a sentence he or she may be most concerned with rewarding a plea bargain, while the judge may be most concerned with using the offender's prior record to make a prediction about success if given a noncustodial or probationary sentence. Representatives of different parts of the system respond to different concerns. This diversity of priorities makes it difficult to effectively change or reform the American criminal justice system.

Resistance to Change

This resistance to change and reform can give the court system a surprising ability to absorb as well as ignore developments in the surrounding political environment and to avoid meaningful alteration in court operations and outputs. More generally, when challenged to change through legislative interventions and organizational innovations, loosely coupled organizations often display a capacity to take on newly created append-ages and policies, while at the same time selectively ignoring their imperatives.

A frequently studied example of a major innovation that seems to have produced little fundamental change in the American criminal courts derives from the first half of this century when probation officers were introduced into the presentencing process. In response to many of the political changes that were associated with the Progressive Era in American politics, with its emphasis on fact finding and social reform, probation departments and probation officers were added to juvenile and adult courts throughout the United States. A major innovation ac-companying this change involved probation officers using casework principles to prepare presentence reports and recommendations that were intended to individualize dispositions through their impact on judges' sentencing decisions. However, although probation officers now regularly make presentence recommendations, there is little evidence that sentencing patterns in North America changed much as a result of this innovation (see Hagan et al., 1979; Rothman, 1980). The loosely coupled structure of North American systems of criminal justice ab-sorbed this innovation with little threat to the established judicial and prosecutorial roles in sentencing.

Yet it is also the case that loosely coupled criminal justice organiza-tions do sometimes change, with important consequences for their op-erations. One salient example of such change involves the periodic attention paid by the criminal justice system to drug law enforcement and its punitive concentration on minorities through most of this cen-tury in the United States. As we will see in later sections of this chapter, drug law enforcement requires a tightening of subsystem operations that begins with proactive policing and ultimately is tied to court imposed sanctions. There is much evidence that over the last decade this has led to a much more punitive response to drug related crime in America.

Reactive and Proactive Policing

Black and Reiss (1970; Reiss, 1971) and Skolnick (1966) have provided two classic analyses of policing in different parts of the United States. These studies emphasize very different aspects of police work, but taken together they provide a unique insight into justice system operations.

Black and Reiss (1970) apply a now well-known distinction introduced in the previous chapter between reactive and proactive police
work, with proactive police work organizing enforcement activity
around initiatives taken by the police in aggressively seeking out crime
rather than simply responding to citizen complaints. The two kinds of
police work are quite different in organization and results, and while
Reiss and Black focus their research on the nature of the more frequent
reactive responses to crime, Skolnick (1966) focuses his research on the
consequences of more aggressively proactive forays into crime.

As a result, Reiss and Black reach different conclusions about modern
policing than Skolnick. Where Black and Reiss tend to see police work as
having a more democratic cast that is often highly routinized in the way
it responds to a wide range of citizen complaints and demands for service, Skolnick tends to see police work as more purposefully focused and
selective in determining a narrower set of targets for its activities. While
reactive policing seems to fit with the "normal" mode of North American
police operations based on loosely coupled processes and outcomes,
proactive policing requires more tightly coupled practices.

More specifically, proactive policing requires a more tightly coupled
organizational response because of the absence of complaints that is the
distinguishing difference between these two modes of modern police
work. In the absence of complaints, it is necessary for the police to develop other sources of information and assistance in developing cases.
Skolnick establishes this point primarily through his observations and
analysis of narcotics law enforcement. Like Reiss and Black, Skolnick
sees narcotics enforcement, and the work of what he more generally calls
law officers, as being quite different from the work of more conventional
patrol officers.

Skolnick notes that to acquire information and cooperation in narcotics work it is necessary to adopt one or more of three kinds of tactics:
going undercover, using techniques of entrapment, or developing informants. The results of doing so are often important not only for narcotics
work, but also as sources of information about other kinds of underworld activities, which make narcotics officers more powerful actors in
the justice system. For example, prosecutors must often rely on narcotics
officers for the information they need in developing cases, and they
therefore are often willing to give these officers extra consideration. The
key forms this consideration takes involve charging decisions and plea
and sentencing bargaining, which both narcotics officers and prosecutors
depend on to develop cooperation and assistance from otherwise unwill-
ing informants and codefendants. Of course, judges too must ultimately

be brought into these arrangements, since judges must ratify and implement the forms that plea and sentence bargains and charge reductions finally take.

Proactive police work therefore involves a tightening of the coupling among the police, prosecutorial, and judicial subsystems. Reactive police work can thrive in a more loosely coupled organizational environment, through its access to and reliance on complainants. However, insofar as a political environment demands a more proactive response to particular kinds of crime in specific times and places, a tightening of subsystem operations will often if not always be necessary. Both kinds of system operations can involve bias, but the selectively focused form of proactive criminal justice may be especially consequential when focused on kinds of crimes that extensively involve minorities. We develop this latter point further when we consider the politics of drug law enforcement in America. We begin by considering the more routine biases involved in more reactive forms of criminal justice activity.

Policing Minority Communities

To better understand policing in America, it is necessary to first know something more about how policing has changed over the past century. Much of this change has involved efforts to professionalize police work by raising educational and training requirements for officers. The research literature suggests that a result of professionalization has been to make the police more formal and bureaucratic in their treatment of minority youths, and in the process the police seem also to have become more inclined to formally arrest large numbers of these youths (Wilson, 1968). It should not be surprising, then, that the police often find minority youth to be resentful, hostile, and threatening, which may further increase the occurrence of harassment and brutality, as well as arrests in minority settings. The highly publicized beatings of Rodney King in Los Angeles and Malice Green in Detroit may only reflect the surface of this sea of hostility.

A Sea of Suspicion

Indeed, suspicion and resentment of the police is common among middle and upper class adult as well as younger African Americans. Prominent accounts of harassment experienced by respected public figures articulate these feelings. A quarter-century ago, the star center of the Boston Celtics basketball team, Bill Russell (1966), wrote in his auto-biography of the harassment he had experienced in encounters with the police. Recently, the Boston Celtic's Dee Brown received an apology from suburban Boston police for "racial implications" in his forcible search by officers looking for a bank robber (*New York Times*, 4 November 1991, VIII:1). Research confirms (Hagan and Albonetti, 1982) that black Americans, especially those who have achieved positions of high status, share a pervasive perception of criminal injustice that is reflective of Russell's and Brown's experiences.

There are many plausible reasons for suspicion and hostility. Research reveals that police fear violence in encounters with minority youths and that this leads them to stereotypically treat many if not most such youths as "symbolic assailants" (Skolnick, 1966). Prejudicial attitudes toward black and other minority Americans are commonplace in the police subculture (Black and Reiss, 1967). A result is that police encounters with minority youths and adults tend to be emotionally charged and confrontational, often involving efforts by the police to "take charge" and "freeze" situations (Reiss and Bordua, 1967), which can counterproductively increase risks of brutality and indiscretion.

Disrespect and Demeanor

Research suggests that adolescents who are disrespectful of the police are at especially high risk of arrest. In a classic study Piliavin and Briar (1964) demonstrated that other than having a prior criminal record, respectful demeanor or "contriteness" was the crucial determinant of police decisions to release or detain suspects (see also Ferdinand and Luchterhand, 1970). In general, police expect to receive more respect than they give, in part because they represent the authority of the law, and probably also because they are older than the youths they often encounter. When white officers are involved, minority youths as well as adults may perceive this as a racially motivated posture or attitude. Sykes and Clark (1975) note that the police attitude constitutes an "asymmetrical status norm," and that when suspects refuse to observe this norm their risks of punitive treatment are increased. A study of over 700 police–suspect encounters in 24 U.S. cities found that suspects displaying antagonism toward the police were much more likely to be detained, that black suspects were more likely to be arrested than whites, and that part of this racial disparity could be explained by the hostility and demeanor of black suspects (Smith and Visher, 1982).

Status-linked expectations can play a role in the treatment of women as well, especially minority women. While it is sometimes thought female delinquents benefit from "chivalrous coddling" by the police, studies suggest that "paternalistic punitiveness" may often be the more pressing problem (McEachern and Bauzer, 1967; Krohn et al., 1983). Visher (1983) suggests that

> . . . when law enforcement officials (for example, police, prosecutors, judges), most of whom are male, interact with female violators, the encounter is transformed into an exchange between a man and a woman. In this situation, appropriate gender behaviors and expectations may become more salient than strictly legal factors in the official sanctioning of female offenders. Indeed, if women fail to conform to traditional female roles, then the assumed bargain is broken and chivalrous treatment is not extended.

Visher and others (for example, Chesney-Lind, 1987) emphasize that "chivalry" is especially unlikely to be extended to young minority women. This is confirmed in field studies of street prostitution (Horowitz and Pottieger, 1991), which indicate that young minority women are routinely harassed by police, taken into custody because they are "known" prostitutes, and sometimes brutalized.

Becoming Streetwise

These experiences produce distrust and suspicion, and feelings of hostility and defiance form the thread that runs through these studies involving police–minority contacts. These studies predate and postdate the American ghetto revolts of the 1960s, and as the Rodney King and Malice Green beatings indicate, the dilemmas of police-minority relations continue to fester. Elijah Anderson (1990:195) expresses some of the core dilemmas involved when he describes the precarious position of young "streetwise" black males in a northeastern U.S. city. He notes that, "in trying to do their job, the police appear to engage in an informal policy of monitoring young Black men as a means of controlling crime, and often they go beyond the bounds of duty" (194). These are the kinds of problems that result for these youths:

> Many youths . . . have reason to fear . . . mistaken identity or harassment, since they might be jailed, if only for a short time. . . . When law-abiding Blacks are ensnared by the criminal justice system, the scenario may proceed as follows. A young man is arbitrarily stopped by the police and questioned. If he cannot effectively negotiate with the officer(s), he may be accused of a crime and arrested. To resolve this situation he needs financial resources,

money for an attorney, . . . [or] he is left to a public defender who may be more interested in going along with the court system than in fighting for a poor Black person. Without legal support, he may well wind up 'doing time' even if he is innocent of the charges brought against him. The next time he is stopped for questioning he will have a record, which will make detention all the more likely. (195–96)

In this context, Anderson reasons that it is not surprising that many black youths develop an "attitude" toward the police.

Police Geography

Anderson's comments about the concentration of policing on youths in minority community settings anticipate another increasingly important kind of research that focuses on the geographical distribution of police work. This research focuses on areas of "offensible space" and processes of "ecological contamination."

Offensible space consists of areas in which the police perceive a disproportionate amount of deviant behavior and accordingly concentrate their patrol resources. In some cases this may be in response to citizen demands that the police "clean up" an area (Black and Reiss, 1970), but in many instances the police themselves will designate "bad" neighborhoods based on their own impressions and past experiences. For example, Black and Reiss (1970:66n) note that

. . . citizens occasionally provide the police with intelligence about patterned juvenile behavior, such as complaints provided by businessmen about recurrent vandalism on their block or recurrent rowdiness on their corner. These may lead the police to increase surveillance in an attempt to 'cleanup' the area.

Smith (1986:316) goes on to suggest that

based on a set of internalized expectations derived from past experience, police divide the population and physical territory they must patrol into readily understandable categories. The result is a process of ecological contamination in which all persons encountered in bad neighborhoods are viewed as possessing the moral liability of the area itself.

Smith observes that the result can be a process of **ecological contamination** in which all residents of affected neighborhoods are stereotyped as potential suspects or threats. Stereotyped areas of offensible space and ecological contamination can encourage proactive and aggressive patterns of police patrol and decision making.

A study designed to assess the impact of police conceptions of offensible space was undertaken in the Canadian community of Westport (Hagan et al., 1978). This study used qualitative and quantitative techniques to show that a neighborhood's delinquency rates can be better explained by police preconceptions and by citizen complaints than by aggregated self-report measures of delinquent behavior. The implication is that the contamination effect of police and citizen conceptions of offensible space can result in the overpolicing and criminalization of stigmatized areas.

Sampson's (1986b) contextual analysis of data gathered in Seattle similarly reveals a stereotyped effect of neighborhood socioeconomic status on the police processing of juveniles that extends beyond differences than could be attributed to self-reported delinquent behavior. Sampson concludes that "the influence . . . is contextual in nature, and stems from an ecological bias with regard to police control, as opposed to a simple individual-level bias against the poor" (1986b). The point is that entire areas are affected by stereotyped conceptions of individuals within them. As Anderson's work discussed earlier suggests, this can lower the threshold at which individuals find themselves subjected to police suspicion and harassment, and this can lead to being detained and arrested apart from anything these individuals otherwise may have done.

Prosecuting Minority Crime

Minority suspects experience increasing risks as they move through the criminal justice system, so it is not surprising that minority defendants are often judged to be uncooperative in this process. Just being caught up in the process can be costly in terms of time lost from school or work, and for this reason one researcher has argued that in this sense "the process is the punishment" (Feeley, 1979).

Bad Bargains

Plea bargaining and charge reduction are the centerpieces at the prosecutorial stage. A high rate of guilty pleas is usually taken as an indication that plea bargaining is common in a court setting (Heumann, 1975), and these rates characteristically have been quite high in most American court settings since the middle of this century (Friedman, 1979). One succinct way of defining *plea bargaining* is as "the exchange of official concessions for the act of self-conviction" (Alschuler, 1979). Often, but not always, the concessions exchanged in plea bargains lead to reduced sentences.

Since, as we have noted, the police often arrest minority suspects on weak evidence and often overcharge them, prosecutors must often simply dismiss weak cases against minority defendants (Petersilia, 1983). However, when cases are not dismissed, minority defendants are less likely to enter guilty pleas and are more likely to go to trial (Petersilia, 1983; LaFree, 1980; Mather, 1979; Uhlman, 1979; Welch et al., 1985; Zatz and Lizotte, 1985). This probably most often results from the combined effects of whites getting better "deals" in the bargaining process (Welch et al., 1985; Zatz, 1985), and from the distrust that minority defendants consequently have for this bargaining process.

When proposing plea bargains, prosecutors may often stereotype strong and weak cases in race-related terms (see Cicourel, 1968; Sudnow, 1965; Myers and Hagan, 1979). For example, these bargains may not only involve considerations of offense seriousness and the quantity and quality of evidence, but also impressions of the credibility of victims and offenders as witnesses. Nonwhite victims tend to be considered less credible witnesses, while white victims, especially of nonwhite defendants, are considered highly credible (Newman, 1966). Many minority defendants are left with difficult choices between the few concessions offered in the form of plea bargains and the risks of going to trial, where refusals to plead guilty are often interpreted as a lack of contrition and therefore deserving of severe treatment.

Criminal Convictions

More generally, minority defendants confront problems shared by many majority group defendants as well: the difficulty of mounting an effective defense. More than a quarter-century ago Abraham Blumberg (1967a,b) drew a classic analogy between the practice of criminal defense work and a criminal confidence game, and there is little reason to think this game has changed much in recent years. Blumberg noted that over time, court officials, prosecutors, and defense lawyers develop working relationships that place the defendant in the role of a potentially disruptive outsider. Several features of court work are said to encourage this situation. First, all actors in the court are under the strain of limited court resources, and they are therefore anxious to move cases through the court system as swiftly as possible. Second, defense lawyers in particular stand to gain financially from handling as many cases as quickly as possible. With this common interest in quickly moving cases along the court docket, Blumberg argues that defense attorneys covertly conspire to encourage their clients to plead guilty. In support of this thesis, Blumberg reports that it is most frequently the lawyer for the defense who suggests first to the defendant that it would be better to plead guilty than to protest his or her innocence. Following this plea, Blumberg suggests that it becomes the further task of the attorney, with the assistance of other members of the court, to in the vernacular of the confidence game, "cool the mark out" by resigning him or her to a putatively reduced sentence.

Recent research by Flemming et al. (1992) in three states does much to reinforce Blumberg's view. These researchers begin by noting that defense attorneys are disadvantaged by standing "in the shadow of their clients' criminal stigma" and by the further fact that although their careers are much influenced by their relationships with other members of the court, they must constantly appear to be in conflict with these court actors on behalf of their clients. The result is that "defense attorneys faced numerous pressures to go along with the courthouse community" and that "both economics and politics militated against vigorous pro-defense actions by attorneys" (158–59).

In the end, Flemming et al. also found that the judges faced by defendants and their attorneys often saw little reason to offer meaningful plea bargains. One public defender commented, "you learn very quickly that the judges in this county, for the most part, consider all clients represented by the public defender's office as guilty. As a consequence, they feel that we have absolutely no bargaining power, or very little" (156). This reality is reflected more vividly in the following account of an off-record plea conference described from the viewpoint of a judge interviewed in this in-depth study.

> Usually there's no record. I'm just sitting there talking to them and in this one case we're kicking around what this kid should get. A lot of times I'll scare the hell out of a kid by starting off saying, "Well, I want penitentiary time on this kid. He's got a couple misdemeanors. He's never gonna make it on probation." And the kid starts to sweat.
>
> Then I say, "You know what happens to you down there? First of all, you're gonna be put in a cell and they'll gang-rape you. You'll have a hell of a time in there. You'll be sucking cocks for three days straight." But a lot of kids you can tell them all you want. A lot of them don't really understand. That's the trouble. You're not talking to people like us. That's the problem. What does get to them? I can't tell because I'm not like them. But I try.
>
> I probably shouldn't talk quite as tough as I do. But when I do it, I do it off the record. I'll say, "Listen, you little son of a bitch. You're a leech. You're

a drag on society. You're running your mother ragged. You're driving your father nuts. You're a leech, a bum." Maybe it affects him, maybe it doesn't. I don't know.

These are general problems that minority defendants often confront along with other defendants in criminal prosecutions that derive from routine and usually reactive forms of law enforcement. Because arrests are proportionately more common in minority communities, these problems fall disproportionately on minority youths. This would likely be true even if selectively focused proactive forms of police work did not further concentrate attention on minority youths. However, these practices gain added significance when they are combined with politically driven proactive law enforcement efforts. For example, these problems become particularly pronounced when they are associated with the periodic "wars against drugs" that have become a recurrent feature of more proactive American law enforcement.

The Prosecutorial Politics of Drug Law Enforcement

As noted in earlier chapters, a concern with drug law enforcement has been a recurrent theme in American politics, dating at least to the turn of the century and the emergence of drug legislation to deal with narcotics and other kinds of drugs (see Musto, 1973). Two contemporary waves of political concern about narcotic drugs occurred during the Nixon administration of the late 1960s and the 1970s, and again in the late 1970s and 1980s during the Reagan and Bush administrations. Peterson and Hagan (1984) provide an analysis that highlights the role of tightened couplings in justice system responses to the changing political environment of the Nixon years.

The Nixon Years

This study divides its attention to the prosecution and sentencing of drug offenders into three periods: (1) from 1963 to 1969, a period of relative calm in the pursuit of drug law violations; (2) from 1969 to 1973, a period of great political activity and public concern in relation to drug use and abuse; and (3) 1974 to 1976, a period of consolidation in which politicians and the public were less preoccupied with drug issues. The middle period in this study is characterized as an antidrug crusade in which well-developed distinctions between "victims" and "villains" within the drug trade were embedded in law and enforcement efforts. The key to the politics of this period was a compromise between conservative and liberal impulses in which "big dealers" were identified as villains, while middle class youth and ordinary black drug users were reconceived as victims. Peterson (1985) points out that this compromise, involving the assignment of a victim status, was made possible by the relative power of middle class parents. The resulting leniency was then generalized to more ordinary drug offenders.

In any case, the consequences of this shifting political environment included an increased punitiveness in the sentencing of big dealers in the period from 1969 to 1973, combined with lenient treatment of more ordinary middle class white and black drug users, and the very severe sentencing of black big dealers. Peterson and Hagan (1984:68) offer the case of Leroy "Nicky" Barnes, summarized in the case study on page 156, as a particularly vivid illustration of this tendency to severely punish black big dealers during the peak of this law enforcement period.

Perhaps the most important aspect of Peterson and Hagan's analysis of this period in the prosecution and sentencing of drug offenders is the apparent role played by plea bargaining during this antidrug crusade. This analysis reveals that big dealers who did not strike bargains, and were also black, received especially severe sentences.

These patterns are consistent with the point we made earlier about the coupling of subsystem operations in periods that involve changes in the political environment and the imposition of political power. To accomplish the political goal of singling out the villainous big dealers in this antidrug crusade, it was necessary to reward cooperating players in the development of major cases, while also imposing especially severe sanctions on those who did not cooperate and/or who were the primary targets of major drug prosecutions. This combination of rewards and punishments, which is characteristic of the kind of proactive narcotics enforcement identified earlier in the work of Skolnick, involves a tightening of police, prosecutorial, and judicial subsystems that is ultimately reflected in the allocation of penal sanctions. The effects of plea bargains identified in this case study—the especially severe treatment of black big dealers who pled not guilty, the lenient treatment of most others, and the overall increases in the ability to account for outcomes—are suggestive of the kinds of departures from "normal" court operations that can accompany important shifts in the political environment, and newly proactive criminal justice operations.

CASE STUDY

The Vilification of a Black Big Dealer

On January 19, 1978, Leroy "Nicky" Barnes was sentenced to life imprisonment without parole on drug conspiracy charges and under the seldom used Continuing Criminal Enterprise provision of the 1970 Federal Drug Act. Regarded as possibly Harlem's biggest drug dealer, Barnes was listed in the New York Police Department's Blue Book of "Black Major Violators." In imposing such a severe sentence, the judge in the case explained that Barnes "is 'a great danger' to the community. . . . His narcotics trafficking affected 'the lives of thousands of people.' And the saddest part of all . . . is that the great majority of people he is affecting are people in his own neighborhood [Harlem]" (*New York Times*, 20 January 1978). This latter comment is consistent with the suggestion that nonwhite big dealers are seen as more villainous, and therefore as deserving more severe penalties, because they offend against an already victimized population. The following comment from a feature magazine article (written prior to Barnes' 1978 conviction) is reflective of the villain status Barnes achieved.

> Whatever the reasons, the failure to make an arrest stick has earned Barnes the street name "Mr. Untouchable." He is not a retiring man. Of medium height, he projects a presence larger than his size. He is muscular and recently shaved the beard he sported for years. He prefers luxurious motor cars and elaborate custom clothing. To the street people, he is a presence. To the police, this symbolic quality is as significant as the crimes they allege he has committed. To them he embodies the new trend in drug trafficking, in which blacks and Hispanics, the new ethnic successors in organized crime, have taken over from their predecessors, the Italian street gangsters (*New York Times Magazine*, 5 June 1977:16).

The Reagan–Bush Years

A number of recent studies have shown that the "war on drugs" during the Reagan and Bush administrations of the 1980s was particularly punitive, especially for young black males (for example, Jackson, 1992; see also Bridges, Crutchfield and Simpson, 1987; Bridges and Crutchfield, 1988). At the core of many of these studies is the thesis that drug crimes represent ". . . overt behavioral manifestations of the very qualities [that] frighten white adults . . ." (Tittle and Curran, 1988:52). During this period the villains of drugs were somewhat more broadly perceived to be "gang" members from a growing "underclass" population composed mainly of black youths (Jackson, 1992:98–100). This has led to the more uniformly punitive prosecution of African-American youths.

Sampson and Laub (1993b) summarize evidence from the 1980s that suggest that the problems of race, class, and drugs have become so closely intertwined that "it is difficult if not impossible to disentangle the various elements of the problem." For example, they note that while the number of arrests for drug abuse violations for white juveniles declined 28 percent in 1985 compared to 1980, there was a 25 percent increase among black juveniles for the same period. During the period from 1985 to 1986 alone, the number of white youths referred to court for drug law violations declined by 6 percent, while the number of referrals for black youth increased 42 percent (Snyder, 1990).

A broader impression of the remarkable changes that have taken place in drug arrests over the past quarter-century is provided in Figure 5.1 and summarized by Blumstein (1993). He notes that since the early 1970s, the arrest rate for whites has been fairly steady at about 300 per 100,000 population. Meanwhile, the rate for nonwhite Americans climbed regularly from 1980 to 1985, when it started to grow exponentially at an approximate annual rate of 15 to 20 percent until 1989, followed by some signs of decline at the turn of the decade. Blumstein concludes that "one can be reasonably confident that if a similar assault was affecting the white community, there would be a strong and effective effort to change either the laws or the enforcement policy"(5).

Sampson and Laub (1993b) are able to demonstrate that underclass poverty and racial inequality measured across more than 200 U.S. counties are significantly related to this pattern of increased punitiveness in the treatment of black youths. They conclude that these outcomes, especially in relation to drug enforcement and the punitive treatment of young black males, are a product of a system in which ". . . juvenile justice outcomes are more tightly coupled when targeted against blacks." The patterns that Sampson and Laub reveal at the arrest and predisposition stages extend to the use of imprisonment and may be representative of a "New Penology."

FIGURE 5.1

Arrest rates for drug offenses, by race, 1965–1991.
(Source: Blumstein, 1993:3)

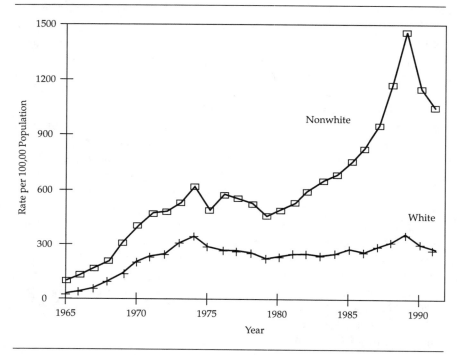

The New Penology and the Expanded Use of Imprisonment

A major development in the sentencing of offenders in recent years has been a shift from an emphasis on rehabilitation and treatment to an emphasis on *incapacitation, deterrence,* and *retribution*. In criminology this transition has involved the resurrection of older theories which emphasize the deterrence of crime and the protection of society, as well as the emergence of newer perspectives that emphasize the efficient use of punishment to manage dangerous populations. This transition is most notably marked by the increased use of institutionalization and incarceration, especially for high-risk minority youths convicted of drug related crimes.

The Growing Numbers

The actual number of persons imprisoned in the United States turns out to be surprisingly difficult to determine, as the "Comparing Imprisonment" case study demonstrates by comparing the process of generating such figures for the United States and Germany. Nonetheless, the aggregate numbers in our state prisons, which hold the majority of our nation's inmates, are themselves dramatic. In little more than a decade, commitments to state prisons increased nationally nearly two and one-half times, from 96,073 in 1974, to 232,969 in 1986. Langan (1991:1568) reports that as of December 31, 1989 state prisons nationwide held a record 610,000 inmates, 63,000 more inmates than a year earlier.

CASE STUDY

Comparing Imprisonment in the United States and Germany

A striking illustration of the loosely coupled form of the U.S. criminal justice system is found in contemporary efforts (for example, Waller and Chan, 1975) to establish what might seem a simple and essential knowledge of the extensiveness of imprisonment in the United States. The most recent and sophisticated attempt to inform this issue is found in the work of James Lynch (1988), who has compared statistics on prison use in England, Canada, the former West Germany, and the United States. The two extremes of this comparison, in terms of use of imprisonment and organizational form, are clearly the United States and Germany. The substantive as well as theoretical importance of this comparison is signaled by the fact that even when a revealing arrest-based calculation of national imprisonment rates is introduced in Lynch's analysis, Germany appears to use incarceration much less frequently than the United States, which indeed may have the highest use of imprisonment per thousand population in the world.

Equally important for our purposes, however, are the striking differences in organizational form that are revealed by the computations that Lynch must undertake to establish these fundamental comparative facts. Lynch begins with the United States, where he notes that responsibility for corrections is shared by local, state, and federal governments, without a unified statistical reporting system. This situation is complicated further when Lynch seeks to establish for what offenses imprisonment is used. The complication is that final charges in the U.S. system are so often the product of charge reductions involved in plea bargaining. The result is that the U.S. system provides no centralized or unified source of information about how many Americans are incarcerated for what crimes.

The result is that Lynch must engage in complicated estimation procedures to generate offense-based imprisonment rates. First, he must estimate how many persons are in local jails rather than the state and federal prisons that generate centralized annual reports. There are no centralized annual reports for local jails. Information on the latter comes from a *Survey of Jail Inmates* whose data are unpublished and available only from the Institute for Political and Social Research at the University of Michigan. Lynch also estimates the local jail population of the United States by using the National Prisoners Statistics (NPS) data on admissions from the Offender-Based Transaction System (OBTS). An indication of the tentativeness of our resulting knowledge of U.S. imprisonment is that the second estimated total for local jails is nearly 50% larger than the first, with a difference of more than a half million people, who may or may not be locked up in local U.S. jails. We simply do not know exactly what this number is.

Contrast this situation with that in Germany and its much more tightly coupled criminal justice system. Lynch (1988:192) first notes that statistics on crime and prison admissions are collected annually and centrally in Germany. Jurisdictions report routinely and there is more uniformity in definitions and collection procedures. Furthermore, prosecutors do not exercise the kind of discretion found in the United States to reduce charges and plea bargain (Langbien, 1979). Calculating an imprisonment rate is therefore far simpler. A variety of different kinds of rates can be calculated, and no comparison can be certain to be accurate given the difficulties with the U.S. figures. Nonetheless, regardless of how the rates are calculated, we find that many more U.S. than German offenders are incarcerated.

Because crime is concentrated so heavily among youth and minorities in American society, the increased use of imprisonment falls most heavily on young minority males. For example, during the 1974–1986 period, the national rate of incarceration for African Americans was more than six times as high as the rate for white Americans (Chilton and Galvin, 1985). At the same time, it is equally apparent that this use of incarceration is heavily focused on drug related crime. In 1991, more than half the inmates in federal prisons and more than a quarter of the inmates in state prisons were there on drug charges. A decade earlier less than 10 percent of prisoners were convicted of drug charges. Blumstein (1993:5–7) reports that in 1991 drug offenders represented nearly half of the new commitments to New York state prisons and about one-third of the overall state prison population.

It is difficult but nonetheless important to obtain some idea of how the use of imprisonment in the United States compares to that in other nations of the world. A Norwegian criminologist, Nils Christie (1993), recently has completed a comprehensive comparison of trends in imprisonment across countries. As noted in Figure 5.2, there is substantial variation even within Western Europe. The United Kingdom hovers near the top of the list of Western European countries, with rates of about 100 persons imprisoned per 100,000 population; Germany is near the middle at 78, and countries as diverse as Cyprus, Iceland, and the Netherlands are at the bottom with rates of imprisonment about half this size. Table 5.1 extends attention beyond Western Europe to Eastern European countries, including the former U.S.S.R, Poland, and Hungary, and into North America with Canada and the United States. Most striking in this table is the way the U.S.S.R. and the United States stand out and as well have changed over the approximate last decade. In 1979, the United States had an imprisonment rate that probably more than doubled any country in Western Europe, at 230 per 100,000, while the Soviet rate was 660 per 100,000 population. A decade later, in 1989, the Soviet rate is estimated to have dropped by nearly half to 353, while the U.S. rate increased to 426, about four times the highest Western European figure. The U.S. figure was 504 in 1991.

Perhaps most disconcerting are comparisons Christie makes between the United States and South Africa. Christie reports that overall in 1989 South Africa imprisoned 333 persons per 100,000 population. Not only is the U.S. rate of imprisonment higher, but Christie cites the work of Mauer (1991; 1992) to demonstrate that this use of incarceration in the United States is even more concentrated against blacks than it is in South Africa.

Half the prison population in the United States is black, with about half a million African-American males currently in prison or jail. In Table 5.2 we see that this translates into a black rate of incarceration of

FIGURE 5.2

Prison figures in selected European countries, 1990, per 100,000 inhabitants. *(Source: Christie, 1993:28)*

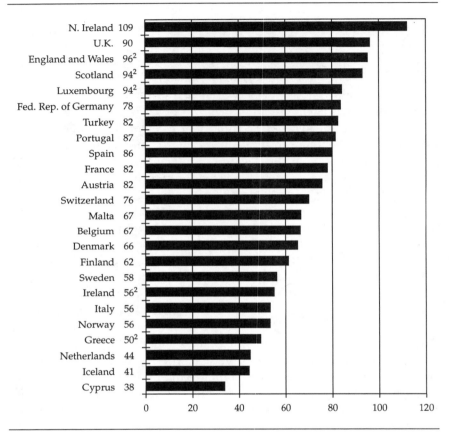

TABLE 5.1

Prison figures from U.S.S.R., Poland, Hungary, Canada, and United States, 1979–1991

	1979	*1989*	*1991*
U.S.S.R.	660	353	
Poland	300	107	
Hungary	134		
Canada	100	111	
United States	230	426	504

Source: Christie (1993:29)

TABLE 5.2

Black male rates of incarcerations in the
United States and South Africa, 1989 and 1990

	United States	South Africa
Black male population 1989	14,625,000	15,050,642
Black male inmates 1989	454,724	109,739
Rate of incarceration per 100,000 1989	3,109	729
Black male inmates 1990	499,871	107,202
Rate of incarceration per 100,000 1990	3,370	681

Source: Christie (1993:119)

over 3,000 per 100,000 population, compared to about 681 per hundred thousand population in South Africa. The figures for South Africa are appalling, but the U.S. figures are astounding.

The New Penology

Malcolm Feeley and Jonathan Simon (1992) recently have argued that such trends are reflective of a **New Penology** that involves a changed way of thinking about crime and punishment in America. Like the economic and political perspectives discussed in Chapter 3 of this book, the New Penology is much concerned with efficiency. However, the New Penology is also distinguished by its shift away from a concern with the individual and the causes of his or her involvement with crime. The new focus is on *subgroups* or *aggregations* of individuals and their *risks* of crime, which are to be *managed* efficiently by means of *selective incapacitation* through imprisonment. The highlighted terms form the language of a New Penology that is used to target categories and subpopulations rather than individuals for penal attention.

Feeley and Simon suggest that these target categories and subpopulations are sometimes identified technocratically as "high-rate offenders" or "career criminals," and at other times more substantively with terms such as "the underclass" or "dangerous class." The terms themselves need not be malicious and can in other contexts and for some purposes be useful (see Hagan, 1992). Their dangers lie more in their association with policies such as selective incapacitation directed at particular groups, including young black drug offenders.

The policy of selective incapacitation is succinctly defined in the following way:

> This approach proposes a sentencing scheme in which lengths of sentence depend not upon the nature of the criminal offense or upon an assessment of the character of the offender, but upon risk profiles. Its objectives are to identify high-risk offenders and to maintain long-term control over them while investing in shorter terms and less intrusive control over lower risk offenders. (Feeley and Simon, 1992:458)

Support for a policy of **selective incapacitation** seems largely to be based on an exaggerated optimism about the crime reducing prospects of withdrawing a large proportion of very active offenders from the larger population. A National Research Council panel on "Research on Criminal Careers" (Blumstein et al., 1978) undertook an evaluation of research on selective incapacitation and concluded that despite the concentration of much crime among some highly active offenders, it would not be possible to reduce crime significantly without very substantial increases in prison populations. This is because (1) the capacity to predict future careers in crime is limited, (2) there is relatively little specialization by type of crime, (3) most criminal careers are brief, and (4) new offenders quickly replace those who are removed from the general population. This may be especially true of drug crime because

> incapacitation removes crimes from the street only if the crimes leave the street with the offender. This should work with the pathological rapist. If, however, there is a ready buyer in the street, removing his or her favorite drug seller will simply mean that a substitute will move in, and the replacement continues to provide the desired drugs. It may take some time for recruitment and training, but experience shows that the amount of time is rarely more than a few days. (Blumstein, 1993:7)

Yet these deficiencies do not seem to have deterred the War on Drugs in America. In fact, Feeley and Simon point out that one of the characteristics of the New Penology is a tendency to focus on its own internal operations in ways that may seem concerned with efficiency but lose track of larger social purposes. A result is that we have dramatically increased prison populations as well as continuing large-scale drug problems.

Politicized Sentencing

There is no doubt that the War on Drugs is a political phenomenon that has produced a major increase in the use of imprisonment that is heavily focused on minority youths. Blumstein (1993) points out that in the 1992 presidential debates all three candidates took the same stern stance in calling for severe sanctions for drug crime: "lacking any better alternative to propose, they merely . . . [advocate increasing] the sanctions, not so much because they think it will work, but because they have come to realize that it is an effective way to relieve the political pressure" (9). The result is increasingly tough laws directed against users as well as traffickers and substantial increases in the proportion of drug offenders sent to prison.

Much of this increased severity has been introduced through measures proposed as reforms for disparities in sentencing practices that have included racial discrimination. These measures include such provisions as rules and guidelines for plea bargaining, mandatory and minimum sentences, statutory determinate sentencing, **presumptive** or **prescriptive sentencing** guidelines, and the establishment of sentencing councils. Most of these measures are built around notions of numerical equality (introduced at the outset of this chapter) and involve tightening the internal structure or coupling of the criminal justice system by insisting, with very few exceptions, on the same sentences being imposed for what are identified as the same crimes. Often this is associated with elevated required sentences, so that, for example, the severity of punishment for drug sales is increased to a level comparable to that for homicide.

The distortion of the claim that such changes in sentencing laws have actually made criminal justice more equal is revealed in a number of ways. For example, Alschuler (1991) has convincingly argued that while sentencing guidelines have been advocated as a means toward more equal justice, in reality they are based upon "rough aggregations and statistical averages," which actually mask notable differences among offenders and offenses. He concludes that the effect of the sentencing guidelines movement has produced "a changed attitude toward sentencing—one that looks to collections of cases and to social harm rather than to individual offenders and punishments they deserve . . . [and rather than] the circumstances of their cases" (951). The sentencing guidelines movement is in this sense a reflection of the New Penology's focus on risks posed by particular subpopulations.

A striking illustration of how statutory sentencing provisions of this kind can be focused selectively on a minority group is provided by a recent Minnesota Supreme Court ruling (cited in Blumstein, 1993:4n). This ruling declared unconstitutional a state statute that stipulated a presumptive sentence of 48 months for possession of three grams of crack cocaine. Elsewhere, possession of ten grams of powder cocaine was defined as warranting a presumptive sentence of only 12 months. Crack and powder cocaine are pharmacologically identical, but in 1988 all of those offenders sentenced in Minnesota under the crack cocaine statute were black, while two-thirds of those sentenced under the powder cocaine statute were white. Black defendants therefore received dramatically longer sentences under these presumptive provisions. The court held that there was no rational basis for this differential treatment of blacks and whites, and that based on constitutional grounds of equal protection, the legislative distinction was racially discriminatory in its impact.

Even when sentencing guidelines and presumptive and prescriptive sentencing statutes are not so obviously slanted to treat minorities more severely, the cumulative effect is still to do so. These sentencing provisions make imprisonment more likely for young minority males in much the same way that the professionalization of police work increased risks of arrest for these youths (Wilson, 1968): that is, because so many minority suspects are swept into the system, more young minority males are imprisoned through an evenhandedness that includes increased severity.

Chesney-Lind (1987) points out that this type of evenhandedness also has been extended to women such that in recent years judges also have been sentencing women to prison in record numbers. She reports (124) that, "between 1974 and 1984, for example, the number of girls and women arrested increased by 203 percent . . . and the number of women in prison jumped 258 percent (considerably steeper than the male increase of 199 percent)." Again, even if this involves an evenhandedness that extends to white as well as nonwhite women, the biggest effect will be felt by young minority women who encounter the system in disproportionate numbers. Black women constitute the majority of female prisoners (Chilton and Galvin, 1985).

Failure to Reduce Crime

There is little reason to believe that the increased use of imprisonment in America has reduced crime, and there is evidence, considered next, that imprisonment increases the likelihood of criminal involvement among offenders when they are released. For example, spending time in prison can have the effect of solidifying networks of association that make unemployment and continued involvement in crime more likely. **Ethnographic research** suggests that racial associations and conflicts are imported into prison from home communities and perpetuate gang activity within these settings (Lockwood, 1980). These continuing associations maintain connections with ethnic vice industries and deviance service centers, which in this way can extend into prisons and persist until release back into the community (Jacobs, 1977; Moore et al., 1978). These underground markets continue to serve as alternatives to conventional employment upon release from prison.

Meanwhile, incarceration, or even prolonged processing through the criminal justice system, can date legitimate job skills and networks of contact for conventional employment. As well, attitudes and interests that signal employability to prospective employers may be undermined and otherwise discouraged, while attitudes of distrust and hostility increase. Anderson (1990) notes that while factory jobs in the manufacturing sector once allowed for a toughness of demeanor among young minority males, such attitudes are a disability in the new jobs of the service economy. Juvenile and criminal justice system contact, especially imprisonment, seem to be a part of the process that perpetuates these attitudes. While the threat or prospect of severe sanctions may help to deter some members of majority groups from contemplating crime, there is more evidence that for minority group members the effect instead is to increase embeddedness in crime networks and attitudes of defiance that increase involvement in crime (Hagan, 1993; Sherman, 1993).

Doing Justice by Reallocating Resources

The New Penology is built, like the economic and political perspectives we considered in Chapter 3, on dubious assumptions about efficiency. A criminal justice system that imprisons such a large share of the population who return so frequently to prison cannot be regarded as efficient. The injustice of this inefficiency is compounded by its concentration on minority youths. The politics of the New Penology have selected minority subgroups for selective incapacitation through imprisonment. This has involved a tightening of connections between police and prosecutorial and judicial subsystems oriented to the more proactive and selective concentration on drug involved offenders from minority communities. Among the results are rates of imprisonment that are among the highest in the world, including rates of imprisonment for African Americans that exceed those for blacks in South Africa.

These facts make the situation of the United States unique. The criminal justice system of the United States has historically and characteristically been a loosely coupled enterprise. Subsystems have tended to insist on their autonomy and to resist innovations and interventions that would diminish this independence. However, the intensity of political demands for more stringent responses to crime in America has combined with the New Penology to force a more consistent and punitive use of criminal sanctions.

Feeley and Simon (1992:457n) note how distinct this American response to crime is by comparing its language and emphasis to that in Sweden and Japan. A language of therapy and rehabilitation is common in Sweden, with an emphasis on seeing the offender as improperly socialized and in need of rehabilitative therapy. The language in Japan is of moral responsibility, with an emphasis on the offender as being morally deficient and in need of moral reeducation in responsibility to the community. In contrast, the new language in the United States is of efficient management, with an emergent emphasis on handling large numbers of offenders by classifying them into subpopulations, which are identified as being especially dangerous and in need of selective incapacitation through imprisonment. This has resulted not only in an exponential growth in the imprisonment of young minority offenders, but also in the development of a widened range of coercive sanctions that include boot camps, electronic surveillance and house arrest, high security "campuses" for drug users, and intensive forms of parole and probation.

The premise of the new sociology of crime and disrepute is that resources currently invested in such coercive innovations could be better reallocated to job creation strategies, day care centers, parent and job training programs, and other forms of capital reinvestment in America's distressed and low-income communities. However, it is also necessary to invest in youths who come into conflict with law. Our juvenile and criminal justice systems are overcrowded and expensive, as well as inefficient in their reliance on institutionalization and imprisonment. They are not reducing crime and they aggravate the suspicion and hostility of minority citizens toward government. Except in the case of violent offenders, there is evidence that many Americans support a broadened use of noninstitutional sanctions which would reduce system contact and costs (see Doble, 1987). The most effective treatment programs are made available outside of the formal institutions of the juvenile justice system (Lipsey, 1991). These tend to be skill-oriented, nonpunitive programs that operate as alternatives to justice system involvements that are socially as well as fiscally inefficient.

Epilogue

This book has emphasized the unique and disturbing dimensions of crime in America. The new sociology of crime and disrepute locates some of the sources of our crime problems in growing disparities of income and wealth that are linked to minority group membership, along with pervasive residential segregation and growing concentrations of poverty in American society. Many citizens accept these features of American society in the 1990s as inevitable reflections of a social inequality that is necessary to stimulate and reward economic productivity. Yet the economic gains have proven elusive and the costs of inequality include high levels of crime and punishment that probably make even the most brazen among us uneasy.

Race-linked inequalities of poverty, segregation, and discrimination increasingly pervade the array of institutional settings where minority, and especially black and white Americans meet. In particular, because community-level policing practices in ghetto settings display discriminatory patterns, and because nonetheless the justice system is expected to embody high standards of fairness and equal treatment, justice system interactions have become especially difficult forums for black–white relations. The final chapter of this book cited disturbing evidence that American juvenile and criminal justice systems are perceived with suspicion, distrust, animosity, and despair by minority citizens, who are too often stereotypically treated as suspects by the police and others. This negative atmosphere is likely intensified by the increasing experience of imprisonment by minority youths. Many disadvantaged minority youths grow up in environments of animosity toward the justice system. It is not surprising that when these youths come into conflict with the law they have attitudes that aggravate their contacts with the system and its agents.

The large-scale use of arrest and imprisonment is incredibly costly in financial terms. Current estimates are that it costs over $15,000 per year to keep the average prisoner in jail. It is probably impossible to calculate the lost social and economic contributions of such persons to society. It is no less difficult to calculate, but perhaps more easily recognized that a growing fear of crime and an increasing alarm about the demoralization of our cities is an added cost of street crime in American society. This fear feeds on itself and is reflected in the proliferation of guns in American society, for purposes of protection as well as predation.

The number of guns in the United States has more than doubled over the past two decades, from less than 100 million prior to 1970, to about 200 million in 1990. In 1992, the citizens of Los Angeles County alone purchased over 100,000 guns. We may have more guns than citizens in the United States. Many of these weapons are owned for self-protection, and this kind of legal gun ownership increases with income and fear of crime. Gun ownership for self-protection is the tip of a private security industry that includes private policing and an abundance of home security devices that range from complicated locks, sensing devices, bars on windows and doors, to high tech alarm systems. These are all signs of a growing class fortification against crime that is a postindustrial counterpart to the protected havens probably more often associated in most Americans' minds with the homes of drug lords in corrupt and developing nations. We live in a society that is ominously polarized around issues of criminal inequality.

The concentration of poverty and inequality along racial and ethnic lines of residential segregation may once have been thought to keep whites separate and safe from blacks in American society. However, the more recent and unintended consequence of this history may be a society that is more dangerous than ever before and uniquely violent among Western nations. The irony is that policies and practices that residentially segregate and concentrate race and poverty also produce increasing problems of crime that threaten to explode beyond the boundaries in which they form. Recognizing this, white as well as minority Americans increasingly arm and otherwise attempt to secure themselves within their homes and communities.

Yet a recurring urban nightmare looms below the surface of American society troubling its citizens in a variety of urban folktales, such as *The Bonfires of the Vanities, Do the Right Thing, Grand Canyon,* and *Boys 'n the Hood,* in which unsuspecting individuals become the alarmed and vulnerable subjects of the polarization of fear and violence that stalk our city streets. Issues of inequality and crime are no longer of interest to sociologists alone. These issues are at the heart of growing concerns about the quality of life available to citizens in this society, whether white, black, male, female, poor, or affluent.

Bibliography

Addams, Jane. 1912. *A New Conscience and an Ancient Evil*. New York: MacMillan.

Adler, Freda. 1975. *Sisters in Crime*. New York: McGraw-Hill.

Aguirre, B. E., E. L. Quaranfell, and J. Mendoza. 1988. "The Collective Behavior of Fads: The Characteristics, Effects, and Career of Streaking." *American Sociological Review* 53:569–84.

Akers, Ronald. 1977. *Deviant Behavior: A Social Learning Approach*. Belmont, Calif.: Wadsworth.

Allan, Emilie. 1985. *Crime and the Labor Market*. Ph.D. dissertation. Pennsylvania State University.

Allan, Emilie, and Darrell Steffensmeier. 1989. "Youth, Underemployment, and Property Crime: Differential Effects of Job Availability and Job Quality on Juvenile and Young Adult Arrest Rates." *American Sociological Review* 54:107–23.

Alschuler, Albert. 1979. "Plea Bargaining and Its History." *Law & Society Review* 13:211–45.

———. 1991. "The Failure of Sentencing Guidelines: A Plea for Less Aggregation." *University of Chicago Law Review* 58:901–51.

Anderson, Elijah. 1990. *Streetwise: Race, Class and Change in an Urban Community*. Chicago: University of Chicago Press.

Arnold, Bruce, and John Hagan. 1992. "Careers of Misconduct." *American Sociological Review* 57:771–801.

Asch, P., and J. J. Seneca. 1969. "Is Collusion Profitable?" *Review of Economics and Statistics* 58:1–12.

Averitt, Robert. 1968. *The Dual Economy*. New York: W. W. Norton.

———. 1992. "The New Structuralism." *Contemporary Sociology* 21:650–53.

Baker, Wayne. 1984. "The Social Structure of a National Securities Market." *American Journal of Sociology* 89:775–811.

Balbus, Issac. 1973. *The Dialectics of Legal Repression*. New York: Russell Sage.

Balkwell, James. 1990. "Ethnic Inequality and the Rate of Homicide." *Social Forces* 69:53–70.

Banfield, Edward. 1968. *The Unheavenly City*. Boston: Little, Brown.

Baron, James N., and William T. Bielby. 1980. "Bringing the Firms Back In: Stratification, Segmentation, and the Organization of Work." *American Sociological Review* 45:737–65.

Baumhart, Raymond. 1961. "How Ethical Are Businessmen?" *Harvard Business Review* 39:5–176.

Becker, Gary. 1964. *Human Capital.* New York: Columbia University Press.

Becker, Howard. 1963. *Outsiders: Studies in the Sociology of Deviance.* New York: Free Press.

Benson, M. L. 1989. "The Influence of Class Position on the Formal and Informal Sanctioning of White-Collar Offenders." *Sociological Quarterly* 30:465–79.

Benson, M. L., W. J. Maakestad, F. T. Cullen, and G. Geis. 1988. "District Attorneys and Corporate Crime: Surveying the Prosecutorial Gatekeepers." *Criminology* 26:505–18.

Berk, Richard, Harold Braskman, and Selma Lesser. 1977. *A Measure of Justice: An Empirical Study of Changes in the Calif. Penal Code, 1955–1971.* New York: Academic Press.

Bickford, A., and Douglas Massey. 1991. "Segregation in the Second Ghetto: Racial and Ethnic Segregation in American Public Housing." *Social Forces* 69:1011–36.

Black, Donald, and Albert J. Reiss. 1967. "Patterns of Behavior in Police–Citizen Transactions." *Studies in Crime and Law Enforcement in Major Metropolitan Areas, Field Surveys III, Vol. 2, President's Commission on Law Enforcement in Major Metropolitan Areas.* Washington, D.C.: U.S. Government Printing Office.

———. 1970. "Police Control of Juveniles." *American Sociological Review* 35:63–77.

Blau, Judith, and Peter Blau. 1982. "The Cost of Inequality: Metropolitan Structure and Violent Crime." *American Sociological Review* 47:114–28.

Blau, Peter, and Otis Duncan. 1967. *The American Occupational Structure.* New York: Wiley.

Blumberg, Abraham. 1967a. "The Practice of Law as a Confidence Game." *Law & Society Review* (January):15–39.

———. 1967b. *Criminal Justice.* Chicago: Quadrangle Books.

Blumstein, Alfred. 1993. "Making Rationality Relevant." *Criminology* 31:1–16.

Blumstein, Alfred, and Jacqueline Cohen. 1987. "Characterizing Criminal Careers." *Science* 237:985–99.

Blumstein, Alfred, Jacqueline Cohen, and Daniel Nagin. 1978. *Deterrence and Incapacitation: Estimating the Effects of Criminal Sanctions on Crime Rates.* Washington, D.C.: National Academy of Sciences.

Bonger, William. 1916. *Criminality and Economic Conditions.* Boston: Little, Brown.

Bonnie, Richard, and Charles Whitebread. 1974. *The Marihuana Conviction.* Charles Hesville: University of Virginia Press.

Boritch, Helen, and John Hagan. 1987. "Crime and the Changing Forms of Class Control: Policing Public Order in 'Toronto the Good,' 1859–1955." *Social Forces* 66:307–35.

———. 1990. "Men, Women and a Century of Crime in Toronto: Gender, Class and Patterns of Social Control, 1859–1955." *Criminology* 28:567–95.

Bound, John, and Richard Freeman. 1992. "What Went Wrong? The Erosion of Relative Earnings and Employment Among Young Black Men in the 1980s." *Quarterly Journal of Economics* 201–30.

Bourdieu, Pierre. 1986. "The Forms of Capital." In J. G. Richardson (Ed.), *Handbook of Theory and Research for the Sociology of Education*. New York: Greenwood Press.

Braithwaite, John. 1981. "The Myth of Social Class and Criminality Reconsidered." *American Sociological Review* 46:36–57.

———. 1984. *Corporate Crime in the Pharmaceutical Industry*. London: Routledge.

———. 1993. "Crime and the Average American." *Law & Society Review* 27:215–32.

Brenner, S. S., and E. A. Molander. 1977. "Is the Ethics of Business Changing?" *Harvard Business Review* 55:57–71.

Bridges, George, and Robert Crutchfield. 1988. "Law, Social Standing and Racial Disparities in Imprisonment." *Social Forces* 66:699–724.

Bridges, George, Robert Crutchfield, and Edith Simpson. 1987. "Crime, Social Structure and Criminal Punishment: White and Nonwhite Rates of Imprisonment." *Social Problems* 34:345–61.

Bureau of Justice Statistics. 1985. *The Prevalence of Imprisonment. U.S. Department of Justice Special Report*. Washington, D.C.: U.S. Government Printing Office.

Bursik, Robert. 1989. "Political Decisionmaking and Ecological Models of Delinquency: Conflict and Consensus." In S. Messner, M. Krohn, and A. Liska (Eds.), *Theoretical Integration in the Study of Deviance and Crime*. Albany: State University of New York Press.

Bursik, Robert, and Harold Grasmick. 1993a. *Neighborhoods and Crime*. New York: Lexington Books.

———. 1993b. "Economic Deprivation and Neighborhood Crime Rates, 1960–1980." *Law & Society Review* 27:263–84.

Cahalan, Don. 1970. *Problem Drinkers*. San Francisco: Jossey-Boss.

Cantor, D., and K. Land. 1985. "Unemployment and Crime Rates in the Post–World War II United States: A Theoretical and Empirical Analysis." *American Sociological Review* 50:317–23.

Centerwall, B. 1984. "Race, Socioeconomic Status and Domestic Homicide, Atlanta, 1971–2." *American Journal of Public Health* 74:813–15.

Chambliss, William. 1964. "A Sociological Analysis of the Law of Vagrancy." *Social Problems* 12:67–77.

———. 1972. *Box Man: A Professional Thief's Journey*. New York: Harper & Row.

Chambliss, William, and Robert Seidman. 1971. *Law, Order and Power*. Reading, Mass.: Addison-Wesley.

Chesney-Lind, Meda. 1987. "Female Offenders: Paternalism Re-examined." In Laura Crites and Winifred Hepperle (Eds.), *Women, the Courts and Equality*. Newbury Park, Calif.: Sage.

Chesney-Lind, Meda, and Randall Sheldon. 1992. *Girls, Delinquency and Juvenile Justice*. Pacific Grove, Calif.: Brooks/Cole.

Chilton, Roland, and J. Galvin. 1985. "Race, Crime and Criminal Justice." *Crime and Delinquency* 31:3–14.

Chiricos, Theodore G. 1987. "Rates of Crime and Unemployment: An Analysis of Aggregate Research Evidence." *Social Problems* 34:187–212.

Christie, Nils. 1993. *Crime Control as Industry*. London: Routledge.

Cicourel, Aaron. 1968. *The Social Organization of Juvenile Justice*. New York: Wiley.

Clairmont, Donald. 1974. "The Development of a Deviance Service Center." In Jack Haas and Bill Shaffir (Eds.), *Decency and Deviance*. Toronto: McClelland and Stewart.

Clinard, Marshall. 1952. *The Black Market: A Study of White Collar Crime*. New York: Holt, Rinehart.

Clinard, Marshall, and Peter Yeager. 1980. *Corporate Crime*. New York: Free Press.

Cloward, Richard, and Lloyd Ohlin. 1960. *Delinquency and Opportunity: A Theory of Delinquent Gangs*. New York: Free Press of Glencoe.

Cohen, Albert. 1955. *Delinquent Boys*. New York: Free Press of Glencoe.

Cohen, Lawrence, and Marcus Felson. 1979. "Social Change and Crime Rate Trends: A Routine Activity Approach." *American Sociological Review* 44:588–608.

Cohen, Lawrence, and Richard Machalek. 1988. "A General Theory of Expropriative Crime: An Evolutionary Ecological Approach." *American Journal of Sociology* 94:465–501.

Coleman, James S. 1974. *Power and the Structure of Society*. New York: W. W. Norton.

———. 1988. "Social Capital in the Creation of Human Capital." *American Journal of Sociology* 94:S95–120.

———. 1990. *Foundations of Social Theory*. Cambridge, Mass.: Harvard University Press.

Coleman, James W. 1985. *The Criminal Elite: The Sociology of White Collar Crime*. 2d ed. New York: St. Martin's Press.

———. 1987. "Toward an Integrated Theory of White-Collar Crime." *American Journal of Sociology* 93:406–39.

Colvin, Mark, and John Pauly. 1983. "A Critique of Criminology: Toward an Integrated Theory of Delinquency Production." *American Journal of Sociology* 89:512–52.

Cressey, Donald. 1965. "The Respectable Criminal: Why Some of Our Best Friends are Crooks." *Transaction* 2:12–15.

————. 1971. *Other People's Money: A Study of the Social Psychology of Embezzlement.* Glencoe, Ill.: Free Press.

Crowe, Cameron. 1981. *Fast Times at Ridgemont High.* New York: Simon & Schuster.

Crutchfield, Robert. 1989. "Labor Stratification and Violent Crime." *Social Forces* 68:589–612.

Cullen, Francis. 1988. "Were Cloward and Ohlin Strain Theorists? Delinquency and Opportunity Revisited." *Journal of Research in Crime and Delinquency* 25:214–41.

Cullen, Francis, Martha Larson, and Richard Mathers. 1985. "Having Money and Delinquency Involvement: The Neglect of Power in Delinquency Theory." *Criminal Justice and Behavior* 12(2):171–92.

Cullen, Francis, Bruce Link, and Craig Polanzi. 1982. "The Seriousness of Crime Revisited: Have Attitudes toward White Collar Crime Changed?" *Criminology* 20:83–102.

Curry, G. David, and Irving Spergel. 1988. "Gang Homicide, Delinquency and Community." *Criminology* 26:381.

Daly, Kathleen. 1989. "Gender and Varieties of White-Collar Crime." *Criminology* 27:769–93.

Davis, Kingsly, and Wilbert Moore. 1945. "Some Principles of Stratification." *American Sociological Review* 10:242–47.

DiMaggio, Paul. 1982. "Cultural Capital and School Success: The Impact of Status Culture Participation on the Grades of U.S. High School Students." *American Sociological Review* 47:189–201.

————. 1987. "Classification in Art." *American Sociological Review* 52:440–55.

DiMaggio, Paul, and John Mohr. 1985. "Cultural Capital, Educational Attainment and Marital Selection." *American Journal of Sociology* 90:1231–61.

Doble, J. 1987. *Crime and Punishment: The Public's View.* New York: Public Agenda Foundation.

Drake, St. Clair, and Horace Clayton. 1945. *Black Metropolis: A Study of Negro Life in a Northern City.* New York: Harcourt, Brace.

Durkheim, Emile. 1951 (1897). *Suicide.* Translated by John Spaulding and George Simpson. Glencoe, Ill.: Free Press of Glencoe.

Duster, Troy. 1970. *The Legislation of Morality: Law, Drugs and Moral Judgment.* New York: Free Press.

Eisenstein, James, and Herbert Jacob. 1977. *Felony Justice: An Organizational Analysis of Criminal Courts.* Boston: Little, Brown.

Elliott, Delbert, and Susan Ageton. 1980. "Reconciling Race and Class Differences in Self-Reported and Official Estimates of Delinquency." *American Sociological Review* 45:95–110.

Ennis, P. H. 1967. *Criminal Victimization in the United States: A Report of a National Survey.* Washington, D.C.: U.S. Government Printing Office.

Erlanger, Howard. 1979. "Estrangement, Machismo and Gang Violence." *Social Science Quarterly* 60:235–48.

Ermann, M. David, and Richard Lundman. 1978. *Corporate and Governmental Deviance: Problems of Organizational Behavior in Contemporary Society*. New York: Oxford University Press.

———. 1982. *Corporate Deviance*. New York: Holt, Rinehart & Winston.

Fagan, Jeffrey. 1993. "Drug Selling and Licit Income in Distressed Neighborhoods: The Economic Lives of Street-Level Drug Users and Dealers." In A. Harrell and G. Peterson (Eds.), *Drugs, Crime and Social Isolation*. Washington, D.C.: Urban Institute Press.

Fantel, Hans. 1989. "Tape-Copying Decks Improve Their Act." *New York Times* 2 (July 9):27.

Farberman, Harvey. 1975. "A Criminogenic Market Structure: The Automobile Industry." *Sociological Quarterly* 16:438–57.

Farley, R., and W. R. Allen. 1987. *The Color Line and the Quality of Life in America*. New York: Russell Sage Foundation.

Feeley, Malcolm. 1979. *The Process of the Punishment*. New York: Russell Sage Foundation.

Feeley, Malcolm, and Jonathon Simon. 1992. "The New Penology: Notes on the Emerging Strategy of Corrections and Implications." *Criminology* 30:449–74.

Ferdinand, Theodore, and Elmer Luchterhand. 1970. "Inner-City Youth, the Police, the Juvenile Court and Justice." *Social Problems* 17:510–27.

Fingerhut, L. A., and J. C. Kleinman. 1990. "Firearm Mortality among Children and Youth." Advance data from *Vital and Health Statistics, No. 178*.

Flemming, Roy, Peter Nardulli, and James Eisenstein. 1992. *The Craft of Justice: Politics and Work in Criminal Court Communities*. Philadelphia: University of Pennsylvania Press.

Franklin, Alice. 1979. "Criminality in the Workplace: A Comparison of Male and Female Offenders." In Freda Adler and Rita Simon (Eds.), *The Criminology of Deviant Women*. Boston: Houghton Mifflin.

Freeman, Richard. 1991. "Crime and the Economic Status of Disadvantaged Young Men." Paper presented to the Conference on Urban Labor Markets and Labor Mobility. Warrenton, Va.

Friedman, Lawrence. 1979. "Plea Bargaining in Historical Perspective." *Law & Society Review* 13:247–59.

Gans, Herbert. 1990. "Deconstructing the Underclass: The Term's Danger as a Planning Concept." *Journal of the American Planning Association* 56:271–77.

Garfinkel, Harold. 1956. "Conditions of Successful Degradation Ceremonies." *American Journal of Sociology* 61:420–24.

Geis, Gilbert. 1962. "Toward a Delineation of White-Collar Offenses." *Sociological Inquiry* 32:160–71.

———. 1975. "Victimization Patterns in White Collar Crime." In Israel Drapkin and Emilio Viano (Eds.), *Victimology: A New Focus*, Vol. 5: *Exploiters and*

Exploited: The Dynamics of Victimization (pp. 89–105). Lexington, Mass.: Lexington Books.

————. 1984. "White-Collar Crime and Corporate Crime." In Robert F. Meier (Ed.), *Major Forms of Crime*. Newbury Park, Calif.: Sage.

Geis, Gilbert, and Robert Meier. 1977. *White Collar Crime*. New York: Wiley.

Ghodsian, M., and C. Power. 1987. "Alcohol Consumption Between the Ages of 16 and 23 in Britain: A Longitudinal Study." *British Journal of Addiction* 82:175–80.

Gibbs, Jack P. 1986. "Punishment and Deterrence: Theory, Research and Penal Policy." In Leon Lipson and Stanton Wheeler (Eds.), *Law and the Social Sciences*. New York: Russell Sage Foundation.

Gillis, A. R. 1989. "Crime and State Surveillance in Nineteenth Century France." *American Journal of Sociology* 95:307–41.

Glassman, R. B. 1973. "Persistence and Loose Coupling in Living Systems." *Behavioral Science* 83–98.

Glueck, Sheldon, and Elenor Glueck. 1950. *Unravelling Juvenile Delinquency*. Cambridge, Mass.: Harvard University Press.

————. 1968. *Delinquents and Nondelinquents in Perspective*. Cambridge, Mass.: Harvard University Press.

Glyn, Andrew. 1992. "The Costs of Stability: The Advanced Capitalist Countries in the 1980s." *New Left Review* 195 (September/October):71–96.

Glyn, Andrew, and David Miliband. 1994. "Equality and Efficiency." Institute for Public Policy Research, London. Paper presented on May 14, 1993 to Conference on Equality and Efficiency.

Goffman, Erving. 1961. *Asylums*. Chicago: Aldine-Atherton.

————. 1963. *Stigma: Notes on the Management of Spoiled Identity*. Englewood Cliffs, N.J.: Prentice-Hall.

Goldin, Claudia, and Robert Margo. 1992. "The Great Compression: The Wage Structure in the United States at Mid-Century." *Quarterly Journal of Economics* CVII (February):1–34.

Goode, William. 1978. *The Celebration of Heroes: Prestige as a Social Control System*. Berkeley: University of California Press.

Gottfredson, Michael, and Travis Hirschi. 1990. *A General Theory of Crime*. Stanford, Calif.: Stanford University Press.

Granovetter, Mark. 1974. *Getting a Job: A Study of Contacts and Careers*. Cambridge, Mass.: Harvard University Press.

————. 1985. "Economic Action and Social Structure: The Problem of Embeddedness." *American Journal of Sociology* 91:481–510.

Greenberg, David. 1979. "Delinquency and the Age Structure of Society." In S. I. Messinger and E. Bittner (Eds.), *Criminology Review Yearbook*. Newbury Park, Calif.: Sage.

————. 1981. *Crime and Capitalism*. Palo Alto, Calif.: Mayfield.

————. 1985. "Age, Crime and Social Explanation." *American Journal of Sociology* 92:788–816.

Greenwood, Peter. 1982. *Selective Incapacitation*. Santa Monica, Calif.: Rand.

Grogger, J. 1991. "The Effect of Arrest on the Employment Outcomes of Young Men." Unpublished manuscript, University of California, Santa Barbara.

Gurr, Ted R. 1979. "On the History of Violent Crime in Europe and America." In Hugh P. Graham and Ted R. Gurr (Eds.), *Violence in America: Historical and Comparative Perspectives*. Newbury Park, Calif.: Sage.

———. 1981. "Historical Trends in Violent Crimes: A Critical Review of the Evidence." In M. Tonry and N. Morris (Eds.), *Crime and Justice: Annual Review of Research* 3:295–353.

Gusfield, Joseph. 1963. *Symbolic Crusade: Status Politics and the American Temperance Movement*. Urbana: University of Illinois Press.

Hagan, John. 1975. "Explaining Watergate: Toward a Control Theory of Upperworld Crime." In Nicholas Kittric and Jackwell Susman (Eds.), *Legality, Morality and Ethics in Criminal Justice*. New York: Praeger.

———. 1977. *The Disreputable Pleasures*. Toronto: McGraw-Hill Ryerson.

———. 1982. "The Corporate Advantage: The Involvement of Individual and Organizational Victims in the Criminal Justice Process." *Social Forces* 60(4):993–1022.

———. 1991a. *The Disreputable Pleasures: Crime and Deviance in Canada*. Toronto: McGraw-Hill Ryerson.

———. 1991b. "Destiny and Drift: Subcultural Preferences, Status Attainments and the Risks and Rewards of Youth." *American Sociological Review* 56:567–82.

———. 1992. "The Poverty of a Classless Criminology." *Criminology* 30:1–20.

———. 1993. "The Social Embeddedness in Crime and Unemployment." *Criminology*.

Hagan, John, and Celesta Albonetti. 1982. "Race, Class and the Perception of Criminal Injustice in America." *American Journal of Sociology* 88:329–55.

Hagan, John, and Ilene Bernstein. 1979. "The Sentence Bargaining of Upperworld and Underworld Crime in Ten Federal District Courts." *Law & Society Review* 13:467–78.

Hagan, John, and Kristin Bumiller. 1983. "Making Sense of Sentencing: A Review and Critique of Sentencing Research." In A. Blumstein, J. Cohen, S. E. Martin, and M. H. Toury (Eds.), *Research on Sentencing: The Search for Reform, Vol. II*. Washington, D.C.: National Academy Press.

Hagan, John, A. R. Gillis, and Janet Chan. 1978. "Explaining Official Delinquency: A Spatial Study of Class, Conflict and Control." *Sociological Quarterly* 19:386–98.

Hagan, John, A. R. Gillis, and John Simpson. 1985. "The Class Structure of Gender and Delinquency: Toward a Power-Control Theory of Common Delinquent Behavior." *American Journal of Sociology* 90:1151–78.

———. 1990. "Clarifying and Extending Power-Control Theory." *American Journal of Sociology* 95:1024–37.

Hagan, John, John Hewitt, and Duane Alwin. 1979. "Ceremonial Justice: Crime and Punishment in a Loosely Coupled System. *Social Forces* 58:506–27.

Hagan, John, and Fiona Kay. 1990. "Gender and Delinquency in White-Collar Families: A Power-Control Perspective." *Crime and Delinquency* 36(3):391–407.

Hagan, John, and Jeffrey Leon. 1977. "Rediscovering Delinquency: Social History, Political Ideology and the Sociology of Law." *American Sociological Review* 42:587–98.

Hagan, John, and Ilene Nagel. 1982. "White Collar Crime, White Collar Time: The Sentencing of White Collar Criminals in the Southern District of New York." *American Criminal Law Review* 20(2):259–301.

Hagan, John, Ilene Nagel, and Celesta Albonetti. 1980. "The Differential Sentencing of White Collar Offenders in Ten Federal District Courts." *American Sociological Review* 45:802–20.

Hagan, John, and Alberto Palloni. 1986. "'Club Fed' and the Sentencing of White Collar Offenders Before and After Watergate." *Criminology* 24:603–21.

———. 1990. "The Social Reproduction of a Criminal Class in Working Class London, Circa 1950–80." *American Journal of Sociology* 96:265–99.

Hagan, John, and Patricia Parker. 1985. "White Collar-Crime and Punishment: The Class Structure and Legal Sanctioning of Securities Violations." *American Sociological Review* 50(3):302–16.

Hagan, John, and Ruth Peterson. 1994. "Criminal Inequality in America." In John Hagan and Ruth Peterson (Eds.), *Crime and Inequality*. Stanford, Calif.: Stanford University Press.

Hagan, John, Edward Silva, and John Simpson. 1977. "Conflict and Consensus in the Designation of Deviance." *Social Forces* 56:320–40.

Hagan, John, and Blair Wheaton. 1993. "The Search for Adolescent Role Exits and the Transition to Adulthood.: *Social Forces* 71:955–80.

Hagedorn, John. 1988. *People and Folks: Gangs, Crime and the Underclass in a Rustbelt City*. Chicago: Lake View Press.

Halperin, Morton, Jerry Bergman, Robert Borosage, and Christine Marwick. 1976. *The Lawless State: The Crimes of the U.S. Intelligence Agencies*. Middlesex, England: Penguin.

Harer, Miles, and Darrell Steffensmeier. 1992. "The Differing Effects of Economic Inequality on Black and White Rates of Violence." *Social Forces* 70:1035–54.

Hartung, Frank E. 1950. "White Collar Offenses in the Wholesale Meat Industry in Detroit." *American Journal of Sociology* 56:25–34.

Harvard Law Review. 1976. "Multinational Corporations and Income Allocation Under Section 482 of the Internal Revenue Codes." *Harvard Law Review* 92:1202–38.

Hawkins, Darnel. 1986. *Homicide among Black Americans*. Lauham, Md.: University Press of America.

Hawkins, Keith. 1983. "Bargain and Bluff: Compliance Strategy and Deterrence in the Enforcement of Regulations." *Law & Policy Quarterly* 5:35–73.

Heumann, Milton. 1975. "A Note on Plea Bargaining and Case Pressure." *Law & Society Review* 9:515–28.

Hill, Gary D., and Anthony Harris. 1981. "Changes in the Gender Patterning of Crime, 1953–77: Opportunity v. Identity." *Social Science Quarterly* 62(4):658–71.

Hindelang, Michael. 1974. "The Uniform Crime Reports Revisited." *Journal of Criminal Justice* 2(1):1–17.

———. 1978. "Race and Involvement in Common Law Personal Crimes." *American Sociological Review* 43:93–109.

———. 1979. "Sex Differences in Criminal Activity." *Social Problems* 27:143–56.

Hindelang, Michael, Travis Hirschi, and Joseph Weis. 1981. *Measuring Delinquency*. Newbury Park, Calif.: Sage.

Hinton, S. E. 1967. *Outsiders*. New York: Viking Press.

Hirschi, Travis. 1969. *Causes of Delinquency*. Berkeley: University of California Press.

Hirschi, Travis, and Michael Gottfredson. 1983. "Age and the Explanation of Crime." *American Journal of Sociology* 89:552–84.

Hodson, Randy, and Robert Kaufman. 1982. "Economic Dualism: A Critical Review." *American Sociological Review* 47:727–39.

Hogan, Dennis, and Nan Marie Astone. 1986. "The Transition to Adulthood." *Annual Review of Sociology* 12:109–30.

Hogarth, John. 1971. *Sentencing as a Human Process*. Toronto: University of Toronto Press.

Hollingshead, August. 1949. *Elmtown's Youth: The Impact of Social Class on Adolescents*. New York: Wiley.

Holmes, Kay Ann. 1972. "Reflections by Gaslight: Prostitution in Another Age." *Issues in Criminology* 7:83–101.

Horowitz, R., and A. E. Pottieger. 1991. "Gender Bias in Juvenile Justice Handling of Seriously Crime-Involved Youth." *Journal of Research in Crime and Delinquency* 28:75–100.

Ianni, Francis. 1972. *A Family Business*. New York: Russell Sage Foundation.

———. 1974. *Black Mafia*. New York: Simon & Schuster.

Inciardi, James. 1975. *Careers in Crime*. Chicago: Rand McNally.

Jackson, Pamela Irving. 1992. "Minority Group Threat, Social Context, and Policing." In A. E. Liska (Ed.), *Social Threat and Social Control*. Albany: State University of New York Press.

Jacobs, James. 1977. *Statesville: The Penitentiary in Mass Society*. Chicago: University of Chicago Press.

Jencks, Christopher. 1992. *Rethinking Social Policy: Race, Poverty and the Underclass*. Cambridge, Mass.: Harvard University Press.

Jencks, Christopher, and Susan Mayer. 1990. "The Social Consequences of Growing Up in a Poor Neighborhood." In Laurence Lynn and Michael

McGeary (Eds.), *Inner-City Poverty in the United States*. Washington, D.C.: National Academy Press.

Jessor, Richard, John Donovan, and Frances Costa. 1993. *Beyond Adolescence: Problem Behavior and Young Adult Development*. New York: Cambridge University Press.

Johnson, Richard. 1980. "Social Class and Delinquent Behavior: A New Test." *Criminology* 18:86–93.

Kasarda, J. P. 1989. "Urban Industrial Transition and the Underclass." *Annals of the American Academy of Political and Social Science* 501:26–47.

Katz, Jack. 1980. "The Social Movement against White-Collar Crime." In Egon Bittner and Sheldon Messinger (Eds.), *Criminology Review Yearbook, Vol. 2*. Newbury Park, Calif.: Sage.

Kleck, Gary. 1982. "On the Use of Self-Report Data to Determine Class Distribution of Criminal and Delinquent Behavior." *American Sociological Review* 43:427–33.

Kolko, Gabriel. 1963. *The Triumph of Conservatism: A Reinterpretation of American History, 1900–1916*. New York: Free Press.

Kornhauser, Ruth. 1978. *Social Sources of Delinquency*. Chicago: University of Chicago Press.

Krohn, Marvin, James Curry, and Shirley Nelson-Kilger. 1983. "Is Chivalry Dead?: An Analysis of Changes in Police Dispositions of Males and Females." *Criminology* 21:417–37.

LaFree, Gary. 1980. "The Effect of Sexual Stratification by Race on Official Reactions to Rape." *American Sociological Review* 45:842–54.

———. 1993. "Race and Crime Trends in the United States, 1946–1990." Unpublished paper, University of New Mexico.

LaFree, Gary, Kriss Drass, and Patrick O'Day. 1992. "Race and Crime in Postwar America: Determinants of African-American and White Rates, 1957–1988." *Criminology* 30:157–88.

Land, K., D. Cantor, and S. Russell. 1994. "Unemployment and Crime Rate Fluctuations in the Post–World War II United States: Statistical Time Series Properties and Alternative Models." In John Hagan and Ruth Peterson (Eds.), *Crime and Inequality*. Stanford, Calif.: Stanford University Press.

Land, Kenneth, P. McCall, and Lawrence Cohen. 1990. "Structural Co-variates of Homicide Rates: Are There Any Invariances across Time and Space?" *American Journal of Sociology* 95:922–63.

Lane, Roger. 1980. "Urban Police and Crime in Nineteenth Century America." In N. Morris and M. Tonry (Eds.), *Crime and Justice: An Annual Review of Research* 2:1–44.

Langan, Patrick. 1991. "America's Soaring Prison Population." *Science* 251:1568–73.

Langbien, John. 1979. "Understanding the Short History of Plea Bargaining." *Law & Society Review* 13:261–72.

Lemert, Edwin. 1951. *Social Pathology*. New York: McGraw-Hill.

———. 1967. *Human Deviance, Social Problems and Social Control*. Englewood Cliffs, N.J.: Prentice-Hall.

Letkemann, Peter. 1973. *Crime as Work*. Englewood Cliffs, N.J.: Prentice-Hall.

Lewis, Peter. 1989. "Cracking Down on Computer Pirates." *New York Times* 2 (July 9):10.

Light, Ivan. 1977. "The Ethnic Vice Industry, 1880–1944." *American Sociological Review* 42:464–79.

Lipset, Seymour Martin. 1989. *American Exceptionalism/Canadian Distinctiveness*. Toronto: C. D. Howe Institute.

Lipsey, Mark. 1991. "Juvenile Delinquency Treatment: A Meta-Analytic Inquiry into the Variability of Effects." In *Meta-Analysis for Explanation: A Casebook*. New York: Russell Sage Foundation.

Lockwood, D. 1980. *Prison Sexual Violence*. New York: Elsevier.

Lowry, P., S. Hassig, R. Gunn, and J. Mathison. 1988. "Homicide Victims in New Orleans: Recent Trends." *American Journal of Epidemiology* 128:1130–36.

Lynch, James. 1988. "A Comparison of Prison Use in England, Canada, West Germany and the United States: A Limited Test of the Punitive Hypothesis." *Journal of Criminal Law and Criminology* 79:180–210.

Lynxwiler, John, Neal Shaver, and Donald Clelland. 1983. "The Organization and Impact of Inspector Discretion in a Regulatory Bureaucracy." *Social Problems* 30:425–36.

Malinowski, Bronislaw. 1959. *Crime and Custom in Savage Society*. Paterson, N.J.: Littlefield, Adams.

Mann, Kenneth. 1985. *Defending White-Collar Crime: A Portrait of Attorneys at Work*. New Haven: Yale University Press.

Mann, Kenneth, Stanton Wheeler, and Austin Sarat. 1980. "Sentencing the White Collar Offender." *American Criminal Law Review* 17(4):479.

Margolin, Stephen, and Juliet Schor. 1990. *The End of the Golden Age*. Oxford: Clarendon Press.

Marks, Carole. 1991. "The Urban Underclass." *Annual Review of Sociology* 17:445–66.

Massey, Douglas. 1990. "American Apartheid: Segregation and the Making of the Underclass." *American Journal of Sociology* 96:329–57.

Massey, Douglas, and Nancy Denton. 1993. *American Apartheid: Segregation and the Making of the Underclass*. Cambridge, Mass.: Harvard University Press.

Mather, Lynn. 1979. *Plea Bargaining or Trial? The Process of Criminal Case Disposition*. Lexington, Mass.: Lexington.

Matsueda, Ross, and Karen Heimer. 1987. "Race, Family Structure and Delinquency: A Test of Differential Association and Social Control Theories." *American Sociological Review* 52:826–40.

Matza, David. 1964. *Delinquency and Drift*. New York: Wiley.

Matza, David, and Gresham Sykes. 1961. "Juvenile Delinquency and Subterranean Values." *American Sociological Review* 26:712–20.

Mauer, Marc. 1991. *Americans Behind Bars: A Comparison of International Rates of Incarceration.* Washington, D.C.

———. 1992. *Americans Behind Bars: One Year Later.* Washington, D.C.

McBarnett, Doreen. 1991. "Whiter Than White Collar Crime: Tax, Fraud Insurance and the Management of Stigma." *British Journal of Sociology* 42:323–44.

McEachern, A.W., and Riva Bauzer. 1967. "Factors Related to Disposition in Juvenile Police Contacts." In Malcolm Klein and Barbara Myerhoff (Eds.), *Juvenile Gangs in Context: Theory, Research and Action.* Englewood Cliffs, N.J.: Prentice-Hall.

Merton, Robert. 1938. "Social Structure and Anomie." *American Sociological Review* 3:672–82.

Messner, Steven. 1989. "Economic Discrimination and Societal Homicide Rates: Further Evidence on the Cost of Inequality." *American Sociological Review* 54:597–611.

Messner, Steven, and Reid Golden. 1992. "Racial Inequality and Racially Disaggregated Homicide Rates: An Assessment of Alternative Theoretical Explanations." *Criminology* 30:421–47.

Messner, Steven, and Richard Rosenfeld. 1993. *Crime and the American Dream.* Belmont, Calif.: Wadsworth.

Messner, Steven, and Robert Sampson. 1991. "The Sex Ratio, Family Disruption, and Rates of Violent Crime: The Paradox of Demographic Structure." *Social Forces* 69(3):693–713.

Meyer, John, and Brian Rowan. 1977. "Institutionalized Organizations: Formal Structure as Myth and Ceremony." *American Journal of Sociology* 83:340–63.

Miller, Walter. 1958. "Lower Class Culture as a Generating Milieu of Gang Delinquency." *Journal of Social Issues* 14:5–19.

Mills, C. Wright. 1943. "The Professional Ideology of Social Pathologists." *American Journal of Sociology* 49:165–80.

———. 1956. *The Power Elite.* New York: Oxford University Press.

Moffitt, Terrie. 1993. "Adolescence—Limited and Life-Course Persistent Antisocial Behavior: A Developmental Taxonomy." *Psychological Review.*

Monkkonen, Eric. 1981. *Police in Urban America, 1860–1920.* New York: Cambridge.

———. 1993. "Racial Factors in New York City Homicides, 1800–1874." Unpublished paper, University of Calif. at Los Angeles.

Moore, Joan. 1991. *Going Down to the Barrio: Homeboys and Homegirls in Change.* Philadelphia: Temple University Press.

Moore, Joan, with Robert Garcia, Carlos Garcia, Luis Cerda, and Frank Valencia. 1978. *Homeboys: Gangs, Drugs and Prison in the Barrios of Los Angeles.* Philadelphia: Temple University Press.

Mosher, Clayton, and John Hagan. 1993. "Constituting Class and Crime in Upper Canada: The Sentencing of Narcotics Offenders, circa 1908–1953." *Social Forces.*

Munford, R. S., R. Kazew, R. Feldman, and R. Stivers. 1976. "Homicide Trends in Atlanta." *American Journal of Public Health* 14:213–21.

Musto, David. 1973. *The American Disease: Origins of Narcotic Control.* New Haven: Yale.

Myers, Martha, and John Hagan. 1979. "Private and Public Trouble: Prosecutors and the Allocation of Court Resources." *Social Problems* 26:439–51.

Myers, Martha, and S. Talarico. 1987. *The Social Contexts of Criminal Sentencing.* New York: Springer-Verlag.

Nagorski, Zygmunt. 1989. "Yes, Socrates, Ethics Can Be Taught." *New York Times* (February 12):F2.

National Opinion Research Center. 1987. *General Social Surveys, 1972–1987: Cumulative Codebook.* Chicago: National Opinion Research Center.

National Research Council. 1989. *A Common Destiny: Blacks and American Society.* Washington, D.C.: National Academy Press.

Nettler, Gwynn. 1978. *Explaining Crime.* New York: McGraw-Hill.

———. 1979. "Criminal Justice." *Annual Review of Sociology* 5:27–52.

Newcomb, M. D., and P. M. Bentler. 1988. *Consequences of Adolescent Drug Use: Impact on the Lives of Young Adults.* Newbury Park, Calif.: Sage.

Newman, Donald. 1966. *Conviction: The Determination of Guilt or Innocence Without Trial.* Boston: American Bar Association.

Newman, Gramae. 1976. *Comparative Deviance.* New York: Elsevier.

Newton, G. D., and F. E. Zimring. 1969. *Firearms and Violence in American Life.* Washington, D.C.: U.S. Government Printing Office.

Nye, F. Ivan, and James F. Short. 1957. "Scaling Delinquent Behavior." *American Sociological Review* 22:326–32.

O'Hare, William, Kelvin Pollard, Taynai Mann, and Mary Kent. 1991. "African Americans in the 1990s." *Population Bulletin* 46:1.

Okun, Arthur. 1975. *Equality and Efficiency: The Big Tradeoff.* Washington, D.C.: The Brookings Institution.

Padilla, Felix. 1992. *The Gang as an American Enterprise.* New Brunswick, N.J.: Rutgers University Press.

Passas, Nikos, and Richard Groskin. 1993. "BCCI and the Federal Authorities: Regulatory Anesthesia and the Limits of Criminal Law." Paper presented at the 1993 annual meeting of the Society for the Study of Social Problems, Miami Beach, Fla.

Petersilia, Joan. 1983. *Racial Disparities in the Criminal Justice System.* Santa Monica, Calif.: Rand.

Peterson, Ruth. 1985. "Discriminatory Decision-Making at the Legislative Level: An Analysis of the Comprehensive Drug Abuse, Prevention and Control Act of 1970." *Law & Human Behavior* 9:243–70.

Peterson, Ruth, and John Hagan. 1984. "Changing Conceptions of Race: The Sentencing of Drug Offenders in an American City, 1963–76." *American Sociological Review* 49:56–71.

Peterson, Ruth, and Lauren Krivo. 1993. "Racial Segregation and Black Urban Homicide." *Social Forces* 71:1001–28.

Piliavin, Irving, and Scott Briar. 1964. "Police Encounters with Juveniles." *American Journal of Sociology* 70:206–14.

Platt, Anthony. 1969. *The Child Savers: The Invention of Delinquency*. Chicago: University of Chicago Press.

Playboy Advisor. 1975. "The Alka-Seltzer Screw." *Playboy* 22(February):35.

Pontell, Henry, and Kitty Calavita. 1993. "Bilking Bankers and Bad Debts: White-Collar Crime and the Savings and Loan Crisis." In Kip Schlegel and David Weisburd (Eds.), *White-Collar Crime Reconsidered*. Boston: Northeastern University Press.

Posner, Richard A. 1980. "Optimal Sentences for White Collar Criminals." *American Criminal Law Review* 409–18.

Pound, Roscoe. 1930. *Criminal Justice in America*. New York: Henry Holt.

Presidential Transcripts. 1974. *The White House Transcripts*. New York: Viking Press.

Quinney, Richard. 1970. *The Social Reality of Crime*. Boston: Little, Brown.

Rawls, J. 1971. *A Theory of Justice*. Cambridge, Mass.: Harvard University Press.

Reasons, Charles. 1974. "The Politics of Drugs: An Inquiry into the Sociology of Social Problems," *Sociological Quarterly* 15:381–404.

Reasons, C., L. Ross, and C. Paterson. 1981. *Assault on the Worker: Occupational Health and Safety in Canada*. Toronto: Butterworths.

Reiss, Albert. 1971. *The Police and the Public*. New Haven: Yale University Press.

Reiss, Albert. 1981. "Foreword: Towards a Revitalization of Theory and Research on Victimization by Crime." *Journal of Criminal Law and Criminology* 72:704–13.

Reiss, Albert, and David Bordua. 1967. "Organization and Environment: A Perspective on the Municipal Police." In David Bordua (Ed.), *The Police: Six Sociological Essays*. New York: Wiley.

Reiss, Albert, and Jeffrey Roth. 1993. *Understanding and Preventing Violence*. Washington, D.C.: National Academy Press.

Reuter, P., R. MacCoun, and P. Murphy. 1990. "Money from Crime." Report R-3894. Santa Monica, Calif.: Rand.

Revenga, Ana. 1992. "Exporting Jobs? The Impact of Import Competition on Employment and Wages in U.S. Manufacturing." *Quarterly Journal of Economics* 255–82.

Robins, Lee. 1966. *Deviant Children Grown Up*. Baltimore, Md.: Williams & Wilkins.

Robinson, W. S. 1950. "Ecological Correlation and the Behavior of Individuals." *American Sociological Review* 15:351–7.

Rose, H., and P. McClain. 1990. *Race, Place and Risk: Black Homicide in Urban America*. Albany, N.Y.: SUNY Press.

Ross, E. A. 1901. *Social Control*. New York: Macmillan.

———. 1909. *Sin and Society*. Boston: Houghton Mifflin.

Rossi, Peter, Emily Waite, Christine Bose, and Richard Berk. 1974. "The Seriousness of Crimes: Normative Structure and Individual Differences." *American Sociological Review* 39:224–37.

Rothman, David. 1980. *Conscience and Convenience: The Asylum and Its Alternatives in Progressive America*. Boston: Little, Brown.

Rusche, George, and Otto Kirchheimer. 1939. *Punishment and Social Structure*. New York: Columbia.

Russell, William Felton, as told to William McSweeny. 1966. *Go Up to Glory*. New York: Coward-McCann.

Sampson, Robert. 1985. "Race and Criminal Violence: A Demographically Disaggregated Analysis of Urban Homicide." *Crime and Delinquency* 31:47–82.

———. 1986a. "Effects of Inequality, Heterogeneity, and Urbanization on Intergroup Victimization." *Social Science Quarterly* 67:751–66.

———. 1986b. "Effects of Socioeconomic Context on Official Reaction to Juvenile Delinquency." *American Sociological Review* 51:876–86.

———. 1987. "Urban Black Violence: The Effect of Male Joblessness and Family Disruption." *American Journal of Sociology* 93:348–82.

———. 1993. "Linking Place and Time: Dynamic Contextualism and the Future of Criminological Inquiry." *Journal of Research in Crime and Delinquency* 4:426–44.

Sampson, Robert, and W. Byron Groves. 1989. "Community Structure and Crime: Testing Social Disorganization Theory of Crime." *American Journal of Sociology* 94:174.

Sampson, Robert, and John Laub. 1990. "Stability and Change in Crime and Deviance over the Life Course: The Salience of Adult Social Bonds." *American Sociological Review* 55:609–27.

———. 1993a. *Crime in the Making*. Cambridge, Mass.: Harvard University Press.

———. 1993b. "Structural Variations in Juvenile Court Processing: Inequality, the Underclass and Social Control." *Law & Society Review* 27:285–312.

Sampson, Robert, and William Wilson. 1994. "Toward a Theory of Race, Crime and Urban Inequality." In John Hagan and Ruth Peterson (Eds.), *Crime and Inequality*. Stanford, Calif.: Stanford University Press.

Sanchez-Jankowski, Martin. 1992. *Islands in the Stream*. Los Angeles: University of California Press.

Schrager, Laura, and James F. Short. 1978. "Toward a Sociology of Organizational Crime." *Social Problems* 25(4):407–19.

Schultz, Theodore. 1961. "Investment in Human Capital." *American Economic Review* 51:1–17.

Schwartz, Richard, and Jerome Skolnick. 1964. "Two Studies of Legal Stigma." In Howard Becker (Ed.), *The Other Side: Perspectives on Deviance*. New York: Free Press.

Sellin, Thorsten. 1935. "Race Prejudice in the Administration of Justice." *American Journal of Sociology* 41:312–17.

———. 1938. *Culture Conflict and Crime*. New York: Social Science Research Council.

Sellin, Thorsten, and Marvin Wolfgang. 1964. *The Measurement of Delinquency*. New York: Wiley.

Shapiro, Susan. 1980. "Thinking About White Collar Crime: Matters of Conceptualization and Research." In *Research on White Collar Crime*. Washington, D.C.: National Institute of Justice.

———. 1984. *The Wayward Capitalists*. New Haven: Yale University Press.

———. 1990. "Collaring the Crime, Not the Criminal: Reconsidering the Concept of White-Collar Crime." *American Sociological Review* 55:346–66.

Shaw, Clifford, and Henry McKay. 1931. *Social Factors in Juvenile Delinquency*. Washington, D.C.: National Commission of Law Observance and Enforcement.

Shearing, Clifford, Susan Addario, and Phillip Stenning. 1985. "Why Organizational Charts Cannot Be Trusted: Rehabilitating Realism in Sociology." Paper presented at a Symposium on Qualitative Research: Ethnographic/Interactionist Perspectives. University of Waterloo (May 15–17).

Sherman, Lawrence. 1993. "Defiance, Deterrence and Irrelevance: A Theory of the Criminal Sanction." *Journal of Research in Crime and Delinquency*.

Short, James F. 1994. *Poverty, Ethnicity and Violent Crime*. Boulder, Colo.: Westview Press. Forthcoming.

Simon, Rita. 1975. *Women and Crime*. Lexington, Mass.: Lexington Press.

Simpson, Sally. 1986. "The Depression of Antitrust: Testing a Multilevel, Longitudinal Model of Profit-Squeeze." *American Sociological Review* 51:859–75.

———. 1991. "Caste, Class, and Violent Crime: Explaining Difference in Female Offending." *Criminology* 29:115–35.

Skogan, Wesley. 1986a. "Methodological Issues in the Study of Victimization." In Ezat Fattah (Ed.), *Crime Policy to Victim Policy*. New York: St. Martin's Press.

———. 1986b. "Fear of Crime and Neighborhood Change." In A. J. Reiss and M. Tonry (Eds.), *Communities and Crime*. Chicago: University of Chicago Press.

———. 1990. *Disorder and Decline: Crime and the Spiral of Decay in American Neighborhoods*. New York: Free Press.

Skogan, Wesley, and M. G. Maxfield. 1981. *Coping with Crime: Individual and Neighborhood Reactions*. Newbury Park, Calif.: Sage.

Skolnick, Jerome. 1966. *Justice without Trial*. New York: Wiley.

Smith, Douglas. 1986. "The Neighborhood Context of Police Behavior." In Albert J. Reiss and Michael Tonry (Eds.), *Communities and Cities*. Chicago: University of Chicago Press.

Smith, Douglas, and Christy Visher. 1980. "Sex and Involvement in Deviance/Crime: A Quantitative Review of the Empirical Literature." *American Sociological Review* 45(4):691–701.

———. 1982. "Street Level Justice: Situational Determinants of Police Arrest Decisions." *Social Problems* 29:167–77.

Snyder, Howard. 1990. *Growth in Minority Detentions Attributed to Drug Law Violators*. Washington, D.C.: Office of Juvenile Justice & Delinquency Prevention, U.S. Department of Justice.

Spergel, Irving. 1964. *Racketville, Slumtown, Haulberg*. Chicago: University of Chicago Press.

Spitzer, Steven. 1975. "Toward a Marxian Theory of Deviance." *Social Problems* 22:638–51.

Steffensmeier, Darrell. 1980. "Sex Differences in Patterns of Adult Crimes, 1965–77: A Review and Assessment." *Social Forces* 57:566–84.

Steffensmeier, Darrell, and Emilie Allan. 1991. "Gender, Age and Crime." In Joseph Sheley (Ed.), *Criminology*. Belmont, Calif.: Wadsworth.

Stewart, James. 1991. *Den of Thieves*. New York: Simon & Schuster.

Stone, Christopher. 1975. *Where the Law Ends: The Social Control of Corporate Behavior*. New York: Harper & Row.

Sudnow, David. 1965. "Normal Crimes: Sociological Features of the Penal Code in a Public Defender Office." *Social Problems* (Winter):255–76.

Sullivan, Mercer. 1989. *Getting Paid: Youth Crime and Work in the Inner City*. Ithaca, New York: Cornell University Press.

Sutherland, Edwin. 1924. *Criminology*. Philadelphia: Lippincott.

———. 1937. *The Professional Thief*. Chicago: University of Chicago Press.

———. 1940. "White Collar Criminality." *American Sociological Review* 5:1–12.

———. 1945. "Is 'White Collar Crime' Crime?" *American Sociological Review* 10:132–39.

———. 1949. *White Collar Crime*. New York: Dryden.

Sutton, John. 1988. *Stubborn Children: Controlling Delinquency in the United States, 1640–1981*. Los Angeles: University of California Press.

Swartz, Joel. 1978. "Silent Killers at Work." In M. David Ermann and Richard Lundman (Eds.), *Corporate and Governmental Deviance*. New York: Oxford University Press.

Swigert, Victoria Lynn, and Ronald Farrell. 1980. "Corporate Homicide: Definitional Processes in the Creation of Deviance." *Law & Society Review* 125:161–82.

Sykes, Gresham, and David Matza. 1957. "Techniques of Neutralization: A Theory of Delinquency." *American Sociological Review* 22:664–70.

Sykes, Richard, and John Clark. 1975. "A Theory of Deference Exchange in Police Civilian Encounters." *American Journal of Sociology* 81:584–600.

Tannenbaum, Franklin. 1938. *Crime and the Community*. Boston: Ginn.

Tappan, Paul. 1947. "Who Is the Criminal?" *American Sociological Review* 12:96–102.

Taylor, Ian, Paul Walton, and Jock Young. 1973. *The New Criminology: For A Social Theory of Deviance*. London: Routledge.

Taylor, Ralph, and Jeanette Covington. 1988. "Neighborhood Changes in Ecology and Violence." *Criminology* 26:553.

Terry, Charles, and Mildred Pellens. 1970. *The Opium Problem*. Montclair, N.J.: Patterson Smith.

Thompson, Hunter. 1967. *Hell's Angels*. New York: Ballantine.

Thornberry, Terrence, and Margaret Farnsworth. 1982. "Social Correlates of Criminal Involvement: Further Evidence on the Relationship Between Social Status and Criminal Behavior." *American Sociological Review* 47:505–18.

Timberlake, James. 1963. *Prohibition and the Progressive Movement: 1900–1920*. Cambridge, Mass.: Harvard.

Tittle, Charles, and Debra Curran. 1988. "Contingencies for Dispositional Disparities in Juvenile Justice." *Social Forces* 67:23.

Tittle, Charles, and Robert Meier. 1990. "Specifying the SES Delinquency Relationship." *Criminology* 28:271–99.

Tittle, Charles, W. J. Villemez, and Douglas Smith. 1978. "The Myth of Social Class and Criminality: An Empirical Assessment of the Empirical Evidence." *American Sociological Review* 47:505–18.

Toby, Jackson. 1974. "The Socialization of Control of Deviant Motivation." In Daniel Glaser (Ed.), *Handbook of Criminology*. Chicago: Rand McNally.

Turk, Austin. 1969. *Criminality and the Legal Order*. Chicago: Rand McNally.

———. 1976. "Law, Conflict and Order: From Theorizing Toward Theories." *Canadian Review of Sociology and Anthropology* 13:282–94.

———. 1982. *Political Criminality*. Newbury Park, Calif.: Sage.

Turner, George Kibbe. 1907. "The City of Chicago: A Study of Great Immoralities." *McClure's Magazine*, April:575.

Uhlman, Thomas. 1979. *Racial Justice: Black Judges and Defendants in an Urban Trial Court*. Lexington, Mass.: Lexington.

van Dijk, Jan, Pat Mayhew, and Martin Killias. 1990. *Experiences of Crime across the World: Key Findings from the 1989 International Crime Survey*. Deventer, Netherlands: Kluwer Law and Taxation Publishers.

Veblen, Thorstein. 1899. *The Theory of the Leisure Class*. New York: Viking Press.

Vold, George. 1958. *Theoretical Criminology*. New York: Oxford University Press.

Visher, Christy. 1983. "Gender, Police Arrest Decisions, and Notions of Chivalry." *Criminology* 21:5–28.

Wacquant, L. D., and William J. Wilson. 1989. "The Costs of Racial and Class Exclusion in the Inner City." *Annals of the American Academy of Political and Social Science* 501:8–25.

Waller, Irvin, and Janet Chan. 1975. "Prison Use: A Canadian and International Comparison." *Criminal Law Quarterly* 47–71.

Ward, David, and Charles Tittle. 1993. "Deterrence or Labelling: The Effects of Informal Sanctions." *Deviant Behavior* 14:43–64.

Warr, Mark. 1985. "Fear of Rape Among Urban Women." *Social Problems* 32:238–50.

Weick, Karl. 1976. "Educational Organizations as Loosely Coupled Systems." *Administrative Science Quarterly* 21:1–19.

Weisburd, David, Elin Waring, and Stanton Wheeler. 1990. "Class, Status and the Punishment of White-Collar Criminals." *Law and Social Inquiry* 15(2):223–46.

Weisburd, David, Stanton Wheeler, Elin Waring, and Nancy Bode. 1991. *Crimes of the Middle Classes: White-Collar Offenders in the Federal Courts.* New Haven, Connecticut: Yale University Press.

Welch, Susan, John Gruhl, and Cassia Spohn. 1985. "Convicting and Sentencing Differences Among Black, Hispanic, and White Males in Six Localities." *Justice Quarterly* 2:67–80.

Wheeler, Stanton. 1976. "Trends and Problems in the Sociological Study of Crime." *Social Problems* 23:525–34.

Wheeler, Stanton, and Michael Rothman. 1982. "The Organization as Weapon in White Collar Crime." *Michigan Law Review* 80(7):1403–26.

Wheeler, Stanton, David Weisburd, and Nancy Bode. 1982. "Sentencing the White Collar Offender: Rhetoric and Reality." *American Sociological Review* 47:641–59.

Wilkins, Leslie. 1964. *Social Deviance.* London: Tavistock.

Williams, Kirk, and Robert Flewelling. 1987. "The Social Production of Criminal Homicide: A Comparative Study of Disaggregated Rates in American Cities." *American Sociological Review* 53:421–31.

Williams, Terry. 1989. *The Cocaine Kids.* New York: Addison-Wesley.

Willis, Paul. 1977. *Learning to Labour.* London: Gower.

———. 1990. *Common Culture.* Boulder, Colo.: Westview Press.

Wilson, James Q. 1968. *Varieties of Police Behavior.* Cambridge: Harvard University Press.

Wilson, William J. 1987. *The Truly Disadvantaged: The Inner City, the Underclass, and Public Policy.* Chicago: University of Chicago Press.

———. 1991. "Studying Inner-City Social Dislocations: The Challenge of Public Agenda Research." *American Sociological Review* 56:1–14.

Wolfgang, Marvin. 1972. *Delinquency in a Birth Cohort*. Chicago: University of Chicago Press.

Wolfgang, Marvin, and Mark Riedel. 1973. "Race, Judicial Discretion, and the Death Penalty." *The Annals of the American Academy of Political and Social Science* 407:119.

World Bank. 1991. *World Development Report 1991*.

Yeager, Peter. 1991. *The Limits of Law: The Public Regulation of Private Pollution*. New York: Cambridge University Press.

———. 1994. "Law, Crime and Inequality." In John Hagan and Ruth Peterson (Eds.), *Crime and Inequality*. Stanford, Calif.: Stanford University Press.

Young, Jock, and Roger Matthews. 1992. *Rethinking Criminology: The Realist Debate*. London: Sage.

Zatz, Marjorie. 1985. "Pleas, Priors and Prison: Racial/Ethnic Differences in Sentencing." *Social Science Research* 14:169–93.

Zatz, Marjorie, and William Chambliss. 1993. *Making Law: Law, the State and Structural Contradictions*. Bloomington: Indiana University Press.

Zatz, Marjorie, and Alan Lizotte. 1985. "The Timing of Court Processing: Toward Linking Theory and Method." *Criminology* 23:313–35.

Zeitz, Dorothy. 1981. *Women Who Embezzle or Defraud: A Study of Women Convicted Felons*. New York: Praeger.

Glossary/Index

Italic page numbers indicate references to figures in the text.